An Index to Anglo-American Psalmody In Modern Critical Editions

Recent Researches in Music

A-R Editions publishes seven series of critical editions, spanning the history of Western music, American music, and oral traditions.

Recent Researches in the Music of the Middle Ages and Early Renaissance
Charles M. Atkinson, general editor

Recent Researches in the Music of the Renaissance
James Haar, general editor

Recent Researches in the Music of the Baroque Era
Christoph Wolff, general editor

Recent Researches in the Music of the Classical Era
Eugene K. Wolf, general editor

Recent Researches in the Music of the Nineteenth and Early Twentieth Centuries
Rufus Hallmark, general editor

Recent Researches in American Music
John M. Graziano, general editor

Recent Researches in the Oral Traditions of Music
Philip V. Bohlman, general editor

Each edition in *Recent Researches* is devoted to works by a single composer or to a single genre. The content is chosen for its high quality and historical importance, and each edition includes a substantial introduction and critical report. The music is engraved according to the highest standards of production using the proprietary software MusE, owned by MusicNotes, Inc.

For information on establishing a standing order to any of our series, or for editorial guidelines on submitting proposals, please contact:

A-R Editions, Inc.
Madison, Wisconsin 53717

800 736-0070 (U.S. book orders)
608 836-9000 (phone)
608 831-8200 (fax)
http://www.areditions.com

An Index to Anglo-American Psalmody in Modern Critical Editions

Karl and Marie Kroeger

A-R Editions, Inc.
Madison

A-R Editions, Inc., Madison, Wisconsin 53717
© 2000 by A-R Editions, Inc.

Printed in the United States of America

ISBN 0-89579-471-3
ISSN 0147-0078

♾ The paper used in this publication meets the minimum
requirements of the American National Standard for
Information Sciences—Permanence of Paper for Printed
Library Materials, ANSI Z39.48-1984.

Contents

Introduction

An Index to Anglo-American Psalmody in Modern Critical Editions (hereafter referred to as Psalmody Index) provides access to a historical repertory that has become increasingly important to both scholars and performers over the past quarter century. Psalmody, the religious music of most British and American churches from the mid-sixteenth to the early nineteenth centuries, is a special category of vocal music with its own composers, musical forms, and compositional style. Designed originally to provide a musical vehicle for congregational participation in divine services, over time psalmody came to embrace many other functions, both sacred and secular. In many areas of Britain and America during those two and a half centuries, it was the popular music of the rural people. As Irving Lowens noted, "this music was much more than a church song sung only of a Sunday morning in church—it was a music of the out-of-doors, of the kitchen hearth, of the blacksmith's forge, and even of the tavern" (Lowens 280).

During the years between about 1535 and 1820, the psalmody repertory grew into an enormous body of vocal and choral music approaching some 20,000 items (see Temperley, *Hymn Tune Index*). It consisted of psalm and hymn tunes intended for congregational singing, and fuging tunes, set pieces, and anthems for a trained choir of singers. (The characteristics of these forms are discussed in the "Guide to the Index.") Most of the composers, particularly during the eighteenth and early nineteenth centuries, stood outside the realm of art music of the day. Some were church organists in the cities and larger towns of Britain and America; others were farmers, mechanics, tradesmen, teachers, or clergymen with a talent for music and a desire to express themselves creatively by making new pieces for religious use. Many were singing masters, some of whom traveled from place to place offering the young people instruction in music reading and choral singing. Particularly in rural areas, where organized entertainment was rare, their singing schools were popular and productive pastimes. They often compiled collections of music (tunebooks) for use in their schools, frequently containing pieces that they themselves had composed. These psalmodists, as they were called, usually lacked the extensive vocal and instrumental training of the art-music composers of the day and were self-taught in the craft of musical composition. They adopted compositional procedures based on Renaissance choral practices that permitted them to compose music for unaccompanied choirs, admirably fitted to the needs and capacities of the modestly trained singers. After about 1820, changes in musical taste and aesthetic perception caused much of this music to be discarded by succeeding generations of church musicians.

In America, while the aesthetic and cultural changes mentioned above caused much of the earlier music to be scorned, an interesting phenomenon occurred: some of this music was anthologized in retrospective collections devoted largely to this repertory. Tunebooks such as *The Stoughton Collection* (Boston, 1829), *The Billings and Holden Collection* (Boston, 1836), *The Antiquarian* (Boston, 1849), and *Continental Harmony* (Boston, 1857) offered the old-time music in modern dress. Apparently, it was fun to sing and enough demand existed for the music of American composers William Billings, Daniel Read, Oliver Holden, and their contemporaries to make these publications profitable. Adding to the attraction were the performances of "Father" Robert Kemp and his troop of singers who toured widely in the 1850s and 1860s presenting "Old Folks Concerts." These performances, featuring old-fashioned dress and rustic accents, brought the music out of the sanctuary and parlor and into the theater as pure entertainment. Kemp compiled a small collection of sacred and secular pieces performed in his shows, first published in 1860, which went through editions in 1874, 1889, 1917, and ca. 1932. In 1930, William Arms Fisher edited a small collection of psalmody for the upcoming George Washington Bicentennial (1932), entitled *Ye Olde New-England Psalm-Tunes*, which catered to the curiosity about earlier life and times aroused by the Washington Bicentennial celebrations.

Little serious attention was paid to psalmody, however, until after the Second World War. Prior to about 1950, music historians tended to look dismissively upon this repertory. It did not aspire to high musical art, it often did not conform to the accepted principles of tonal harmony, and its composers stood far outside the European musical mainstream that seemed so significant at that time. After the war, musicologists, such as Allen P. Britten, Alan C. Buechner, Ralph T. Daniel, and others, investigated important aspects of the psalmody tradition in doctoral dissertations. In the 1950s and early 1960s, Irving Lowens published a number of thought-provoking articles on psalmody in scholarly journals. These scholars laid the foundations for the future developments in psalmody scholarship.

In 1964, W. Thomas Marrocco and Harold Gleason co-compiled the anthology *Music in America*, which presented examples of both sacred and secular music to 1865 in accurate editions. Richard Crawford began his important work in psalmody in 1968 by publishing a biography of the singing master, Andrew Law, based on his doctoral dissertation. Interest in psalmody as a cultural phenomenon was growing, with serious and perceptive scholars entering the field, bringing with them fresh insights into the traditions and times and new understandings of the composers' lives and methods.

The American Revolution Bicentennial in 1976 was a major impetus that brought psalmody to the fore. This event focused public attention as never before on the cultural activities of two centuries earlier, a large part of which was devoted to music. Urged on by the American Revolution Bicentennial Commission, many performing organizations included earlier American music in their programming. It soon became clear that choirs held a distinct advantage over most other performing groups, because of the significant and substantial body of choral music—psalmody—that fitted their needs with little adaptation and made a favorable impression on listeners. Over the three decades between the end of the Second World War and the Bicentennial celebrations, some performing editions of some tunes and anthems by early American composers had been published, and music publishers hastened to add more to those resources.

As their contribution to the Bicentennial, the American Musicological Society and the Colonial Society of Massachusetts planned the publication of the first scholarly edition of the collected works of an American composer. *Gesamtausgaben*, long an important part of European musical scholarship, had conferred on such masters as Bach, Handel, Palestrina, Mozart, Beethoven, and Schubert critical collected editions of their music carefully scrutinized by distinguished scholars. America's debut in this field was *The Complete Works of William Billings*, unquestionably the most important American psalmodist of his era. The edition was proposed and planned by Hans Nathan, a scholar who had done notable work on Billings and other aspects of early American music. Nathan edited volume 2 of the edition, published in 1977, but discontinued his editorial efforts shortly thereafter. Karl Kroeger completed the edition

over the next thirteen years, the final volume appearing in 1990.

The British psalmody traditions, which had received scant notice from scholars, were given a detailed exploration by Nicholas Temperley in his path-breaking *Music of the English Parish Church* (Cambridge, 1979), in two volumes, the second being a carefully edited anthology of representative pieces of British parish church music. In 1984 Richard Crawford published *The Core Repertory of Early American Psalmody*, an anthology of the 101 pieces most often appearing in American tunebooks through 1810, over half of which were imports from British psalmody.

The 1990s saw a significant expansion of American psalmody published in scholarly editions, and again the American Musicological Society played an important role. It sponsored *Music of the United States of America*, a series of musical monuments which, at present, includes Daniel Read, *Collected Works*, edited by Karl Kroeger (1995) and Timothy Swan, *Psalmody and Secular Songs*, edited by Nym Cooke (1997). A-R Editions' series, *Recent Researches in American Music*, which had earlier carried Richard Crawford's *Core Repertory* anthology, brought out David Warren Steel's *Collected Works* of Stephen Jenks (Madison, 1995) and Karl Kroeger's anthology, *Early American Anthems* (Madison, 2000). Finally, Garland Publications issued *Music of the New American Nation* (New York, 1995–99), a fifteen-volume compendium of the collected music of twenty-three important American psalmodists under the general editorship of Karl Kroeger.

Thus, at the onset of the twenty-first century, the critically edited collected works of twenty-seven early American composers of sacred music are available for performance and study. Additionally, two anthologies, Crawford's *Core Repertory* and Kroeger's *Early American Anthems*, contain samples of music of other composers of the era. The whole of the published repertory today consists of about 2000 individual pieces. The Psalmody Index provides access to this body of music by tune name, composer, tune type, first line of text, text source, and subject of the text. Details of the index and a guide to its use are presented in the following section.

An Index to
Anglo-American
Psalmody
in Modern
Critical Editions

Guide to the Index

The Psalmody Index consists of a main index, alphabetically arranged by Tune Name, followed by five subsidiary indexes, which provide access to various details in the main index. The main index is arranged alphabetically, as indicated, by the name that the tune is known by. The following example shows a typical entry for a tune.

ABINGTON
1   ft L.M. Stone, J
    Who is this fair one in distress
    Sources. MNAN10/3, WH1/78
    Topic. Solomon's Song

The first item is the tune name, in small capital type. Under this designation appear all pieces with this name in the published repertory. The first line of the tune entry begins with the tune identification number, followed by the tune type, the poetic meter, and composer's name. The next line contains the first line of the text set by the composer. The third line, *Sources,* gives the modern collection that contains the tune and the poet or source of text. The final line contains the topic or subject of the hymn. Further details of the entries are given in the discussion that follows. The meanings of the abbreviations are found in the lists of abbreviations given later in this guide.

Tune Identification Number

The entry for an individual tune begins with the tune identification number, a unique number assigned to that tune that identifies it in the subsidiary indexes.

Tune Name

The tune name, the primary identifier for the piece, was usually given by the composer at the time of composition and seldom changed through the various states in which the tune may appear (e.g., the composer's manuscript, a manuscript copy by some other person, a printed copy in a tunebook). A composer seldom gave the same tune name to more than one of his compositions, although other composers frequently used this name for one of their works. Thus, under a single tune name, several compositions by different composers may be listed. Since the Psalmody Index includes only works that appear in modern critical editions, multiple printings of a tune by the same composer may also appear. For example, William Billings's popular ANTHEM FOR EASTER was printed three times in recent years: first in Richard Crawford's *The Core Repertory of Early American Psalmody* (Madison, 1984), then in *The Complete Works of William Billings,* Vol. 3 (Boston, 1986), and, finally, in Karl Kroeger's anthology of *Early American Anthems,* Part 1 (Madison, 2000). Each printing is given a separate entry in the index. All entries under a single tune name are alphabetical by composer, and for several printings of the same piece, they are further arranged by the collections in which they were published. The tune names are listed in the index as they appear in the collections that contain them. Variant spellings for the same tune by the same composer may exist and are treated as different tune names. For example, William Croft's tune, ST. ANNE, is entered by that name as found in Crawford's *Core Repertory,* but it was called ST. ANN'S by William Billings when he published his arrangement of the tune, and is found by that name in the Billings *Complete Works,* Vol. 3. The popular tune OLD HUNDRED appears under both that name and PSALM 100 [OLD] as given in the collections that contain it. On the few occasions when a composer did give the same name to different tunes, the tune name is followed by [I] and [II] to distinguish between them (e.g., ADVENT [I] and ADVENT [II] by Supply Belcher).

The tune name itself may or may not carry topical significance. Often it is a place name, like BOSTON, NEW HAVEN, CHINA, RUSSIA, ASIA, or EUROPE. Just why the composer chose this particular name is unknown (in some instances, he may have wished to honor a particular town where he taught a singing school by naming a tune after it). In other cases, the tune name reflects the subject content of the hymn that the composer set. For example, JUDGMENT, a name given to at least five different tunes, sets texts related to the biblically prophesied Day of Judgment; CRUCIFIXION, used by four composers, sets texts dealing with Christ's crucifixion and death; and INVITATION, used by six composers, sets texts which invite the reader/singer to a better life in Christ. Some tune names honored famous men of the day (e.g., WASHINGTON, ADAMS, JEFFERSON), and some seem to have been made up from euphonious syllables that seem to carry no meaning (e.g., ARNON, DENSTON, ORLAND).

Tune Type

Following the tune name is an abbreviation for the type of piece the tune represents. There are six tune types identified in the index:

pt   Plain tune: a syllabic setting of a single stanza of the hymn, without word repetition, lengthy melismas, or other devices.

xt   Extended tune: uses some means to increase the tune's length, often word repetition or the reiteration of the final line of text to different music.

ft   Fuging tune: a setting of the text containing a polyphonic section in which the words are sung at different times by the voices, causing verbal conflict.

an   Anthem: an extended, non-strophic setting of a text, which may be biblical, liturgical, prose, or poetry, or a combination of these elements. An anthem is usually defined as a setting of biblical or liturgical prose, with the term set piece used for extended, non-strophic settings of poetry. However, American composers of psalmody often mixed verse with prose, or even set entire poems to music, calling their compositions anthems. Here they are taken at their word: if the composer called his work an anthem, it is so designated in the index.

sp   Set piece: non-strophic settings of poetry that are not called anthems by their composers, but have tune names similar to plain, extended, and fuging tunes.

canon   A relatively rare tune type, designates a piece, usually notated on a single line of music, in which all voices sing the same melody but starting at designated time intervals after the first voice.

Poetic Meter

The poetic meter that the tune is intended to serve is the next element in the entry. Text substitution was still an important performance practice in eighteenth- and early-nineteenth-century America, and familiar tunes were often printed in tunebooks with different words, or sometimes with no accompanying text at all. The latter invited the singer to sing any words that fit the musical mood and meter. The complete text of a hymn was seldom given in a tunebook. Singers could find additional stanzas of common hymns in the many editions of various hymn collections available at the time. There were four generally used designations for the standard metrical patterns found in the hymns of the day:

C.M.   Common Meter: a four-line stanza in iambic meter, alternating eight and six syllables per line.

L.M.   Long Meter: a four-line stanza in iambic meter, but each line containing eight syllables.

S.M.   Short Meter: a four-line stanza in iambic meter, the first, second, and fourth lines having six syllables, the third having eight.

P.M.   Particular Meter: used to designate any metrical pattern that does not conform to the three listed above. Since anthems and set pieces were not adapted for strophic singing, they are not usually given meter designations, and this field is omitted for these musical forms.

Composer

The name of the composer of that particular setting (surname followed by the initial letter of the first name) follows the poetic meter. If the composer is unknown, the abbreviation "Anon." is used.

First Line of Text

The second line of the index entry provides the first line of the text that is set to the tune. If the text is poetry, this is the complete first line of the first stanza that the composer set. Since composers sometimes began their settings with later stanzas of the hymn, this may not always be the first line of the hymn as the poet framed it. If the text is prose, the first line consists of as many words as are necessary to make reasonably good sense, but may not include all of the text in the first line of the source. Capitalization and interior punctuation are retained, but final punctuation marks are omitted.

Modern Edition

The first element listed under Sources is an abbreviation for the modern collection in which the work appears. The numbers following the abbreviation designate the starting page number of the piece; for multi-volume compilations the volume number and a slash precede the page number. For example, MNAN10/3 means page 3 in volume 10 of *Music of the New American Nation*. The collections indexed are the following:

AA   *Early American Anthems*, ed. Karl Kroeger, 2 vols. (Madison, 2000).

CR   *The Core Repertory of Early American Psalmody*, ed. Richard Crawford (Madison, 1984).

DR   Daniel Read, *Collected Works*, ed. Karl Kroeger (Madison, 1995).

MNAN   *Music of the New American Nation*, Karl Kroeger, general editor, 15 vols. (New York, 1995–99).

SJ   Stephen Jenks, *The Collected Works*, ed. David Warren Steel (Madison, 1996).

TS   Timothy Swan, *Psalmody and Secular Songs*, ed. Nym Cooke (Madison, 1997). [N.B.: the secular songs have not been indexed.]

WB   *The Complete Works of William Billings*, ed. Karl Kroeger and Hans Nathan, 4 vols. (Boston, 1977–90).

Source of Text

The final element listed under *Sources* is the identification of the poet or the source of the text. If the poet is known, his or her name is given—the surname followed by the initial letter of the first name. If the attribution is uncertain, the name is followed by a question mark. For hymns where the poet is unknown, the abbreviation "Anon." is used.

Titles for well-known collections and text sources are abbreviated in the index and are to be interpreted according to the following list:

BarP   Joel Barlow. *Dr. Watts's Imitation of the Psalms of David,* Corrected and Enlarged, 2d ed. (Hartford: Hudson and Goodwin, 1785).

BCP   Protestant Episcopal Church, *Book of Common Prayer* (New York: Evert Duyckinck, 1809).

BCPP   Protestant Episcopal Church, *Book of Common Prayer* (New York: Evert Duyckinck, 1809). Psalms.

BelP   Jeremy Belknap, *Sacred Poetry* (Boston, 1795).

Bible   *The Holy Bible* (Boston: Thomas and Andrews, 1814).

BP   *The Holy Bible* (Boston: Thomas and Andrews, 1814). Psalms.

BPB   [The Bay Psalm Book] *Psalms, Hymns and Spiritual Songs of the Old and New Testament,* 21st ed. (Boston, 1726).

DP   Timothy Dwight, *The Psalms of David . . . by I. Watts . . . A New Edition* (Albany: Whiting, Backus, & Whiting, 1804).

NV   Nicholas Brady and Nahum Tate, *A New Version of the Psalms* (London: J. Roberts, 1749).

OV   Thomas Sternhold, John Hopkins, *et al., The Booke of Psalms* (London: Companie of Stationers, 1612).

RCH   James Relly and John Relly, *Christian Hymns* (Burlington [N. J.]: Isaac Collins, 1776).

SP   [Edward Millar], *Psalms of David . . . [for the Church of Scotland]* (Edinburgh: Andrew Hart, 1635).

WDMS   Isaac Watts, *Divine and Moral Songs,* 16th ed. (Philadelphia: Joseph Crukshank), 1773.

WH1   Isaac Watts, *Hymns and Spiritual Songs,* Book 1 (Boston: Samuel T. Armstrong, 1819).

WH2   Isaac Watts, *Hymns and Spiritual Songs,* Book 2 (Boston: Samuel T. Armstrong, 1819).

WH3   Isaac Watts, *Hymns and Spiritual Songs,* Book 3 (Boston: Samuel T. Armstrong, 1819).

WHor   Isaac Watts, *Horae Lyricae,* 10th ed. (New York: Hugh Gaine, 1762).

WP   Isaac Watts, *The Psalms of David Imitated* (Boston: Samuel T. Armstrong, 1819).

The number following the "P" (for Psalm) or "V" (for version of the psalms) is the number of the psalm; the number following the "H" is the hymn number. For example, BarP108 means Psalm 108 in Joel Barlow's *Imitation of the Psalms of David.* For Watts's psalms, which appear in various parts and in different meters, the number following the "P" is the psalm number, and that following the slash is the part number. For Watts's hymns, which were published in three books, the number following the "H" is the book number, and that following the slash is the hymn number within that book.

Topic

The final element in the index entry is the topic or subject of the piece. The subjects are mostly those found in James M. Winchell's *An Arrangement of the Psalms, Hymns, and Spiritual Songs of the Rev. Isaac Watts, D.D., to which is added a Supplement . . . [of] Hymns,* 2d ed. (Boston, 1820). Winchell, a Baptist minister in Boston, arranged the psalms and hymns of Watts under topical headings that grouped the poems together by their broad subject content. To Watts's poems, he added a supplement of about 300 popular hymns by Watts, Doddridge, Wesley, and others, similarly grouped by subject. Not all of the texts set by American composers are found in Winchell's collection. For example, none of the versifications in Brady and Tate's *A New Version of the Psalms* are included, nor are any of the hymns in James and John Relly's *Christian Hymns.* Many other hymns and versions of the psalms are also not found there. For poems not in Winchell's collection, the compilers of this index have assigned topics from Winchell's arrangement as best they could according to their understanding of the subjects of these hymns.

Some of Winchell's topics have been slightly altered or modernized. For example, Winchell's "Incarnation of Christ" has been changed to "Birth of Christ." His "Ascension and Exaltation of Christ" is used when the ascension is an element of the hymn, but when Christ is exalted on other occasions, only "Exaltation of Christ" is employed. Some topics have been shortened. For example, Winchell's "Settlement and Beauty of the Church" is given simply as "Beauty of the Church"; his "Afflictions, Persecutions, and Complaints of the Church" becomes "Afflictions of the Church"; "Safety, Deliverance, and Triumph of the Church" is given as "Safety and Triumph of the Church."

The subjects in Winchell's arrangement consist of the following topics:

The Perfections of God
Creation and Providence
Universal Praise
Scripture
Christ
    Birth of
    Life and Ministry of
    Sufferings and Death of
    Resurrection of
    Ascension and Exaltation of
    Exaltation of
    Intercession of
    Dominion of
    Characters and Offices of
    Addresses to
Doctrines of the Gospel
    Adoption
    Atonement
    Communion with God
    Depravity and Fall of Man

Grace
Election
Justification
Pardon
Perseverance
Redemption
Regeneration
Salvation
Sanctification
Law and Gospel
    Moral Law
    Gospel
    Invitations and Promises
The Holy Spirit
    Graces of
        Faith
        Fear and Hope
        Humility
        Joy and Rejoicing
        Knowledge
        Liberality
        Love
        Prudence
        Repentance
        Resignation
        Sincerity
        Trust and Confidence
    Addresses to the Holy Spirit
Christian
Saints and Sinners
Worship
    Public
    Lord's Day
The World
The Church
    Jewish Church
    Christian Church
    Beauty of
    Afflictions of
    Safety and Triumph of
    Prayer and Praise for
    Church Meetings
    Missionary Meetings
Baptism
The Lord's Supper
Solomon's Song
Times and Seasons
    Morning and Evening
    Seasons of the Year
    Youth and Old Age
    Thanksgiving

Magistracy
    Sickness and Recovery
Time and Eternity
Death and Resurrection
Day of Judgment
Hell and Heaven
Doxologies
    Hosannas to Christ

Not all texts could be fitted into Winchell's classification scheme. Anthems, for example, are given names of the occasions for which they were intended to be used (Christmas, Easter, Funeral, Ordination, etc.). Patriotic and Masonic hymns, verses for New Year's celebrations, and a few secular poems in the repertory also found no place in Winchell's arrangement. Thus, the compilers of the index have supplemented Winchell's subjects to take these topics into account.

Additions to Winchell's Subject List

The following topics have been added to Winchell's list:

Charity
Christmas
Communion
Dedication
Easter
Fast Day
Funeral
Marriage
Masonic
Music
New Year
Ordination
Patriotic
Secular

Subsidiary Indexes

The five subsidiary indexes provide access to information contained in the main index. The subsidiary indexes are: Composer, Tune Type, First Line, Author and Text Source, and Topic. All are arranged alphabetically by the element indexed and refer to the main index by the tune identification number. The Tune Type index is further arranged by the poetic meter of the tune, so that one finds, for example, Extended Tune C.M., Extended Tune L.M., Extended Tune P.M., and Extended Tune S.M. Watts's psalms in the Authors and Text Sources index are supplied with poetic meter indications when necessary to distinguish between different metrical versions of the same psalm.

Bibliography

Billings, William. *The Complete Works of William Billings.* 4 vols. Ed. by Karl Kroeger and Hans Nathan. Boston: American Musicological Society and The Colonial Society of Massachusetts, 1977–90.

The Billings and Holden Collection of Ancient Psalmody. Boston: Marsh, Capen, and Lyon, 1836; supplement, Boston: Kidder and Wright, 1838.

Britten, Allen P. "Theoretical Introductions in American Tunebooks to 1800." Ph.D. diss., University of Michigan, 1949.

Britten, Allen P., Irving Lowens, and Richard Crawford. *American Sacred Music Imprints, 1698–1810: A Bibliography.* Worcester: American Antiquarian Society, 1990.

Buechner, Alan C. "Yankee Singing Schools and the Golden Age of Choral Music in New England." Ed.D. diss., Harvard University, 1960.

Continental Harmony. Boston: O. Ditson, 1857.

Crawford, Richard. *Andrew Law, American Psalmodist.* Evanston: Northwestern University Press, 1968.

———, ed. *The Core Repertory of Early American Psalmody.* Recent Researches in American Music, vols. 11–12. Madison: A-R Editions, 1984.

Daniel, Ralph T. *The Anthem in New England to 1800.* Evanston: Northwestern University Press, 1966.

Father Kemp's Old Folks Concert Music. Boston: O. Ditson, 1860 (with editions in 1874, 1888, 1917, and ca.1932).

Fisher, William Arms. *Ye Olde New-England Psalm Tunes.* Boston: O. Ditson, 1930.

Jenks, Stephen. *Collected Works.* Ed. by David Warren Steel. Recent Researches in American Music, vol. 18. Madison: A-R Editions, 1995.

Kroeger, Karl, ed. *Early American Anthems.* Recent Researches in American Music, vols. 36–37. Madison: A-R Editions, 2000.

Lowens, Irving. *Music and Musicians in Early America.* New York: Norton, 1964.

Marrocco, W. Thomas, and Harold Gleason. *Music in America: An Anthology for the Landing of the Pilgrims to the Close of the Civil War, 1620–1865.* New York: Norton, 1964.

Marshall, Leonard. *The Antiquarian.* Boston: C. H. Keith, 1849.

Music of the New American Nation. 15 vols. General editor, Karl Kroeger. New York: Garland, 1995–99.

New Grove Dictionary of American Music, s.v. "Psalmody" by Richard Crawford.

New Grove Dictionary of Music and Musicians, s.v. "Psalmody" by Nicholas Temperley and Richard Crawford.

Read, Daniel. *Collected Works.* Ed. by Karl Kroeger. Recent Researches in American Music, vol. 24. Madison: A-R Editions, 1995.

Stoughton Collection of Church Music. Boston: Marsh, Capen, and Lyon, 1829.

Swan, Timothy. *Psalmody and Secular Songs.* Ed. by Nym Cooke. Recent Researches in American Music, vol. 26. Madison: A-R Editions, 1997.

Temperley, Nicholas. *The Hymn Tune Index.* 4 vols. Oxford: Oxford University Press, 1998.

———. *Music of the English Parish Church.* 2 vols. Cambridge: Cambridge University Press, 1979.

Winchell, James M. *An Arrangement of the Psalms, Hymns, and Spiritual Songs of the Rev. Isaac Watts, D.D., to which is Added a Supplement . . . of More than Three Hundred Hymns.* 2d ed. Boston: Richardson & Lord, and Cummings & Hilliard, 1820.

Tune Name

ABINGTON

1   ft L.M. Stone, J
Who is this fair one in distress
Sources. MNAN10/3, WH1/78
Topic. Solomon's Song

ABYSINA

2   xt P.M. French, J
Greatly belov'd, of God approv'd
Sources. MNAN9/3, RCH5
Topic. Sufferings and Death of Christ

ACCEPTANCE

3   xt C.M. Holden, O
When midnight darkness veils the skies
Sources. MNAN13/3, WP119/2
Topic. Worship

ACTON

4   xt L.M. Belknap, D
Farewell, bright soul, a short farewell
Sources. MNAN14/3, WHor
Topic. Death and Resurrection

5   pt C.M. Wood, A
Vain man, thy fond pursuits forbear
Sources. MNAN6/3, Hart, J
Topic. Death and Resurrection

ADAMS

6   xt P.M. Billings, W
To spend one sacred day
Sources. WB4/228, WP84
Topic. Public Worship

7   ft C.M. Read, D
Why did the nations join to slay
Sources. DR2, WP2
Topic. Intercession of Christ

ADDISON

8   ft P.M. Gillet, A
How pleasant 'tis to see
Sources. MNAN2/65, WP133
Topic. Public Worship

9   xt C.M. Holden, O
Thy mercy sweetens ev'ry soil
Sources. MNAN13/4, Addison, J
Topic. Fear and Hope

ADESTE FIDELES

10   xt L.M. Wade, J
Lord, 'tis a pleasant thing to stand
Sources. CR1, WP92/2
Topic. The Christian Church

ADIEU

11   xt C.M. Jenks, S
Far from our friends and country dear
Sources. SJ3, BelP137
Topic. Afflictions of the Church

ADMIRATION

12   ft L.M. Babcock, L?
Infinite grace! Almighty charms
Sources. MNAN11/134, WHor
Topic. Sufferings and Death of Christ

13   ft L.M. Belcher, S
Ye sons of men with joy record
Sources. MNAN5/3, Doddridge, P
Topic. Creation and Providence

14   ft C.M. Edson, L Jr
Our life contains a thousand strings
Sources. MNAN3/47, WH2/19
Topic. Creation and Providence

ADMONITION

15   ft P.M. Read, D
Sinners, awake betimes; ye fools be wise
Sources. DR4, WP50/2
Topic. Day of Judgment

ADORATION

16   pt P.M. Benham, A
O God of my salvation hear
Sources. MNAN8/3, BarP88
Topic. Fear and Hope

17   ft L.M. Billings, W
      To God the father, God the son
      Sources. WB3/109, WH3/32
      Topic. Doxology

18   pt C.M. Bull, A
      Songs of immortal praise belong
      Sources. MNAN1/3, WP111/1
      Topic. Perfections of God

ADVENT

19   pt P.M. Bull, A
      The God of glory sends his summons forth
      Sources. MNAN1/4, WP50/2
      Topic. Day of Judgment

ADVENT [I]

20   ft C.M. Belcher, S
      The Lord descended from above
      Sources. MNAN5/5, OV18
      Topic. Perfections of God

ADVENT [II]

21   ft L.M. Belcher, S
      He comes! he comes! the judge severe
      Sources. MNAN5/8, Wesley, C
      Topic. Day of Judgment

ADVICE

22   an Newcomb, W
      Now hear the voice which wisdom cries
      Sources. AA2/135, Anon.
      Topic. Prudence

AETNA

23   pt P.M. Edson, L
      The God of glory sends his summons forth
      Sources. MNAN3/3, WP50/2
      Topic. Day of Judgment

AFRICA

24   pt C.M. Billings, W
      Now shall my inward joys arise
      Sources. WB1/88, WH1/39
      Topic. Safety and Triumph of the Church

25   pt C.M. Billings, W
      Now shall my inward joys arise
      Sources. WB2/46, WH1/39
      Topic. Safety and Triumph of the Church

ALARM

26   pt C.M. Jenks, S
      Why do we mourn departing friends
      Sources. SJ4, WH2/3
      Topic. Death and Resurrection

ALBANY

27   pt C.M. Billings, W
      How long wilt thou forget me, Lord
      Sources. WB1/98, NV13
      Topic. Christian

28   ft S.M. Edson, L
      Behold the morning sun
      Sources. MNAN3/6, WP19/2
      Topic. Lord's Day

29   ft S.M. Olmsted, T
      Raise your triumphant songs
      Sources. MNAN15/85, WH2/104
      Topic. Perfections of God

30   pt C.M. Read, D
      No, I shall envy them no more
      Sources. DR6, WH2/56
      Topic. The World

ALEXANDRIA

31   xt L.M. Gillet, A
      My spirit sinks within me, Lord
      Sources. MNAN2/66, WP42
      Topic. Fear and Hope

ALIBAMA

32   pt L.M. Holden, O
      Hark! 'tis the trumpet's piercing sound
      Sources. MNAN13/5, Anon.
      Topic. Day of Judgment

ALL SAINTS

33   xt L.M. Gillet, A
      This life's a dream, an empty show
      Sources. MNAN2/70, WP17
      Topic. Saints and Sinners

34   pt L.M. Knapp, W
      The heav'ns declare thy glory, Lord
      Sources. CR2, NV19
      Topic. Scripture

ALPHA

35   pt S.M. Belcher, S
      My soul, repeat his praise
      Sources. MNAN5/9, WP103/2
      Topic. Perfections of God

36   xt C.M. Holden, O
      When faith presents the saviour's death
      Sources. MNAN13/6, Hervey, J
      Topic. Faith

AMANDA

37   pt L.M. Gillet, A
      Death, like an overflowing stream
      Sources. MNAN2/71, WP90
      Topic. Death and Resurrection

38 xt L.M. Morgan, J
Death, like an overflowing stream
Sources. MNAN7/120, WP90
Topic. Death and Resurrection

AMBOY

39 pt P.M. Read, D
I am not concern'd to know
Sources. DR7, WHor
Topic. Prudence

AMELIA

40 xt L.M. Woodruff, M
Lord, I am vile, conceiv'd in sin
Sources. MNAN8/57, WP51/2
Topic. Depravity and Fall of Man

AMEN

41 sp Holden, O
Now unto the king eternal
Sources. MNAN13/7, Bible
Topic. Doxology

AMENIA

42 ft C.M. Chandler, S
Teach me the measure of my days
Sources. MNAN2/139, WP39/2
Topic. Time and Eternity

AMERICA

43 pt P.M. Billings, W
To thee the tuneful anthem soars
Sources. WB1/40, Byles, M
Topic. Safety and Triumph of the Church

44 pt P.M. Billings, W
Come let us sing unto the Lord
Sources. WB2/50, Billings, W
Topic. Universal Praise

45 ft L.M. Jenks, S
But there's a brighter world on high
Sources. SJ5, WP24
Topic. Ascension and Exaltation of Christ

46 ft C.M. West, E
When God reveal'd his gracious name
Sources. MNAN7/3, WP126
Topic. Church Meetings

AMHERST

47 pt P.M. Belknap, D
Begin, my soul, th'exalted lay
Sources. MNAN14/4, Ogilvy, J
Topic. Universal Praise

48 xt P.M. Billings, W
Ye boundless realms of joy
Sources. CR3, NV148
Topic. Universal Praise

49 xt P.M. Billings, W
To God, the mighty Lord
Sources. WB1/182, NV136
Topic. The Jewish Church

50 xt P.M. Billings, W
To God, the mighty Lord
Sources. WB2/54, NV136
Topic. The Jewish Church

AMIENS

51 xt S.M. Holden, O
Welcome, sweet day of rest
Sources. MNAN13/8, WH2/14
Topic. Worship

AMITY

52 ft P.M. Read, D
How pleas'd and blest was I
Sources. DR8, WP122
Topic. Public Worship

AMOSKEAG

53 ft C.M. Holyoke, S
Zion rejoice and Judah sing
Sources. MNAN12/3, WH2/111
Topic. Thanksgiving

AMSTERDAM

54 xt P.M. Anon.
Rise, my soul, and stretch thy wings
Sources. CR5, Seagrave, R
Topic. Christian

ANDOVER

55 xt P.M. Babcock, S
My redeemer, let me be
Sources. MNAN11/3, RCH17
Topic. Redemption

56 pt C.M. Billings, W
O God, we praise thee and confess
Sources. WB1/234, Tate, N
Topic. Universal Praise

57 ft C.M. Billings, W
Awake my heart, arise my tongue
Sources. WB3/105, WH1/20
Topic. Pardon

58 ft C.M. Wood, A
My passions fly to seek their king
Sources. MNAN6/4, WHor
Topic. Communion with God

ANGELS HYMN

59 pt L.M. Gibbons, O
O come, loud anthems let us sing
Sources. CR6, NV95
Topic. Worship

ANGOLA

   60   pt C.M. Belknap, D
        Down from the top of earthly bliss
        Sources. MNAN14/6, WH2/96
        Topic. Election

ANNAPOLIS

   61   ft C.M. Read, D
        Awake, ye saints, to praise your king
        Sources. DR10, WP135
        Topic. Perfections of God

ANNIVERSARY DIRGE

   62   sp Holden, O
        Is this the anniversary so dear
        Sources. MNAN13/177, Harris, T
        Topic. Secular

ANTHEM

   63   an Babcock, S
        Comfort ye, comfort ye, my people
        Sources. MNAN11/4, Bible
        Topic. Fast Day

   64   an Babcock, S
        Lord, thou hast been our dwelling place
        Sources. MNAN11/11, BP90
        Topic. Fast Day

   65   an Babcock, S
        O come, let us sing unto the Lord
        Sources. MNAN11/14, Bible
        Topic. Thanksgiving

   66   an Babcock, S
        Remember now thy creator in the days of thy youth
        Sources. MNAN11/18, Bible
        Topic. Funeral

   67   an Benham, A
        Holy, holy, holy Lord God almighty
        Sources. MNAN8/4, Bible
        Topic. Thanksgiving

   68   an Billings, W
        And I saw a mighty angel proclaiming
        Sources. WB3/46, Bible
        Topic. Day of Judgment

   69   an Billings, W
        As the hart panteth after the waterbrooks
        Sources. WB1/138, BP42
        Topic. Fear and Hope

   70   an Billings, W
        Blessed is he that considereth the poor
        Sources. WB1/340, BP34&41
        Topic. Charity

   71   an Billings, W
        Blessed is he that considereth the poor
        Sources. WB3/35, Bible
        Topic. Charity

   72   an Billings, W
        Except the Lord build the house
        Sources. WB3/236, BCPP127
        Topic. Dedication

   73   an Billings, W
        Hark! hear you not a cheerful noise
        Sources. WB4/173, Billings?
        Topic. Christmas

   74   an Billings, W
        Hear, hear, O heav'ns, and give ear, O earth
        Sources. WB4/47, Bible
        Topic. Thanksgiving

   75   an Billings, W
        Hear my pray'r, O Lord my God
        Sources. WB1/293, BP143
        Topic. Fast Day

   76   an Billings, W
        Hear my pray'r, O Lord my God
        Sources. WB2/118, BP143
        Topic. Fast Day

   77   an Billings, W
        I am come into my garden, my sister, my spouse
        Sources. WB4/113, Bible
        Topic. Solomon's Song

   78   an Billings, W
        I am the rose of Sharon and the lily of the vallies
        Sources. WB2/216, Bible
        Topic. Solomon's Song

   79   an Billings, W
        I charge you, O ye daughters of Jerusalem
        Sources. WB4/233, Bible
        Topic. Solomon's Song

   80   an Billings, W
        Is any afflicted, let him pray
        Sources. WB2/128, Bible
        Topic. Thanksgiving

   81   an Billings, W
        Let ev'ry mortal ear attend
        Sources. WB3/120, WH1/7
        Topic. Communion

   82   an Billings, W
        Lift up your eyes, ye sons of light
        Sources. WB3/177, WH2/43
        Topic. Ascension and Exaltation of Christ

   83   an Billings, W
        O clap your hands and shout for joy
        Sources. WB3/252, Morton, P
        Topic. Thanksgiving

   84   an Billings, W
        O God, my heart is fixed; I will sing and give praise
        Sources. WB4/264, BP108
        Topic. Thanksgiving

85 an Billings, W
O praise the Lord of heaven
Sources. WB4/39, BCPP148
Topic. Thanksgiving

86 an Billings, W
O thou, to whom all creatures bow
Sources. WB4/157, NV8/Bible
Topic. Ordination

87 an Billings, W
Praise the Lord, O my soul
Sources. WB3/336, BCPP103
Topic. Thanksgiving

88 an Billings, W
Sanctify a fast; call a solemn assembly
Sources. WB4/278, Bible
Topic. Fast Day

89 an Billings, W
Sing praises to the Lord, O ye saints of his
Sources. WB4/103, BP30
Topic. Thanksgiving

90 an Billings, W
Sing ye merrily unto God our strength
Sources. WB2/184, BCPP81
Topic. Thanksgiving

91 an Billings, W
The beauty of Israel is slain
Sources. WB3/24, Bible
Topic. Funeral

92 an Billings, W
The Lord descended from above
Sources. WB1/191, OV18
Topic. Perfections of God

93 an Billings, W
The Lord is king and is clothed with majesty
Sources. WB1/124, BP93
Topic. Creation and Providence

94 an Billings, W
Thou, O God, art praised in Sion
Sources. WB3/17, BCPP65
Topic. Thanksgiving

95 an Billings, W
We have heard with our ears
Sources. WB4/127, BP44
Topic. Thanksgiving

96 an Billings, W
When the Lord turn'd again the captivity of Zion
Sources. WB4/239, BCPP126
Topic. Fast Day

97 an Billings, W
Who is this that cometh from Edom
Sources. WB3/84, Bible
Topic. Easter

98 an Carpenter, E
Sing, O daughter of Sion
Sources. AA2/95, Bible
Topic. Thanksgiving

99 an Chandler, S
Hear, O heav'ns, give ear, O earth
Sources. MNAN2/141, Bible
Topic. Fast Day

100 an Cole, J
O praise the Lord, all ye nations
Sources. AA2/112, BP11
Topic. Universal Praise

101 an Doolittle, E
Ho, ev'ryone that thirsteth
Sources. MNAN15/3, Bible
Topic. Invitations and Promises

102 an Forbush, A
Behold I bring you glad tidings
Sources. AA1/123, Bible
Topic. Christmas

103 an Jenks, S
Ho, ev'ryone that thirsteth
Sources. SJ28, Bible
Topic. Invitations and Promises

104 an Jenks, S
I heard a voice from heav'n, saying unto me
Sources. SJ254, Bible
Topic. Funeral

105 an Kimball, J
O come, sing unto the Lord
Sources. MNAN12/127, BP95
Topic. Thanksgiving

106 an Kimball, J
O Lord, thou art my God, and I will exalt thee
Sources. MNAN12/134, Bible
Topic. Thanksgiving

107 an Lee, T
Behold, how good and pleasant it is
Sources. AA2/124, BP133/122
Topic. Love

108 an Moors, H
Sing unto God, ye kingdoms of the earth
Sources. AA2/131, BP68
Topic. Perfections of God

109 an Read, D
Down steers the bass with grave majestic air
Sources. DR185, Byles, M
Topic. Secular

110 an Read, D
Hear our pray'r, O Lord our God
Sources. DR191, BP143
Topic. Fast Day

111 an Read, D
I know that my redeemer lives
Sources. DR195, Bible
Topic. Easter

112 an Read, D
It is better to go to the house of mourning
Sources. DR200, Bible
Topic. Funeral

113 an Read, D
O praise the Lord, O my soul
Sources. DR292, BP103
Topic. Universal Praise

114 an Read, D
O be joyful in the Lord, all ye lands
Sources. DR202, BCPP100
Topic. Thanksgiving

115 an Read, D
O praise the Lord, O my soul
Sources. DR208, BP103
Topic. Universal Praise

116 an Read, D
There were shepherds abiding in the fields
Sources. DR212, Bible
Topic. Christmas

117 an Read, D
Let not your heart be troubled
Sources. AA2/142, Bible
Topic. Faith

118 an Tuckey, W
Jehovah reigns, let all the earth rejoice
Sources. AA2/155, NV97
Topic. Universal Praise

ANTHEM, AN

119 an Edson, L Jr
The beauty of my native land
Sources. MNAN3/48, WHor
Topic. Trust and Confidence

120 an French, J
Descend from heav'n, celestial dove
Sources. MNAN9/15, Anon.
Topic. Ordination

121 an Lyon, J
Let the shrill trumpet's warlike voice
Sources. AA2/129, NV150
Topic. Universal Praise

122 an Palfray, W
Bless the Lord, O my soul
Sources. AA2/137, Bible
Topic. Thanksgiving

123 an Stone, J
Unto us a child is born
Sources. AA1/134, Bible
Topic. Christmas

ANTHEM NO.1

124 an Mann, E
I was glad when they said unto me
Sources. MNAN4/58, Bible
Topic. Dedication

ANTHEM I

125 an Bull, A
Praise the Lord, O my soul
Sources. MNAN1/8, BCPP104
Topic. Thanksgiving

ANTHEM II

126 an Bull, A
O praise God in his holiness
Sources. MNAN1/11, BCPP150
Topic. Universal Praise

ANTHEM III

127 an Bull, A
Thou art my portion, O Lord
Sources. MNAN1/14, BCPP119
Topic. Sincerity

ANTHEM IV

128 an Bull, A
O be joyful in the Lord, all ye lands
Sources. MNAN1/18, BCPP100
Topic. Thanksgiving

ANTHEM V

129 an Bull, A
Arise, shine, O Zion, for thy light is come
Sources. MNAN1/23, Bible
Topic. Perfections of God

ANTHEM VI

130 an Bull, A
O sing unto the Lord a new song
Sources. MNAN1/26, BCPP96
Topic. Thanksgiving

ANTHEM VII

131 an Bull, A
O Lord, thou art God from everlasting
Sources. MNAN1/31, BCPP90
Topic. Fast Day

ANTHEM VIII

132 an Bull, A
Behold I bring you tidings, good tidings
Sources. AA1/117, Bible
Topic. Christmas

133 an Bull, A
Behold, I bring you tidings, good tidings
Sources. MNAN1/33, Bible
Topic. Christmas

ANTHEM IX

134   an Bull, A
       Arise, O Lord, arise into thy resting place
       Sources. MNAN1/37, BCPP132
       Topic. Ordination

ANTHEM X

135   an Bull, A
       O Lord, thou hast searched me out
       Sources. MNAN1/41, BCPP139
       Topic. Communion with God

ANTHEM XI

136   an Bull, A
       Ponder my words, O Lord
       Sources. MNAN1/45, BCPP5
       Topic. Fast Day

ANTHEM XII

137   an Bull, A
       O Lord, revive thy work in the midst of the years
       Sources. MNAN1/49, Bible
       Topic. Perfections of God

ANTHEM COMPOSED FOR A MARRIAGE

138   an Sweeny, G
       Blessed are they that fear the Lord
       Sources. AA2/89, BP128
       Topic. Marriage

ANTHEM FOR A CHARITY MEETING, AN

139   an Kimball, J
       Blessed is he that considereth the poor
       Sources. AA2/79, BP41
       Topic. Charity

ANTHEM FOR A FAST DAY

140   an Holyoke, S
       Hear our pray'r, O Lord our God
       Sources. AA1/181, BP143
       Topic. Fast Day

ANTHEM FOR A PUBLIC THANKSGIVING

141   an Robbins, C
       O give thanks unto the Lord
       Sources. AA1/99, Bible
       Topic. Thanksgiving

ANTHEM FOR DEDICATION

142   an Jenks, S
       Hail! glorious day, Hail! the assembled throng
       Sources. SJ8, Cleaveland, P
       Topic. Dedication

143   an Mann, E
       Where shall we go to seek and find
       Sources. MNAN4/133, WP132
       Topic. Dedication

ANTHEM FOR DEDICATION OR ORDINATION

144   an Lane, I
       Where shall we go to seek and find
       Sources. AA2/9, WP132
       Topic. Dedication

ANTHEM FOR EASTER

145   an Billings, W
       The Lord is ris'n indeed, Hallelujah
       Sources. CR8, Young, E
       Topic. Easter

ANTHEM FOR EASTER, AN

146   an Belcher, S
       Angels, roll the rock away
       Sources. MNAN5/10, Scott, T
       Topic. Easter

147   an Belknap, D
       See from the dungeon of the dead
       Sources. MNAN14/7, Anon.
       Topic. Easter

148   an Billings, W
       The Lord is ris'n indeed, Hallelujah
       Sources. WB3/245, Young, E
       Topic. Easter

149   an Billings, W
       The Lord is ris'n indeed, Hallelujah
       Sources. AA1/143, Young, E
       Topic. Easter

ANTHEM FOR FAST DAY, AN

150   an Billings, W
       Mourn, mourn, pharaoh and Ahab prevail in our land
       Sources. WB4/217, Bible/Billings
       Topic. Fast Day

151   an Billings, W
       Mourn, mourn, pharaoh and Ahab prevail in our land
       Sources. AA1/171, Bible/Billings
       Topic. Fast Day

152   an Holden, O
       O thou that hearest pray'r, unto thee
       Sources. MNAN13/10, Bible
       Topic. Fast Day

ANTHEM FOR ORDINATION, AN

153   an Terril, I
       Sing, O ye heav'ns, and be joyful, O earth
       Sources. AA2/52, Bible
       Topic. Ordination

ANTHEM FOR THANKSGIVING

154   an Frost, R
       O give thanks unto the Lord
       Sources. AA1/20, Bible
       Topic. Thanksgiving

155   an Holyoke, S
       O be joyful in the Lord, all ye lands
       Sources. AA1/64, BCPP100
       Topic. Thanksgiving

156   an Maxim, A
       Grateful songs and anthems bring
       Sources. AA1/81, Dodd, W
       Topic. Thanksgiving

157   an Merrill, D
       Grateful songs and anthems bring
       Sources. AA1/85, Dodd, W
       Topic. Thanksgiving

ANTHEM FOR THANKSGIVING, AN

158   an Janes, W
       Come, let us sing a new-made song
       Sources. AA1/70, BP95
       Topic. Thanksgiving

159   an Jenks, S
       Come, let us sing a new made song
       Sources. SJ18, Bible
       Topic. Thanksgiving

160   an Newhall, J
       Hail! joyful day, hail! ye harmonious choir
       Sources. AA1/92, Anon.
       Topic. Thanksgiving

161   an Cooper, W
       The Lord hath done great things for us
       Sources. AA1/10, Bible
       Topic. Thanksgiving

162   an Gram, H
       We'll sing to God with one accord
       Sources. AA1/24, Anon.
       Topic. Thanksgiving

ANTHEM FROM PSALM 119, AN

163   an French, J
       Righteous art thou, O Lord, and upright
       Sources. MNAN9/5, Bible
       Topic. Fast Day

ANTHEM FROM THE 150TH PSALM

164   an Swan, T
       Let the shrill trumpet's warlike voice
       Sources. TS2, NV150
       Topic. Universal Praise

ANTHEM IN MEMORY OF GOV. HANCOCK

165   an Rogerson, R
       Know ye not that there is a great man fall'n
       Sources. AA2/147, Anon.
       Topic. Funeral

ANTHEM OF PRAISE

166   an Herrick, J
       O praise ye the Lord
       Sources. AA2/121, BP150
       Topic. Universal Praise

ANTHEM OF PRAISE, AN

167   an Belcher, S
       Make a joyful noise unto the Lord
       Sources. MNAN5/14, BP100
       Topic. Thanksgiving

168   an West, E
       The mighty Lord, the Lord hath spoken
       Sources. MNAN7/4, Bible
       Topic. Thanksgiving

ANTHEM PERFORMED AT THE OPENING

169   an Selby, W
       Behold, he is my salvation
       Sources. AA2/18, Bible
       Topic. Dedication

ANTHEM SUNG AT THE DEDICATION

170   an Brown, B
       Hail, glorious day, hail, the assembled throng
       Sources. AA2/3, Cleaveland, P
       Topic. Dedication

ANTHEM TO FUNERAL THOUGHT

171   an Frost
       Hark! from the tombs a doleful sound
       Sources. AA2/63, WH2/63
       Topic. Funeral

APPEARANCE

172   ft L.M. Belcher, S
       The voice of my beloved sounds
       Sources. MNAN5/19, WH1/69
       Topic. Solomon's Song

APPLETON

173   xt L.M. Swan, T
       Now to the Lord a noble song
       Sources. TS16, WH2/47
       Topic. Christ

ARABIA

174   xt C.M. Wood, A
       Sweet muse, descend and bless the shade
       Sources. MNAN6/5, Anon.
       Topic. Secular

ARCHANGEL

175   pt P.M. Gillet, A
       The God of glory sends his summons forth
       Sources. MNAN2/73, WP50/2
       Topic. Day of Judgment

ARGYLE

176   xt P.M. Doolittle, E
How tedious and tasteless the hours
Sources. MNAN15/7, Newton, J
Topic. Trust and Confidence

ARISE

177   xt C.M. Jenks, S
Arise my soul, my joyful pow'rs
Sources. SJ256, WH2/82
Topic. Redemption

ARMENIA

178   xt P.M. Jenks, S
Lord of the worlds above
Sources. SJ32, WP84
Topic. Public Worship

ARNHEIM

179   pt L.M. Holyoke, S
Now for a tune of lofty praise
Sources. MNAN12/5, WH2/43
Topic. Ascension and Exaltation of Christ

ARNON

180   xt C.M. Swan, T
Great God, to thine almighty love
Sources. TS18, Steele, A
Topic. Perfections of God

ASCENSION

181   xt P.M. French, J
Hail the day that sees him rise
Sources. MNAN9/22, Wesley, C
Topic. Ascension and Exaltation of Christ

182   sp Wood, A
Jesus our triumphant head
Sources. MNAN6/6, Hart, J
Topic. Ascension and Exaltation of Christ

ASHBURNHAM

183   pt P.M. Kimball, J
O praise ye the Lord, prepare your glad voice
Sources. MNAN12/142, NV149
Topic. Universal Praise

ASHBY

184   pt P.M. Kimball, J
To spend one sacred day
Sources. MNAN12/143, WP84
Topic. Public Worship

ASHFORD

185   sp Babcock, S
Jesus is become at length
Sources. MNAN11/22, Newton, J
Topic. Exaltation of Christ

186   xt L.M. Belknap, D
Loud let the tuneful trumpet sound
Sources. MNAN14/10, Doddridge, P
Topic. Salvation

187   xt C.M. Billings, W
The Lord himself, the mighty Lord
Sources. WB1/314, NV23
Topic. Communion with God

188   pt C.M. Doolittle, E
With earnest longings of the mind
Sources. MNAN15/8, WP42
Topic. Fear and Hope

ASHHAM

189   pt L.M. Billings, W
Thou whom my soul admires above
Sources. WB2/150, WH1/67
Topic. Solomon's Song

190   pt L.M. Billings, W
Thou whom my soul admires above
Sources. WB3/278, WH1/67
Topic. Solomon's Song

ASIA

191   pt S.M. Billings, W
Defend me, Lord, from shame
Sources. WB1/214, NV31
Topic. Faith

192   pt S.M. Billings, W
Let sinners take their course
Sources. WB2/304, WP55
Topic. Worship

193   ft S.M. Read, D
When man grows bold in sin
Sources. DR12, WP36
Topic. Perfections of God

ASPIRATION

194   ft P.M. French, J
Weary world, when will it end
Sources. MNAN9/24, Wesley, C
Topic. Resignation

195   ft C.M. Wood, A
'Tis pure delight without alloy
Sources. MNAN6/9, WHor
Topic. Joy and Rejoicing

ASSOCIATION

196   xt P.M. French, J
Content, thou dear object of all our desires
Sources. MNAN9/26, Anon.
Topic. Secular

ASSURANCE

197   ft C.M. Billings, W
       Now shall my head be lifted high
       Sources. WB3/14, WP27/1
       Topic. Public Worship

ATHENS

198   pt P.M. French, J
       Touch, heav'nly word, O touch those cur'ous souls
       Sources. MNAN9/27, Anon.
       Topic. Gospel

ATONEMENT

199   ft L.M. Doolittle, E
       Yet, gracious God, thy pow'r and love
       Sources. MNAN15/10, WP69/1
       Topic. Sufferings and Death of Christ

ATTENTION

200   ft C.M. Benham, A
       Hark! from the tombs a doleful sound
       Sources. MNAN8/10, WH2/63
       Topic. Death and Resurrection

201   pt C.M. Doolittle, E
       Hark! the glad sound, the saviour comes
       Sources. MNAN15/12, Doddridge, P
       Topic. Life and Ministry of Christ

202   ft P.M. French, J
       Cease awhile ye winds to blow
       Sources. MNAN9/29, Anon.
       Topic. Secular

203   ft C.M. Jenks, S
       Unite my roving thoughts, unite
       Sources. SJ257, Doddridge, P
       Topic. Faith

ATTLEBOROUGH

204   pt S.M. Billings, W
       To God the only wise
       Sources. WB1/210, WH1/51
       Topic. Perseverance

205   xt C.M. Stone, J
       When all thy mercies, O my God
       Sources. MNAN10/4, Addison, J
       Topic. Creation and Providence

AUGUSTA

206   pt P.M. Gillet, A
       O tell me no more of this world's vain store
       Sources. MNAN2/77, Gambold, J
       Topic. Grace

AURORA

207   ft S.M. Billings, W
       Awake, my soul, awake
       Sources. WB2/37, Billings
       Topic. Morning and Evening

208   pt C.M. Doolittle, E
       Lord, in the morning thou shalt hear
       Sources. MNAN15/13, WP5
       Topic. Lord's Day

AUSPICIOUS MORN

209   xt C.M. Babcock, S
       Again the Lord of life and light
       Sources. MNAN11/24, Barbauld, A
       Topic. Worship

210   xt P.M. Holden, O
       No war or battle's sound
       Sources. MNAN13/13, Milton, J
       Topic. Birth of Christ

AUSTRIA

211   sp Holyoke, S
       Ye that obey th'immortal king
       Sources. MNAN12/7, WP134
       Topic. Public Worship

AUTUMN

212   xt L.M. Belknap, D
       'Twas spring, 'twas summer, all was gay
       Sources. MNAN14/12, Anon.
       Topic. Seasons of the Year

AYLESBURY

213   pt S.M. Anon.
       The Lord my shepherd is
       Sources. CR14, WP23
       Topic. Communion with God

BABEL

214   xt P.M. Babcock, S
       Sitting by the streams that glide
       Sources. MNAN11/25, Anon.
       Topic. Afflictions of the Church

215   ft C.M. French, J
       O all ye nations, praise the Lord
       Sources. MNAN9/30, WP117
       Topic. The Christian Church

BABEL'S STREAMS

216   xt C.M. Jenks, S
       By Babel's streams we sat and wept
       Sources. SJ34, SP137

       Topic. Afflictions of the Church

217   xt C.M. Jenks, S
       By Babel's streams we sat and wept
       Sources. SJ258, SP137
       Topic. Afflictions of the Church

BABYLON

218   xt P.M. Benham, A
       Along the banks where Babel's current flows
       Sources. MNAN8/11, BarP137
       Topic. Afflictions of the Church

219 ft P.M. French, J
Along the banks where Babel's current flows
Sources. MNAN9/33, BarP137
Topic. Afflictions of the Church

220 sp West, E
Come sing us one of Zion's songs
Sources. MNAN7/12, Anon.
Topic. Redemption

BABYLON [I]

221 ft P.M. Gillet, A
Along the banks where Babel's current flows
Sources. MNAN2/78, BarP137
Topic. Afflictions of the Church

BABYLON [II]

222 xt P.M. Gillet, A
Along the banks where Babel's current flows
Sources. MNAN2/81, BarP137
Topic. Afflictions of the Church

BAGGADUCE

223 ft L.M. French, J
Broad is the road that leads to death
Sources. MNAN9/35, WH2/158
Topic. Depravity and Fall of Man

BALLOON

224 xt L.M. Swan, T
Behold, I fall before thy face
Sources. TS19, WP51/2
Topic. Depravity and Fall of Man

225 xt L.M. Swan, T
Behold, I fall before thy face
Sources. TS301, WP51/2
Topic. Depravity and Fall of Man

BALTIC

226 pt S.M. Edson, L Jr
But I with all my cares
Sources. MNAN3/52, WP55
Topic. Worship

BALTIMORE

227 xt P.M. Billings, W
Father of mercies
Sources. WB2/165, Billings, W
Topic. Perfections of God

BANCROFT

228 xt C.M. Brownson, O
Of justice and of grace I sing
Sources. MNAN2/3, WP101
Topic. Family Worship

BANGOR

229 pt C.M. Tans'ur, W
Teach me the measure of my days
Sources. CR16, WP39/2
Topic. Time and Eternity

230 pt C.M. Tans'ur, W
In God the Lord I put my trust
Sources. WB3/342, OV11
Topic. Faith

BAPTISM

231 xt P.M. Billings, W
O! how doth God our souls surprise
Sources. WB3/188, RCH15
Topic. Baptism

BARNEY

232 pt L.M. Read, D
Kind is the speech of Christ our Lord
Sources. DR14, WH1/73
Topic. Solomon's Song

BARNSTABLE

233 xt P.M. Read, D
Hail the day that saw him rise
Sources. DR16, Wesley, C
Topic. Ascension and Exaltation of Christ

234 xt P.M. Read, D
Hail the day that saw him rise
Sources. DR245, Wesley, C
Topic. Ascension and Exaltation of Christ

BARRE

235 pt C.M. Billings, W
How glorious is our heav'nly king
Sources. WB1/243, WDMS
Topic. Universal Praise

BARRINGTON

236 ft C.M. Read, D
How long wilt thou forget me, Lord
Sources. DR19, NV13
Topic. Christian

237 ft C.M. Read, D
How long wilt thou forget me, Lord
Sources. DR247, NV13
Topic. Christian

238 xt L.M. Stone, J
Sov'reign of life, before thine eye
Sources. MNAN10/6, Doddridge, P
Topic. Fear and Hope

BARRY

239 pt C.M. Billings, W
How glorious is our heav'nly king
Sources. WB3/280, WDMS
Topic. Universal Praise

BATH

240 pt L.M. Anon.
Nature with open volume stands
Sources. CR17, WH3/10
Topic. The Lord's Supper

241   pt P.M. Belcher, S
Not to our names, thou only just and true
Sources. MNAN5/21, WP115
Topic. Perfections of God

BEAUFORT

242   pt C.M. Woodruff, M
How vain are all things here below
Sources. MNAN8/59, WH2/48
Topic. Christian

BEAUTY

243   ft L.M. French, J
We are a garden, wall'd around
Sources. MNAN9/37, WH1/74
Topic. Solomon's Song

244   xt S.M. Jenks, S
O let thy God and king
Sources. SJ260, WP45
Topic. Beauty of the Church

BEDFORD

245   pt P.M. Belknap, D
The God of glory sends his summons forth
Sources. MNAN14/14, WP50/2
Topic. Day of Judgment

246   pt S.M. Billings, W
Behold what wond'rous grace
Sources. WB3/281, WH1/64
Topic. Adoption

247   pt C.M. Brownson, O
My never ceasing songs shall show
Sources. MNAN2/4, WP89/1
Topic. Perfections of God

248   ft S.M. Edson, L Jr
To bless thy chosen race
Sources. MNAN3/53, NV67
Topic. Joy and Rejoicing

249   xt S.M. Jenks, S
How beauteous are their feet
Sources. SJ35, WH1/10
Topic. Law and Gospel

250   pt C.M. Wheall, W
Praise ye the Lord with hymns of joy
Sources. CR18, NV147
Topic. Creation and Providence

BELFAST

251   pt C.M. Belknap, D
With flowing eyes and bleeding hearts
Sources. MNAN14/17, Mason, W
Topic. Grace

BELGOROD

252.   xt C.M. French, J
And now the scales have left mine eyes
Sources. MNAN9/39, WH2/81
Topic. Christian

BELLINGHAM

253   xt C.M. Billings, W
Begin my tongue some heav'nly theme
Sources. WB4/78, WH2/69
Topic. Invitations and Promises

254   sp French, J
Come, dearest Lord, descend and dwell
Sources. MNAN9/41, WH1/135
Topic. Worship

BENEFICENCE

255   xt L.M. Billings, W
That man is blest who stands in awe
Sources. WB3/150, NV112
Topic. Liberality

256   xt P.M. Holden, O
Father of our feeble race
Sources. MNAN13/15, Taylor, J
Topic. Love

BENEVOLENCE

257   ft C.M. Billings, W
Happy the man whose tender care
Sources. WB2/213, NV41
Topic. Liberality

BENINGTON

258   pt L.M. Read, D
Had not the Lord, may Israel say
Sources. DR22, WP124
Topic. Thanksgiving

BENINGTON [I]

259   pt L.M. Read, D
Had not the Lord, may Israel say
Sources. DR249, WP124
Topic. Thanksgiving

BENINGTON [II]

260   sp Read, D
He dies! the heav'nly lover dies
Sources. DR250, WHor
Topic. Sufferings and Death of Christ

BENNINGTON

261   pt C.M. Billings, W
Shepherds rejoice, lift up your eyes
Sources. WB3/312, WHor
Topic. Birth of Christ

BERKELEY

262   xt C.M. Kimball, J
Come, let us join our cheerful songs
Sources. MNAN12/145, WH1/62
Topic. Addresses to Christ

BERKLEY

263   xt P.M. Gillet, A
The Lord my pasture shall prepare
Sources. MNAN2/83, Addison, J
Topic. Creation and Providence

BERKLY

264   xt P.M. Gillet, A
Jesus Christ the Lord's anointed
Sources. MNAN2/85, Newton, J
Topic. Characters and Offices of Christ

BERLIN

265   ft P.M. Belknap, D
The Lord Jehovah reigns, His throne
Sources. MNAN14/19, WH2/169
Topic. Perfections of God

266   xt L.M. Billings, W
He dies! the heav'nly lover dies
Sources. WB3/5, WHor
Topic. Sufferings and Death of Christ

267   xt C.M. Read, D
Stoop down my thoughts that use to rise
Sources. DR255, WH2/28
Topic. Death and Resurrection

268   xt L.M. West, E
Where are the mourners, saith the Lord
Sources. MNAN7/16, WH2/154
Topic. Justification

BERNAY

269   ft L.M. Read, D
Kind is the speech of Christ our Lord
Sources. DR256, WH1/73
Topic. Solomon's Song

BERWICK

270   pt L.M. Bull, A
Great God, attend while Zion sings
Sources. MNAN1/54, WP84/2
Topic. Public Worship

271   ft C.M. French, J
Speak, O ye judges of the earth
Sources. MNAN9/44, NV58
Topic. Magistracy

BETHANY

272   ft L.M. French, J
Mourn, mourn, ye saints, who once did see
Sources. MNAN9/46, Anon.
Topic. Sufferings and Death of Christ

BETHEL

273   xt L.M. Holyoke, S
Lord, I will bless thee all my days
Sources. MNAN12/9, WP34/1
Topic. Church Meetings

BETHESDA

274   pt P.M. Anon.
Lord of the worlds above
Sources. CR20, WP84
Topic. Public Worship

275   xt P.M. West, E
If your heart is unbelieving
Sources. MNAN7/17, Anon.
Topic. Faith

BETHLEHEM

276   ft C.M. Billings, W
While shepherds watch their flocks by night
Sources. WB2/207, Tate, N
Topic. Birth of Christ

277   sp West, E
While shepherds watch their flocks by night
Sources. MNAN7/18, Tate, N
Topic. Birth of Christ

BETHSAIDA

278   ft S.M. Holden, O
Beside the gospel pool
Sources. MNAN13/16, Newton, J
Topic. Resignation

BIRD, THE

279   ft C.M. Billings, W
Since I have plac'd my trust in God
Sources. WB3/225, NV11
Topic. Saints and Sinners

BLEEDING LOVE

280   sp Jenks, S
Not all the blood of beasts
Sources. SJ261, WH2/142
Topic. Faith

BLENDON

281   xt C.M. Belknap, D
Our sins, alas! how strong they be
Sources. MNAN14/21, WH2/86
Topic. Hell and Heaven

BLESSING OF THE SPRING

282   ft C.M. Billings, N
       Good is the Lord, the heav'nly king
       Sources. MNAN3/89, WP65/3
       Topic. Seasons of the Year

BLISS

283   ft C.M. Belcher, S
       My thoughts surmount these lower skies
       Sources. MNAN5/24, WH2/162
       Topic. Faith

BLOOMS TO DIE

284   pt L.M. Jenks, S
       So fades the lovely blooming flow'r
       Sources. SJ265, Steele, A
       Topic. Faith

BLUE HILL

285   ft L.M. Belknap, D
       Eternal pow'r, whose high abode
       Sources. MNAN14/22, WHor
       Topic. Universal Praise

BOLSOVER

286   pt L.M. Holyoke, S
       Almighty ruler of the skies
       Sources. MNAN12/10, WP8/1
       Topic. Times and Seasons

BOLTON

287   ft P.M. Billings, W
       Rejoice, the Lord is king
       Sources. WB2/116, Wesley, C
       Topic. Dominion of Christ

288   pt P.M. Brownson, O
       I'll praise my maker with my breath
       Sources. MNAN2/5, WP146
       Topic. Perfections of God

BONDAGE

289   ft P.M. Swan, T
       Along the banks where Babel's current flows
       Sources. TS22, BarP137
       Topic. Afflictions of the Church

BOSTON

290   xt C.M. Billings, W
       Shepherds rejoice, lift up your eyes
       Sources. WB1/120, WHor
       Topic. Birth of Christ

291   xt C.M. Billings, W
       Methinks I see a heav'nly host
       Sources. WB2/40, Billings, W
       Topic. Birth of Christ

292   ft C.M. Edson, L
       My trust is in my heav'nly friend
       Sources. MNAN3/8, WP7
       Topic. Christian

BOXBOROUGH

293   xt S.M. Wood, A
       Like sheep we went astray
       Sources. MNAN6/12, WH1/142
       Topic. Ascension and Exaltation of Christ

BOXFORD

294   ft L.M. Kimball, J
       The lands which long in darkness lay
       Sources. MNAN12/147, WH1/13
       Topic. Characters and Offices of Christ

295   ft S.M. Swan, T
       My sorrows, like a flood
       Sources. TS24, WHor
       Topic. Pardon

BOYLSTON

296   xt P.M. Belknap, D
       Great father of mankind
       Sources. MNAN14/24, Doddridge, P
       Topic. Prayer and Praise for the Church

297   ft C.M. Billings, N
       Sing all ye nations to the Lord
       Sources. MNAN3/91, WP66/1
       Topic. Perfections of God

298   sp Mann, E
       Arise, O king of grace, arise
       Sources. MNAN4/50, WP132
       Topic. The Christian Church

BRADFORD

299   xt C.M. Belknap, D
       These glorious minds, how bright they shine
       Sources. MNAN14/25, WH1/41
       Topic. Hell and Heaven

300   xt C.M. Billings, W
       O for a shout of sacred joy
       Sources. WB3/314, WP47
       Topic. Ascension and Exaltation of Christ

301   xt C.M. Kimball, J
       How short and hasty is our life
       Sources. MNAN12/148, WH2/32
       Topic. Time and Eternity

302   pt P.M. Wood, A
       Uprising from the darksome tomb
       Sources. MNAN6/13, Hart, J
       Topic. Resurrection of Christ

BRAINTREE

303   pt P.M. Billings, W
God is our refuge in distress
Sources. WB1/164, NV46
Topic. The Christian Church

BRANDON

304   sp Holyoke, S
The scatter'd clouds are fled at last
Sources. MNAN12/12, Anon.
Topic. Secular

BRANFORD

305   xt C.M. Benham, A
Save me, O God, the swelling floods
Sources. MNAN8/14, WP69/1
Topic. Sufferings and Death of Christ

BRATTLE SQUARE

306   pt C.M. Billings, W
Come, let us join our cheerful songs
Sources. WB3/148, WH1/62
Topic. Addresses to Christ

BRATTLE STREET

307   xt L.M. Billings, W
With one consent let all the earth
Sources. WB1/107, NV100
Topic. Universal Praise

308   ft L.M. Billings, W
Sweet is the work, my God, my king
Sources. WB3/161, WP92/1
Topic. Lord's Day

BRENT

309   pt L.M. Holyoke, S
Eternal spirit, we confess
Sources. MNAN12/14, WH2/133
Topic. Addresses to the Holy Spirit

BRENTWOOD

310   ft S.M. Kimball, J
Not all the blood of beasts
Sources. MNAN12/150, WH2/142
Topic. Faith

BREST

311   pt L.M. Billings, W
Mercy and judgment are my song
Sources. WB2/280, WP101
Topic. Magistracy

BREVITY

312   pt C.M. Wood, A
Man, born of woman, like a flow'r
Sources. MNAN6/15, Anon.
Topic. Death and Resurrection

BRIDGEPORT

313   ft P.M. Doolittle, E
O God of my salvation hear
Sources. MNAN15/14, BarP88
Topic. Fear and Hope

BRIDGEWATER

314   ft L.M. Edson, L
My soul thy great creator praise
Sources. CR22, WP104
Topic. Creation and Providence

315   ft L.M. Edson, L
O come, loud anthems let us sing
Sources. MNAN3/9, NV95
Topic. Worship

BRIDGWATER

316   pt L.M. Billings, W
Majestyck God, when I descry
Sources. WB1/154, Billings, W
Topic. Creation and Providence

BRIGHT GLORY

317   xt P.M. Jenks, S
Our bondage here shall end
Sources. SJ266, Anon.
Topic. Death and Resurrection

BRIGHT REVERSION

318   xt L.M. Holden, O
When conscious grief laments sincere
Sources. MNAN13/18, Steele, A
Topic. Faith

BRIMFIELD

319   pt S.M. Jenks, S
Sure there's a righteous God
Sources. SJ36, WP73
Topic. Creation and Providence

320   ft C.M. Stone, J
To thine almighty arm we owe
Sources. MNAN10/8, WP18/2
Topic. Thanksgiving

BRISTOL

321   ft L.M. Swan, T
The lofty pillars of the sky
Sources. CR24, Addison, J
Topic. Universal Praise

322   ft L.M. Swan, T
Rejoice, you shining worlds on high
Sources. TS26, WP24
Topic. Ascension and Exaltation of Christ

323   ft L.M. Swan, T
The lofty pillars of the sky
Sources. TS303, Addison, J
Topic. Universal Praise

BRITAIN

324   ft L.M. French, J
Great God, to thee my voice I raise
Sources. MNAN9/48, WDMS
Topic. Thanksgiving

BRITTANIA

325   pt P.M. Edson, L
Begin, my soul, th'exalted lay
Sources. MNAN3/11, Oglivie, J
Topic. Universal Praise

BROAD COVE

326   ft C.M. Billings, W
Time! what an empty vapor 'tis
Sources. WB4/191, WH2/58
Topic. Time and Eternity

BROMSGROVE

327   pt C.M. Anon.
My soul come meditate the day
Sources. CR27, WH2/61
Topic. Death and Resurrection

BROOKFIELD

328   pt L.M. Billings, W
Shall the vile race of flesh and blood
Sources. CR28, WH1/82
Topic. Perfections of God

329   pt L.M. Billings, W
'Twas on that dark, that doleful night
Sources. WB1/64, WH3/1
Topic. The Lord's Supper

330   pt L.M. Billings, W
'Twas on that dark, that doleful night
Sources. WB2/48, WH3/1
Topic. The Lord's Supper

331   pt S.M. Chandler, S
My thirsty, fainting soul
Sources. MNAN2/145, WP63
Topic. Lord's Day

332   ft L.M. Stone, J
Would you behold the works of God
Sources. MNAN10/9, WP107/4
Topic. Creation and Providence

BROOKLINE

333   pt C.M. Billings, W
The heav'ns declare thy glory, Lord
Sources. WB1/42, NV19
Topic. Scripture

334   pt C.M. Billings, W
The heav'ns declare thy glory, Lord
Sources. WB2/300, NV19
Topic. Scripture

BROOKLYN

335   pt L.M. Stone, J
O wash my soul from ev'ry sin
Sources. MNAN10/12, WP51/1
Topic. Christian

BROOKLYNE

336   xt S.M. Jenks, S
Come, sound his praise abroad
Sources. SJ38, WP95
Topic. Worship

BRUNSWICK

337   xt C.M. Billings, W
Stoop down, my thoughts, that use to rise
Sources. WB2/57, WH2/28
Topic. Death and Resurrection

338   pt L.M. Holyoke, S
From age to age exalt his name
Sources. MNAN12/15, WP107/2
Topic. The Jewish Church

BUCKINGHAM

339   pt C.M. Anon.
Lord thou wilt hear me when I pray
Sources. CR29, WP4
Topic. Times and Seasons

340   pt C.M. Anon.
Help, Lord, for good and godly men
Sources. WB3/344, OV12
Topic. Perseverance

BUCKLAND

341   xt P.M. Brownson, O
Th'eternal speaks, all heav'n attends
Sources. MNAN2/7, Anon.
Topic. Redemption

BUNKER HILL

342   xt C.M. Wood, A
We are expos'd all day to die
Sources. MNAN6/16, WP44
Topic. The Christian Church

BURFORD

343   pt C.M. Anon.
Indulgent God, with pitying eyes
Sources. CR30, Doddridge, P
Topic. Redemption

BURLINGTON

344   xt P.M. Billings, W
Canaan promis'd is before
Sources. WB3/210, RCH3
Topic. Faith

345   pt C.M. Holyoke, S
Awake, my soul, to sound his praise
Sources. MNAN12/16, BarP108
Topic. Universal Praise

346   xt C.M. Kimball, J
Let others boast how strong they be
Sources. MNAN12/152, WH2/19
Topic. Creation and Providence

347   pt P.M. Read, D
Disciples of Christ, Ye friends of the lamb
Sources. DR24, Anon.
Topic. Addresses to Christ

BURTON

348   xt L.M. West, E
Lord, what a thoughtless wretch was I
Sources. MNAN7/23, WP73
Topic. The World

BURWICK

349   xt L.M. Swan, T
Now for a tune of lofty praise
Sources. TS28, WH2/43
Topic. Ascension and Exaltation of Christ

BUXTON

350   xt C.M. Belknap, D
Shout to the Lord, ye surging seas
Sources. MNAN14/27, WP148/2
Topic. Universal Praise

351   xt C.M. French, J
Hark! from the tombs a doleful sound
Sources. MNAN9/51, WH2/63
Topic. Death and Resurrection

352   xt S.M. Holyoke, S
Faith! 'tis a precious grace
Sources. MNAN12/17, Beddome, B
Topic. Faith

BYFIELD

353   ft C.M. Kimball, J
Shout to the Lord, and let your joys
Sources. MNAN12/153, WH2/92
Topic. Thanksgiving

BYFORD

354   pt P.M. Brownson, O
Not to our names, thou only just and true
Sources. MNAN2/9, WP115
Topic. Perfections of God

355   pt P.M. Jenks, S
How tedious and tasteless the hours
Sources. SJ268, Newton, J
Topic. Trust and Confidence

CALEDONIA

356   sp Babcock, S
I will praise thee ev'ry day
Sources. MNAN11/26, Newton, J
Topic. Thanksgiving

CALIFORNIA

357   xt C.M. Kimball, J
Thou whom my soul admires above
Sources. MNAN12/155, WH1/67
Topic. Solomon's Song

CALVARY

358   pt C.M. Billings, W
Methinks I see my saviour dear
Sources. WB2/319, Watts?
Topic. Sufferings and Death of Christ

359   pt P.M. Holyoke, S
See the Lord of glory dying
Sources. MNAN12/19, Anon.
Topic. Ascension and Exaltation of Christ

360   ft C.M. Read, D
My thoughts, that often mount the skies
Sources. CR31, WHor
Topic. Death and Resurrection

361   ft C.M. Read, D
My thoughts, that often mount the skies
Sources. DR26, WHor
Topic. Death and Resurrection

362   sp Swan, T
Infinite grief, amazing woe
Sources. TS30, WH2/95
Topic. Christian

CALVERT

363   pt C.M. Doolittle, E
Eat, O my friends, the saviour cries
Sources. MNAN15/16, Stennett, S
Topic. The Lord's Supper

CAMBRIDGE

364   sp Babcock, S
With one consent let all the earth
Sources. MNAN11/28, NV100
Topic. Universal Praise

365   pt P.M. Billings, W
Ye that delight to serve the Lord
Sources. WB1/178, WP113
Topic. Perfections of God

366 pt L.M. Billings, W
Ye that delight to serve the Lord
Sources. WB2/75, WP113
Topic. Perfections of God

367 ft L.M. Brownson, O
Deep in our hearts, let us record
Sources. MNAN2/11, WP69/1
Topic. Sufferings and Death of Christ

CAMDEN

368 xt L.M. Billings, W
My soul thy great creator praise
Sources. WB3/154, WP104
Topic. Creation and Providence

369 xt P.M. Holden, O
The God of glory sends his summons forth
Sources. MNAN13/20, WP50/2
Topic. Day of Judgment

370 xt C.M. Read, D
Out of the deeps of long distress
Sources. DR28, WP130
Topic. Pardon

CANA

371 xt P.M. Babcock, S
Praise to God, immortal praise
Sources. MNAN11/30, Barbauld, A
Topic. Thanksgiving

CANAAN

372. ft C.M. Edson, L
Salvation, O the joyful sound
Sources. MNAN3/13, WH2/88
Topic. Salvation

373 ft L.M. Jenks, S
I send the joys of earth away
Sources. SJ39, WH2/11
Topic. Christian

374 xt C.M. Read, D
There is a land of pure delight
Sources. DR30, WH2/66
Topic. Death and Resurrection

375 xt C.M. Swan, T
How sweet the voice, how sweet the hand
Sources. TS36, Anon.
Topic. Intercession of Christ

CANADA

376. xt L.M. Doolittle, E
Behold, I fall before thy face
Sources. MNAN15/17, WP51/2
Topic. Depravity and Fall of Man

CANDIA

377. ft P.M. Wood, A
The God of glory sends his summons forth
Sources. MNAN6/17, WP50/2
Topic. Day of Judgment

CANNON OF FOUR IN ONE, A

378 canon P.M. French, J
Hark! ye mortals, hear the trumpet
Sources. MNAN9/53, Anon.
Topic. Day of Judgment

CANON OF 4 IN 1, A

379 canon L.M. Billings, W
Now to the pow'r of God supreme
Sources. WB1/177, WH1/137
Topic. Salvation

380 canon L.M. Billings, W
When Jesus wept, the falling tear
Sources. WB1/203, Morton, P
Topic. Sufferings and Death of Christ

381 canon L.M. Billings, W
Thus saith the high and lofty one
Sources. WB1/303, WH1/87
Topic. Invitations and Promises

CANON OF 6 IN ONE, A

382 canon P.M. Billings, W
Wake ev'ry breath, and ev'ry string
Sources. WB1/39, Byles, M
Topic. Universal Praise

CANTERBURY

383 pt C.M. Anon.
Why do we mourn departing friends
Sources. CR33, WH2/3
Topic. Death and Resurrection

CANTON

384 xt P.M. Belcher, S
Glorious Jesus! glorious Jesus
Sources. MNAN5/26, RCH84
Topic. Addresses to Christ

385 pt L.M. Belknap, D
Sweet is the day of sacred rest
Sources. MNAN14/28, WP92/1
Topic. Lord's Day

386 ft C.M. Holden, O
How did my heart rejoice to hear
Sources. MNAN13/23, WP122
Topic. Public Worship

387 ft L.M. Swan, T
When, marching to thy blest abode
Sources. TS39, NV68
Topic. The Jewish Church

CAPTIVITY

388 xt L.M. Belcher, S
When we, our weary limbs to rest
Sources. MNAN5/27, NV137
Topic. Afflictions of the Church

389 ft P.M. Edson, L Jr
Along the banks where Babel's current flows
Sources. MNAN3/54, BarP137
Topic. Afflictions of the Church

390 ft P.M. Jenks, S
Along the banks where Babel's current flows
Sources. SJ41, BarP137
Topic. Afflictions of the Church

391 ft P.M. Woodruff, M
Along the banks where Babel's current flows
Sources. MNAN8/61, BarP137
Topic. Afflictions of the Church

CARDIGAN

392 pt L.M. Holyoke, S
O thou, that hear'st when sinners cry
Sources. MNAN12/20, WP51/3
Topic. Christian

CARLISLE

393 ft C.M. Belknap, D
Now shall my inward joys arise
Sources. MNAN14/29, WH1/39
Topic. Safety and Triumph of the Church

394 xt P.M. Stone, J
Rejoice in glorious hope
Sources. MNAN10/13, Wesley, C
Topic. Trust and Confidence

CARLO

395 ft L.M. Edson, L Jr
Bless, O my soul, the living God
Sources. MNAN3/56, WP103/1
Topic. Perfections of God

CAROL

396 ft C.M. Belcher, S
While shepherds watch'd their flocks by night
Sources. MNAN5/29, Tate, N
Topic. Birth of Christ

CAROLINA

397 ft L.M. French, J
O Israel's shepherd, Joseph's guide
Sources. MNAN9/54, NV80
Topic. Trust and Confidence

CARTHAGENA

398 xt P.M. Holyoke, S
The God of glory sends his summons forth
Sources. MNAN12/22, WP50/2
Topic. Day of Judgment

CASTILE

399 ft P.M. French, J
Come let us sing unto the Lord
Sources. MNAN9/57, Billings, W
Topic. Universal Praise

CASTLE ISLAND

400 pt L.M. French, J
Great God, whom heav'nly hosts obey
Sources. MNAN9/58, Anon.
Topic. Fear and Hope

CELESTIAL

401 xt C.M. West, E
Down by the bank of gentle Thames
Sources. MNAN7/25, WHor
Topic. Secular

CHAMPLAIN

402 sp Holyoke, S
Angels, roll the rock away
Sources. MNAN12/26, Scott, T
Topic. Resurrection of Christ

CHARITY

403 sp Babcock, S
Had I the tongues of Greeks and Jews
Sources. MNAN11/31, WH1/134
Topic. Love

CHARLESTOWN

404 ft C.M. Read, D
When God reveal'd his gracious name
Sources. DR32, WP126
Topic. Church Meetings

CHARLTON

405 xt P.M. French, J
How pleas'd and blest was I
Sources. MNAN9/59, WP122
Topic. Public Worship

406 ft P.M. Stone, J
Yes, the redeemer rose
Sources. MNAN10/15, Doddridge, P
Topic. Resurrection of Christ

CHASTISEMENT

407 pt C.M. Doolittle, E
I know thy judgments, Lord, are right
Sources. MNAN15/19, WP119/14
Topic. Sickness and Recovery

CHATHAM

408 ft P.M. Benham, A
How pleas'd and blest was I
Sources. MNAN8/16, WP122
Topic. Public Worship

CHELSEA

409 pt L.M. Billings, W
He reigns; the Lord, the saviour reigns
Sources. WB1/180, WP97/1
Topic. Day of Judgment

410   pt P.M. Billings, W
       What beauties divine
       Sources. WB3/208, RCH43
       Topic. Redemption

411   xt L.M. Holyoke, S
       Great God, thy glories shall employ
       Sources. MNAN12/45, WH2/167
       Topic. Perfections of God

CHESTER

412   pt C.M. Belcher, S
       How shall the young secure their hearts
       Sources. MNAN5/31, WP119/4
       Topic. Scripture

413   pt L.M. Billings, W
       Let the high heav'ns your songs invite
       Sources. CR34, Doddridge, P
       Topic. Universal Praise

414   pt L.M. Billings, W
       Let tyrants shake their iron rod
       Sources. WB1/321, Billings, W
       Topic. Faith

415   pt L.M. Billings, W
       Let tyrants shake their iron rod
       Sources. WB2/72, Billings, W
       Topic. Faith

CHESTERFIELD

416   pt C.M. Billings, W
       Death may dissolve my body now
       Sources. WB1/224, WH1/27
       Topic. Death and Resurrection

417   ft P.M. Jenks, S
       How pleasant 'tis to see
       Sources. SJ42, WP133
       Topic. Public Worship

CHILD'S REQUEST, THE

418   xt L.M. Edson, L
       Thou giver of my life and joy
       Sources. MNAN3/14, Anon.
       Topic. Humility

CHINA

419   xt L.M. Babcock, S
       Nature, with all her pow'rs shall sing
       Sources. MNAN11/33, WH2/1
       Topic. Thanksgiving

420   ft C.M. French, J
       O praise the Lord with one consent
       Sources. MNAN9/60, NV135
       Topic. Perfections of God

421   pt C.M. Swan, T
       Why should we mourn departing friends
       Sources. TS48, WH2/3
       Topic. Death and Resurrection

CHOCKSETT

422   xt P.M. Billings, W
       Lord of the worlds above
       Sources. WB2/168, WP84
       Topic. Public Worship

CHOICE

423   xt S.M. Jenks, S
       Let sinners take their course
       Sources. SJ269, WP55
       Topic. Worship

CHOSEN RACE

424   ft S.M. Holden, O
       To bless thy chosen race
       Sources. MNAN13/25, NV67
       Topic. Joy and Rejoicing

CHRISTIAN LOVE

425   pt S.M. Jenks, S
       Blest be the tie that binds
       Sources. SJ44, Fawcett, J
       Topic. Love

CHRISTIAN SOLDIER

426   xt S.M. Read, D
       Soldiers of Christ, arise
       Sources. DR34, Wesley, C
       Topic. Trust and Confidence

CHRISTIAN SOLDIER, THE

427   xt P.M. Jenks, S
       O brothers be faithful
       Sources. SJ270, Anon.
       Topic. Perseverance

CHRISTIANITY

428   sp French, J
       'Tis by the faith of joys to come
       Sources. MNAN9/63, WH2/129
       Topic. Faith

CHRISTIAN'S HOPE

429   sp Babcock, S
       Hear what the voice of heav'n proclaims
       Sources. MNAN11/35, WH1/18
       Topic. Death and Resurrection

CHRISTMAS

430   sp Babcock, S
       Shout, shout for joy, rejoice, O earth
       Sources. MNAN11/37, Richards, G
       Topic. Birth of Christ

431   xt S.M. Holden, O
       Behold the grace appears
       Sources. MNAN13/27, WH1/3
       Topic. Birth of Christ

432. xt P.M. Madan, M
Lift up your heads in joyful hope
Sources. CR35, Anon.
Topic. Birth of Christ

CHRISTMAS ANTHEM

433. an Lane, I
Shepherds rejoice, lift up your eyes
Sources. AA1/128, WHor
Topic. Christmas

CHRISTMAS-EVE

434. pt C.M. Doolittle, E
While shepherds watch'd their flocks by night
Sources. MNAN15/21, Tate, N
Topic. Birth of Christ

CHRISTMAS HYMN

435. xt P.M. Mann, E
Hark! how all the welkin rings
Sources. MNAN4/18, Wesley, C
Topic. Birth of Christ

436. xt P.M. Stone, J
O sight of anguish, view it near
Sources. MNAN10/16, Anon.
Topic. Birth of Christ

CHRISTMAS ODE

437. sp Olmsted, T
Great day of grace! when spake th'eternal God
Sources. MNAN15/87, Anon.
Topic. Birth of Christ

CHRISTIAN'S-HOPE

438. xt L.M. Doolittle, E
My flesh shall slumber in the ground
Sources. MNAN15/20, WP17
Topic. Saints and Sinners

CHURCH STREET

439. pt P.M. Jenks, S
O praise ye the Lord, prepare your glad voice
Sources. SJ271, NV149
Topic. Universal Praise

CIRCASSIA

440. xt L.M. Olmsted, T
The voice of my beloved sounds
Sources. MNAN15/90, WH1/69
Topic. Solomon's Song

CLAPBOARDTREE GROVE

441. xt C.M. Belknap, D
The gentle breeze which through the grove
Sources. MNAN14/31, Anon.
Topic. Trust and Confidence

CLAPBOARDTREES

442. ft C.M. Jenks, S
Wave your tall heads, ye lofty pines
Sources. SJ45, WHor
Topic. Universal Praise

CLARADON

443. pt P.M. Swan, T
O come, let us join, together combine
Sources. TS49, Anon.
Topic. Exaltation of Christ

CLAREMONT

444. xt P.M. Billings, W
Arise, and hail the sacred day
Sources. WB4/230, Anon.
Topic. Resurrection of Christ

CLIO

445. pt P.M. Woodruff, M
Come to Jesus, come away
Sources. MNAN8/63, Anon.
Topic. Invitations and Promises

CLOVERHILL

446. xt P.M. Wood, A
Great God, the heav'n's well order'd frame
Sources. MNAN6/21, WP19
Topic. Scripture

COBHAM

447. xt C.M. Billings, W
Teach me the measure of my days
Sources. WB4/276, WP39/2
Topic. Time and Eternity

COELESTIS

448. xt P.M. French, J
Rise, my soul, and stretch thy wings
Sources. MNAN9/66, Seagrave, R
Topic. Christian

COHASSET

449. ft L.M. Billings, W
Life is the time to serve the Lord
Sources. WB4/80, WH1/88
Topic. Time and Eternity

COLCHESTER

450. pt P.M. Brownson, O
Great God, the heav'n's well order'd frame
Sources. MNAN2/12, WP19
Topic. Scripture

451. ft S.M. French, J
Let sinners take their course
Sources. MNAN9/68, WP55
Topic. Worship

452   pt C.M. Tans'ur, W
O, 'twas a joyful sound to hear
Sources. CR37, NV122
Topic. Public Worship

COLESHILL

453   pt C.M. Anon.
Lord, what is man, poor feeble man
Sources. CR38, WP144/2
Topic. Time and Eternity

COLUMBIA

454   xt P.M. Billings, W
Not all the pow'rs on earth
Sources. WB2/182, Billings, W
Topic. Faith

455   xt P.M. Jenks, S
In vain the noisy crowd
Sources. SJ46, WP93/2
Topic. Perfections of God

456   pt P.M. Swan, T
Columbia, trust the Lord; thy foes in vain
Sources. TS51, Anon.
Topic. Patriotic

457   ft L.M. West, E
All ye bright armies of the skies
Sources. MNAN7/27, WP97/2
Topic. Birth of Christ

COLUMBIA'S GUARDIAN SLEEPS

458   xt P.M. Holden, O
What mournful strains invade our ears
Sources. MNAN13/169, Anon.
Topic. Patriotic

COLUMBUS

459   ft S.M. Jenks, S
Thus will the church below
Sources. SJ48, Beddome, B
Topic. Beauty of the Church

COME LORD JESUS

460   sp Woodruff, M
Now let our cheerful eyes survey
Sources. MNAN8/65, WHor
Topic. Day of Judgment

COME YE SINNERS

461   xt P.M. Jenks, S
Come, ye sinners, poor and wretched
Sources. SJ273, Hart, J
Topic. Invitations and Promises

COMMAND

462   pt P.M. French, J
Arise ye bright nations and honor your maker
Sources. MNAN9/69, Anon.
Topic. Thanksgiving

COMMUNION

463   sp French, J
Father, we wait to feel thy grace
Sources. MNAN9/71, WH3/24
Topic. The Lord's Supper

COMPASSION

464   ft S.M. Holden, O
Did Christ o'er sinners weep
Sources. MNAN13/30, Beddome, B
Topic. Atonement

465   pt S.M. Jenks, S
Did Christ o'er sinners die
Sources. SJ49, Beddome, B
Topic. Atonement

466   ft C.M. Jenks, S
How condescending; and how kind
Sources. SJ275, WH3/4
Topic. The Lord's Supper

COMPLAINT

467   xt C.M. Benham, A
O were I like a feather'd dove
Sources. MNAN8/18, WP55
Topic. Christian

468   ft C.M. French, J
Why hast thou cast us off, O God
Sources. MNAN9/73, NV74
Topic. Fear and Hope

469   xt S.M. Jenks, S
My sorrows, like a flood
Sources. SJ50, WHor
Topic. Pardon

470   pt S.M. Jenks, S
My sorrows, like a flood
Sources. SJ277, WHor
Topic. Pardon

471   ft P.M. Read, D
'Twas in a vale where osiers grow
Sources. DR37, WHor
Topic. Sincerity

COMPLAINT, THE

472   ft P.M. Read, D
'Twas in a vale where osiers grow
Sources. DR258, WHor
Topic. Sincerity

CONCERT HALL

473   xt C.M. Swan, T
Let all the just to God, with joy
Sources. TS55, NV33
Topic. Creation and Providence

CONCLUDING ANTHEM, A

474   an Holden, O
      The Lord is good to all, and his tender mercies
      Sources. MNAN13/31, Bible
      Topic. Thanksgiving

CONCORD

475   xt L.M. Belknap, D
      'Tis finish'd! so the saviour cried
      Sources. MNAN14/33, Stennett, S
      Topic. Sufferings and Death of Christ

476   pt C.M. Billings, W
      Lord, hear the voice of my complaint
      Sources. WB1/58, NV64
      Topic. Faith

477   ft S.M. Holden, O
      The hill of Zion yields
      Sources. MNAN13/36, WH2/30
      Topic. Joy and Rejoicing

478   xt C.M. Kimball, J
      Glory to God who walks the sky
      Sources. MNAN12/156, WH2/59
      Topic. Joy and Rejoicing

479   xt P.M. Woodruff, M
      Hail the day that sees him rise
      Sources. MNAN8/70, Wesley, C
      Topic. Ascension and Exaltation of Christ

CONDESCENSION

480   xt L.M. Read, D
      Hark! the redeemer from on high
      Sources. DR40, WH1/70
      Topic. Solomon's Song

CONFESSION

481   sp Jenks, S
      Lord, I am vile, conceived in sin
      Sources. SJ51, WP51/2
      Topic. Depravity and Fall of Man

CONFIDENCE

482   xt L.M. Holden, O
      Now can my soul in God rejoice
      Sources. MNAN13/37, Alline, H
      Topic. Joy and Rejoicing

CONNECTICUT

483   ft P.M. French, J
      Come let us sing unto the Lord
      Sources. MNAN9/76, Billings, W
      Topic. Universal Praise

CONNECTION

484   pt S.M. Billings, W
      Great is the Lord our God
      Sources. WB2/256, WP48
      Topic. The Christian Church

485   pt S.M. Billings, W
      Hail! sacred music hail
      Sources. WB4/296, Billings?
      Topic. Music

CONQUEST

486   xt P.M. Billings, W
      Sing the triumphs of your conqu'ring
      Sources. WB3/198, RCH94
      Topic. Ascension and Exaltation of Christ

CONSECRATION

487   xt P.M. Babcock, S
      Change me, O God, my flesh shall be
      Sources. MNAN11/39, WHor
      Topic. Trust and Confidence

CONSOLATION

488   xt C.M. Billings, W
      He's come, let ev'ry knee be bent
      Sources. WB2/98, Bedford, A
      Topic. Redemption

489   pt P.M. Jenks, S
      Children of the heav'nly king
      Sources. SJ278, Cennick, J
      Topic. Christian

490   xt P.M. Woodruff, M
      What good news the angels bring
      Sources. MNAN8/72, Hammond, W
      Topic. Birth of Christ

CONSONANCE

491   an Billings, W
      Down steers the bass with grave majestic air
      Sources. WB3/113, Byles, M
      Topic. Secular

CONSUMATION

492   pt P.M. Benham, A
      The God of glory sends his summons forth
      Sources. MNAN8/19, WP50/2
      Topic. Day of Judgment

CONSUMMATION

493   xt S.M. Belknap, D
      Behold, with awful pomp
      Sources. MNAN14/35, Hart, J
      Topic. Day of Judgment

CONTENT

494   xt P.M. Belcher, S
      I am not concern'd to know
      Sources. MNAN5/32, WHor
      Topic. Prudence

CONTENTMENT

495   pt S.M. Bull, A
      Welcome, sweet day of rest
      Sources. MNAN1/55, WH2/14
      Topic. Worship

496   ft S.M. French, J
       The Lord my shepherd is
       Sources. MNAN9/77, WP23
       Topic. Communion with God

497   ft S.M. Jenks, S
       Let sinners take their course
       Sources. SJ54, WP55
       Topic. Worship

CONVERSION

498   ft C.M. Belcher, S
       When God reveal'd his gracious name
       Sources. MNAN5/33, WP126
       Topic. Church Meetings

CONVICTION

499   ft C.M. Billings, N
       How long wilt thou forget me, Lord
       Sources. MNAN3/93, NV13
       Topic. Christian

500   xt S.M. French, J
       Alas, my aching heart
       Sources. MNAN9/79, WHor
       Topic. Pardon

COOPERSTOWN

501   ft L.M. Billings, N
       Let Zion praise the mighty God
       Sources. MNAN3/96, WP147/2
       Topic. Seasons of the Year

CORONATION

502   xt C.M. Holden, O
       All hail the pow'r of Jesus' name
       Sources. CR39, Perronet, E
       Topic. Characters and Offices of Christ

503   xt C.M. Holden, O
       All hail the pow'r of Jesus' name
       Sources. MNAN13/39, Perronet, E
       Topic. Characters and Offices of Christ

CORSICA

504   xt C.M. Billings, W
       The Lord almighty is a God
       Sources. WB1/174, Morton, P
       Topic. Perfections of God

COVENTRY

505   xt L.M. French, J
       The sun may set beyond the main
       Sources. MNAN9/81, Anon.
       Topic. Death and Resurrection

506   xt S.M. Olmsted, T
       Far as thy name is known
       Sources. MNAN15/92, WP48/2
       Topic. The Christian Church

507   pt S.M. Read, D
       Let strangers walk around
       Sources. DR42, WP48/2
       Topic. The Christian Church

COWPER

508   ft L.M. Holden, O
       Forgive the song that falls so low
       Sources. MNAN13/40, Cowper, W
       Topic. Humility

CRADLE HYMN

509   ft P.M. Woodruff, M
       Hush, my dear, lie still and slumber
       Sources. MNAN8/74, WDMS
       Topic. Trust and Confidence

CREATION

510   pt L.M. Belcher, S
       The spacious firmament on high
       Sources. MNAN5/34, Addison, J
       Topic. Perfections of God

511   pt C.M. Billings, W
       When I with pleasing wonder stand
       Sources. WB2/276, WP139/2
       Topic. Perfections of God

512   ft C.M. Billings, W
       When I with pleasing wonder stand
       Sources. WB4/67, WP139/2
       Topic. Perfections of God

513   xt P.M. French, J
       Blest be the man whose piercing mind
       Sources. MNAN9/82, Anon.
       Topic. Secular

514   xt P.M. West, E
       God fram'd the globe, he built the skies
       Sources. MNAN7/28, WP96
       Topic. Hell and Heaven

CRETE

515   xt P.M. Babcock, S
       In deep distress I oft have cry'd
       Sources. MNAN11/40, NV120
       Topic. Christian

CROSS

516   xt L.M. Holden, O
       O! the sweet wonders of that cross
       Sources. MNAN13/42, WH3/10
       Topic. The Lord's Supper

CROSS-STREET

517   xt P.M. Billings, W
       The Lord my pasture shall prepare
       Sources. WB4/74, Addison, J
       Topic. Creation and Providence

CROWN OF LOVE

518   xt P.M. Jenks, S
Love divine all loves excelling
Sources. SJ279, Wesley, C
Topic. Love

CRUCIFICTION

519   pt L.M. Billings, W
Mourn, mourn, ye saints as if you see
Sources. WB2/298, Anon.
Topic. Atonement

CRUCIFIXION

520   xt L.M. Babcock, S
Now let our mournful songs record
Sources. MNAN11/42, WP22
Topic. Ascension and Exaltation of Christ

521   ft C.M. Benham, A
Jesus, whom ev'ry saint adores
Sources. MNAN8/23, WP16/2
Topic. Resurrection of Christ

522   ft L.M. Billings, W
Mourn, mourn, ye saints, as if you see
Sources. WB3/228, Anon.
Topic. Atonement

523   xt P.M. Stone, J
Hearts of stone, relent, relent
Sources. MNAN10/18, Wesley, C
Topic. Repentance

CUMBERLAND

524   pt L.M. Belcher, S
He reigns; the Lord, the saviour reigns
Sources. MNAN5/36, WP97/1
Topic. Day of Judgment

525   xt S.M. Benham, A
The Lord, the sov'reign king
Sources. MNAN8/24, WP103/3
Topic. Universal Praise

526   pt C.M. Billings, W
Behold the glories of the lamb
Sources. WB1/94, WH1/1
Topic. Addresses to Christ

CURIOSITY

527   ft P.M. Jenks, S
He fram'd the globe, he built the sky
Sources. SJ56, WP96
Topic. Hell and Heaven

CYPRESS

528   xt C.M. Read, D
Hark! from the tombs a doleful sound
Sources. DR44, WH2/63
Topic. Death and Resurrection

CYRENE

529   pt C.M. Holyoke, S
Christ and his cross is all our theme
Sources. MNAN12/47, WH1/119
Topic. Law and Gospel

CYTHERIA

530   pt P.M. Woodruff, M
The God of glory sends his summons forth
Sources. MNAN8/76, WP50/2
Topic. Day of Judgment

DALSTON

531   pt P.M. Anon.
How pleas'd and blest was I
Sources. CR40, WP122
Topic. Public Worship

DALTON

532   pt C.M. Doolittle, E
Hark! from the tombs a doleful sound
Sources. MNAN15/22, WH2/63
Topic. Death and Resurrection

DANBURY

533   pt S.M. Billings, W
Lord, what a feeble piece
Sources. WB2/310, WP90
Topic. Time and Eternity

534   ft P.M. Edson, L
Great God, the heav'n's well order'd frame
Sources. MNAN3/15, WP19
Topic. Scripture

535   ft S.M. Stone, J
Alas, the brittle clay
Sources. MNAN10/20, WP90
Topic. Time and Eternity

DANVERS

536   ft C.M. Woodruff, M
Let Pharisees of high esteem
Sources. MNAN8/79, WH1/133
Topic. Love

DANVILLE

537   ft C.M. Jenks, S
Save me, O God, the swelling floods
Sources. SJ58, WP69/1
Topic. Sufferings and Death of Christ

DARTMOUTH

538   xt L.M. Belknap, D
Bless'd are the humble souls that see
Sources. MNAN14/36, WH1/102
Topic. Christian

539   xt S.M. Jenks, S
       To bring the glorious news
       Sources. SJ59, WH1/3
       Topic. Birth of Christ

DAUPHIN

540   ft S.M. French, J
       Welcome, sweet day of rest
       Sources. MNAN9/83, WH2/14
       Topic. Worship

DAVID'S HARP

541   ft L.M. Edson, L
       Sweet is the day of sacred rest
       Sources. MNAN3/17, WP92/1
       Topic. Lord's Day

DAVID'S LAMENTATION

542   an Billings, W
       David, the king, was grieved and moved
       Sources. WB2/108, Bible
       Topic. Resignation

DAWN, THE

543   xt L.M. Belcher, S
       Aurora veils her rosy face
       Sources. MNAN5/37, Erskine, R
       Topic. Death and Resurrection

DEATH'S ALARM

544   xt L.M. Benham, A
       Ho, ho, prepare to go with me
       Sources. MNAN8/26, Anon.
       Topic. Death and Resurrection

DEATH'S ALARM [I]

545.   xt C.M. West, E
       The rising morning can't insure
       Sources. MNAN7/30, WH2/8
       Topic. Morning and Evening

DEATH'S ALARM [II]

546.   ft C.M. West, E
       Death, with his warrant in his hand
       Sources. MNAN7/31, Billings, W
       Topic. Death and Resurrection

DECAY

547   ft S.M. Jenks, S
       My days are as the grass
       Sources. SJ62, WP103/2
       Topic. Perfections of God

548   pt S.M. Jenks, S
       And must this body die
       Sources. SJ281, WH2/110
       Topic. Death and Resurrection

DECLARATION

549   ft L.M. French, J
       Thy mercies, Lord, shall be my song
       Sources. MNAN9/84, NV89
       Topic. Grace

DECLINE

550   pt L.M. Jenks, S
       Swift as declining shadows pass
       Sources. SJ282, Anon.
       Topic. Faith

DEDHAM

551   pt L.M. Billings, W
       Life is the time to serve the Lord
       Sources. WB1/170, WH1/88
       Topic. Time and Eternity

552   ft L.M. Billings, W
       Rejoice, ye shining worlds on high
       Sources. WB4/141, WP24
       Topic. Ascension and Exaltation of Christ

DEDICATION

553   an Wood, A
       Where shall we go to seek and find
       Sources. MNAN6/23, WP132
       Topic. Dedication

DEDICATION ANTHEM

554   an French, J
       Lift up your heads, O ye gates
       Sources. MNAN9/87, Bible
       Topic. Dedication

555   an Newhall, J
       Where shall we go to seek and find
       Sources. AA2/13, WP132
       Topic. Dedication

556   an Swan, T
       The Lord reigneth; let the earth rejoice
       Sources. TS57, BP97
       Topic. Dedication

DEDICATORY ANTHEM, A

557   an Holden, O
       Great is the Lord, and greatly to be praised
       Sources. MNAN13/44, BP48
       Topic. Dedication

DEDICATORY HYMN

558   xt L.M. Holden, O
       Let flowing numbers sweetly rise
       Sources. MNAN13/47, Anon.
       Topic. Beauty of the Church

DEDICATORY POEM

559   sp Holden, O
       With joyful hearts and tuneful song
       Sources. MNAN13/49, Lovett, J
       Topic. Prayer and Praise for the Church

DEERFIELD

560   pt C.M. Jenks, S
       Blest are the undefil'd in heart
       Sources. SJ63, WP119/1
       Topic. Saints and Sinners

DEFENCE

561   pt C.M. Bull, A
       In thee, great God, with songs of praise
       Sources. MNAN1/57, WP21
       Topic. Magistracy

DELAWARE

562   xt C.M. Babcock, S
       In awful state the conq'ring God
       Sources. MNAN11/43, WHor
       Topic. Ascension and Exaltation of Christ

563   pt L.M. Billings, W
       Remember, Lord, our mortal state
       Sources. WB2/314, WP89
       Topic. Death and Resurrection

DELIGHT

564   xt S.M. Jenks, S
       O let thy God and king
       Sources. SJ65, WP45
       Topic. Beauty of the Church

DELIVERANCE

565   an Billings, W
       I will love thee, O Lord, my strength
       Sources. WB4/195, BP18
       Topic. Fast Day

566   pt C.M. Holden, O
       Soon shall I quit this mortal shore
       Sources. MNAN13/58, Alline, H
       Topic. Death and Resurrection

567   an West, E
       Arise, O God, in thine anger
       Sources. MNAN7/33, Bible
       Topic. Fast Day

DELLY

568   ft C.M. French, J
       Down headlong from their native skies
       Sources. MNAN9/97, WH2/96
       Topic. Election

DENBIGH

569   ft C.M. Swan, T
       God counts the sorrows of his saints
       Sources. TS305, WP56
       Topic. Christian

DENMARK

570   sp Madan, M
       Before Jehovah's awful throne
       Sources. CR41, WP100/2
       Topic. Universal Praise

571   sp Madan/Mann
       Before Jehovah's awful throne
       Sources. MNAN4/98, WP100/2
       Topic. Universal Praise

DENSTON

572   xt P.M. Holyoke, S
       Lo! he cometh; countless trumpets
       Sources. MNAN12/48, Cennick, J
       Topic. Day of Judgment

DEPARTING FRIENDS

573   pt P.M. Jenks, S
       Friend after friend departs
       Sources. SJ283, Anon.
       Topic. Death and Resurrection

DEPRAVITY

574   xt C.M. Read, D
       By nature all are gone astray
       Sources. DR46, WP14/1
       Topic. Depravity and Fall of Man

DERBY

575   pt P.M. Read, D
       Lord of the worlds above
       Sources. DR48, WP84
       Topic. Public Worship

DESIRE

576   pt P.M. Jenks, S
       Busy, curious, thirsty fly
       Sources. SJ66, Oldys, W
       Topic. Resignation

DESIRE OF NATIONS

577   ft L.M. Holden, O
       Ye heav'nly gates, loose all your chains
       Sources. MNAN13/60, WHor
       Topic. Day of Judgment

DESOLUTION

578   pt P.M. Jenks, S
       Along the banks where Babel's current flows
       Sources. SJ67, BarP137
       Topic. Afflictions of the Church

DESPAIR

579   xt P.M. Morgan, J
       O! now Amanda's dead and gone
       Sources. MNAN7/121, Pope, A
       Topic. Humility

DESPONDENCE

580   xt L.M. Jenks, S
       Arise, my tend'rest thoughts, arise
       Sources. SJ284, Doddridge, P
       Topic. Depravity and Fall of Man

DETROIT

581   xt P.M. Jenks, S
Come thou fount of ev'ry blessing
Sources. SJ69, Robinson, R
Topic. Times and Seasons

DEVER-RILL

582   xt L.M. French, J
Thou, Lord, by strictest search hast known
Sources. MNAN9/99, NV139
Topic. Perfections of God

DEVOTION

583   ft L.M. French, J
Awake, my soul, and with the sun
Sources. MNAN9/101, Ken, T
Topic. Morning and Evening

584   ft L.M. Read, D
Sweet is the day of sacred rest
Sources. DR50, WP92/1
Topic. Lord's Day

DICKINSON

585   pt S.M. Billings, W
To bless thy chosen race
Sources. WB1/262, NV67
Topic. Joy and Rejoicing

DIGBY

586   ft C.M. Swan, T
God counts the sorrows of his saints
Sources. TS86, WP56
Topic. Christian

DIGHTON

587   pt C.M. Billings, W
Adore and tremble, for our God
Sources. WB1/250, WH1/42
Topic. Perfections of God

DIRGE, A

588   sp Holden, O
Hark! she bids her friends adieu
Sources. MNAN13/62, WHor
Topic. Death and Resurrection

589   sp Holden, O
Peace to his soul, the fatal hour is past
Sources. MNAN13/172, Rowson, S
Topic. Funeral

590   pt P.M. Jenks, S
And am I only born to die
Sources. SJ286, Wesley, C
Topic. Death and Resurrection

DIRGE, OR SEPULCHRAL SERVICE, A

591   sp Holden, O
Lo! sorrow reigneth, and the nation mourns
Sources. MNAN13/185, Pasquin, A
Topic. Patriotic

DISCONSOLATION

592   xt C.M. Stone, J
As on some lonely building's top
Sources. MNAN10/21, WP102/1
Topic. Sickness and Recovery

DISSOLUTION

593   xt C.M. Babcock, S
Stoop down, my thoughts, that us'd to rise
Sources. MNAN11/45, WH2/28
Topic. Death and Resurrection

594   xt C.M. Belknap, D
And must this body faint and die
Sources. MNAN14/37, Anon.
Topic. Death and Resurrection

595   xt C.M. Holden, O
Death will dissolve the tend'rest tie
Sources. MNAN13/64, Anon.
Topic. Death and Resurrection

596   ft C.M. West, E
Death may dissolve my body now
Sources. MNAN7/37, WH1/27
Topic. Death and Resurrection

DISSOLUTION [I]

597   ft L.M. French, J
The great, the good, the wise, the just
Sources. MNAN9/104, Anon.
Topic. Death and Resurrection

DISSOLUTION [II]

598   ft P.M. French, J
And is the lovely shadow fled
Sources. MNAN9/105, Wesley, C
Topic. Death and Resurrection

DIVINE LOVE

599   sp Jenks, S
He dies! the friend of sinners dies
Sources. SJ70, WHor
Topic. Sufferings and Death of Christ

DIX-HILLS

600   pt C.M. Holden, O
Too many, Lord, abuse thy grace
Sources. MNAN13/65, Cowper, W
Topic. Saints and Sinners

DOMINION

601   xt P.M. Bull, A
The Lord Jehovah reigns, And royal
Sources. MNAN1/58, WP93/2
Topic. Perfections of God

602   ft C.M. Edson, L
Thy words the raging winds control
Sources. MNAN3/19, WP89/2
Topic. Perfections of God

603 pt P.M. Jenks, S
no text
Sources. SJ287

604 ft L.M. Read, D
Jesus shall reign where'er the sun
Sources. DR52, WP72/2
Topic. The Christian Church

DOOMS DAY

605 ft S.M. Wood, A
Behold, with awful pomp
Sources. MNAN6/29, Hart, J
Topic. Day of Judgment

DOOMSDAY

606 xt S.M. Jenks, S
And will the judge descend
Sources. SJ288, Doddridge, P
Topic. Repentance

DORCHESTER

607 ft L.M. Babcock, S
My God, permit me not to be
Sources. MNAN11/47, WH2/122
Topic. Worship

608 pt C.M. Billings, W
Time! what an empty vapour 'tis
Sources. WB1/284, WH2/58
Topic. Time and Eternity

609 pt C.M. Billings, W
Time! what an empty vapour 'tis
Sources. WB2/60, WH2/58
Topic. Time and Eternity

610 ft L.M. Stone, J
Lord, I am vile, conceiv'd in sin
Sources. MNAN10/23, WP51/2
Topic. Depravity and Fall of Man

DORMANT

611 ft L.M. French, J
Sleep, downy sleep, come close my eyes
Sources. MNAN9/107, Flatman, T
Topic. Regeneration

DOUGLAS

612 xt S.M. Jenks, S
My soul, why weepest thou
Sources. SJ76, Beddome, B
Topic. Repentance

DOUGLASS

613 ft S.M. French, J
And will the God of grace
Sources. MNAN9/108, WP83
Topic. The Christian Church

DOVER

614 pt C.M. Belknap, D
Naked as from the earth we came
Sources. MNAN14/39, WH1/5
Topic. Resignation

615 pt C.M. Read, D
O that the Lord would guide my ways
Sources. DR55, WP119/11
Topic. Sanctification

616 xt L.M. Swan, T
My soul, thy great creator praise
Sources. TS88, WP104
Topic. Creation and Providence

617 xt L.M. Swan, T
My soul, thy great creator praise
Sources. TS307, WP104
Topic. Creation and Providence

DOXOLOGY

618 sp Babcock, S
Now unto the king eternal
Sources. MNAN11/49, Bible
Topic. Doxology

619 sp Mann, E
Now unto the king eternal
Sources. MNAN4/56, Bible
Topic. Doxology

620 ft L.M. Read, D
To God the father, God the son
Sources. DR57, WH3/32
Topic. Doxology

DRESDEN

621 pt P.M. Brownson, O
How pleasant 'tis to see
Sources. MNAN2/14, WP133
Topic. Public Worship

DRYDEN

622 xt C.M. Read, D
My soul, come, meditate the day
Sources. DR59, WH2/61
Topic. Death and Resurrection

DUBLIN

623 pt S.M. Billings, W
Like sheep we went astray
Sources. WB2/306, WH1/142
Topic. Ascension and Exaltation of Christ

624 ft L.M. Swan, T
All you bright armies of the skies
Sources. TS90, WP97/2
Topic. Birth of Christ

DUDLEY

625 pt L.M. Billings, W
How long, O Lord, shall I complain
Sources. WB2/294, WP13
Topic. Christian

DUNKIRK

626 sp Holyoke, S
Come, let us join our cheerful songs
Sources. MNAN12/50, WH1/62
Topic. Addresses to Christ

DUNSTABLE

627 ft C.M. Billings, W
With earnest longings of the mind
Sources. WB2/258, WP42
Topic. Fear and Hope

628 pt C.M. Billings, W
Methinks I see my saviour dear
Sources. WB3/317, Watts?
Topic. Sufferings and Death of Christ

629 pt L.M. Holyoke, S
Methinks the last great day is come
Sources. MNAN12/54, Needham, J
Topic. Day of Judgment

DUNSTAN

630 xt L.M. Madan, M
Jesus shall reign where'er the sun
Sources. CR46, WP72/2
Topic. The Christian Church

DUNSTON

631 xt L.M. French, J
Thou, whom my soul admires above
Sources. MNAN9/110, WH1/67
Topic. Solomon's Song

DURHAM

632 xt P.M. Belknap, D
Think, mighty God, on feeble man
Sources. MNAN14/41, WP89
Topic. Death and Resurrection

633 pt L.M. Brownson, O
Sweet is the work, my God, my king
Sources. MNAN2/16, WP92/1
Topic. Lord's Day

634 pt P.M. Kimball, J
How pleasant 'tis to see
Sources. MNAN12/158, WP133
Topic. Public Worship

DUXBOROUGH

635 pt L.M. Billings, W
In vain the wealthy mortals toil
Sources. WB1/70, WH1/24
Topic. Death and Resurrection

636 pt L.M. Billings, W
In vain the wealthy mortals toil
Sources. WB2/42, WH1/24
Topic. Death and Resurrection

DYING CHRISTIAN, THE

637 sp Harwood, E
Vital spark of heav'nly flame
Sources. CR47, Pope, A
Topic. Death and Resurrection

DYING CHRISTIAN TO HIS SOUL, THE

638 an Billings, W
Vital spark of heav'nly flame
Sources. WB3/130, Pope, A
Topic. Death and Resurrection

DYING CHRISTIAN'S LAST FAREWELL, THE

639 an Billings, W
My friends, I am going a long journey
Sources. WB4/245, Anon.
Topic. Funeral

DYING SAINT, THE

640 xt P.M. Jenks, S
What's this that steals, that steals upon my frame
Sources. SJ290, Anon.
Topic. Death and Resurrection

EAST NEEDHAM

641 ft C.M. Belknap, D
The little hills on ev'ry side
Sources. MNAN14/43, WP65/3
Topic. Seasons of the Year

EAST SUDBURY

642 xt P.M. Billings, W
Ye tribes of Adam join
Sources. WB4/226, WP148
Topic. Universal Praise

EAST WINDSOR

643 pt S.M. Jenks, S
Grace! 'tis a charming sound
Sources. SJ292, Doddridge, P
Topic. Grace

EASTBURY

644 xt S.M. Doolittle, E
When overwhelm'd with grief
Sources. MNAN15/24, WP61
Topic. Christian

EASTFORD

645 xt L.M. French, J
When, marching to thy blest abode
Sources. MNAN9/111, NV68
Topic. The Jewish Church

EASTHAM

646   pt C.M. Billings, W
Christ from the dead is rais'd and made
Sources. WB1/220, Tate, N
Topic. Resurrection of Christ

647   xt C.M. Read, D
'Tis with a mournful pleasure now
Sources. DR61, WP42
Topic. Fear and Hope

EAST-TOWN

648   pt S.M. Billings, W
Behold what wond'rous grace
Sources. WB1/226, WH1/64
Topic. Adoption

ECSTACY

649   ft C.M. Belcher, S
Some seraph, lend your heav'nly tongue
Sources. MNAN5/40, WHor
Topic. Perfections of God

EDEN

650   xt C.M. Billings, W
Those glorious minds, how bright they shine
Sources. WB3/220, WH1/41
Topic. Hell and Heaven

EDENTON

651   pt P.M. Read, D
Lord of the worlds above
Sources. DR63, WP84
Topic. Public Worship

EDENVALE

652   xt P.M. Holyoke, S
Too mean this little globe for me
Sources. MNAN12/55, Anon.
Topic. The World

EDGEWARE

653   pt C.M. Holyoke, S
'Tis not the law of ten commands
Sources. MNAN12/56, WH2/124
Topic. The Jewish Church

EDINBURGH

654   xt L.M. Holyoke, S
Ye heav'ns with sounds of triumph ring
Sources. MNAN12/58, Doddridge, P
Topic. Day of Judgment

655   xt P.M. Kimball, J
O tell me no more of this world's vain store
Sources. MNAN12/159, Gambold, J
Topic. Grace

EDINGTON

656   pt C.M. Jenks, S
Alas! and did my saviour bleed
Sources. SJ77, WH2/9
Topic. Repentance

EDOM

657   ft C.M. West, E
He sends his word and melts the snow
Sources. MNAN7/38, WP147
Topic. Seasons of the Year

EGYPT

658   ft C.M. Billings, W
Come, see the wonders of our God
Sources. WB4/83, WP66/1
Topic. Perfections of God

659   xt C.M. Swan, T
He called for darkness; darkness came
Sources. TS92, NV105
Topic. The Jewish Church

ELDEN

660   pt C.M. Holyoke, S
O God of mercy hear my call
Sources. MNAN12/59, WP51/2
Topic. Repentance

ELECTION

661   pt P.M. Billings, W
Thou art my blest portion, thou dear Nazarene
Sources. WB3/192, RCH29
Topic. Salvation

ELEGY ON THE DEATH OF A . . . LADY

662   sp Wood, A
Ye virgin souls, whose sweet complaint
Sources. MNAN6/30, WHor
Topic. Funeral

ELEVATION

663   ft S.M. Babcock, S
Raise your triumphant songs
Sources. MNAN11/50, WH2/104
Topic. Perfections of God

ELIM

664   xt P.M. Babcock, S
Lift your voice, and thankful sing
Sources. MNAN11/51, Merrick, J
Topic. Universal Praise

ELSTOW

665   pt L.M. Holyoke, S
Ye servants of th'almighty king
Sources. MNAN12/61, WP113
Topic. Perfections of God

EMANCIPATION

666 xt P.M. Belcher, S
Hail! everlasting spring
Sources. MNAN5/42, Doddridge, P
Topic. Grace

EMANUEL

667 xt P.M. Billings, W
As shepherds in Jewry were guarding their sheep
Sources. WB3/59, Billings?
Topic. Birth of Christ

EMMAUS

668 pt L.M. Billings, W
When Jesus wept, a falling tear
Sources. WB2/102, Morton, P
Topic. Sufferings and Death of Christ

ENERGY

669 xt C.M Swan, T
Attend our armies to the fight
Sources. TS101, WP60
Topic. Thanksgiving

ENFIELD

670 xt L.M. Belknap, D
The voice of my beloved sounds
Sources. MNAN14/44, WH1/69
Topic. Solomon's Song

671 xt C.M. Chandler, S
Before the rosy dawn of day
Sources. CR54, Rowe, E
Topic. Morning and Evening

672 xt C.M. Chandler, S
Before the rosy dawn of day
Sources. MNAN2/146, Rowe, E
Topic. Morning and Evening

673 ft L.M. Read, D
Might I enjoy the meanest place
Sources. DR65, WP84/2
Topic. Public Worship

EPHRATAH

674 xt C.M. Babcock, S
While shepherds watch'd their flocks by night
Sources. MNAN11/52, Tate, N
Topic. Birth of Christ

EPPING

675 pt C.M. Holyoke, S
We sing the glories of thy love
Sources. MNAN12/62, WH1/56
Topic. The Christian Church

EQUITY

676 xt C.M. Woodruff, M
Rise, great redeemer, from thy seat
Sources. MNAN8/82, WP9/2
Topic. Creation and Providence

ERIE

677 pt P.M. Holden, O
As lost in lonely grief, I tread
Sources. MNAN13/66, BarP88
Topic. Fear and Hope

ESSEX

678 pt S.M. Billings, W
How beauteous are their feet
Sources. WB1/232, WH1/10
Topic. Law and Gospel

EUGENIO

679 xt P.M. Woodruff, M
What is the blooming tincture of a skin
Sources. MNAN8/83, Anon.
Topic. Secular

EUROCLYDON

680 an Billings, W
They that go down to the sea in ships
Sources. WB3/71, BCPP107
Topic. Thanksgiving

EUROPE

681 ft C.M. Billings, W
Let Whig and Tory all subside
Sources. WB1/317, Billings?
Topic. Universal Praise

682 pt C.M. Billings, W
Let ev'ry mortal ear attend
Sources. WB2/284, WH1/7
Topic. Invitations and Promises

EVENING HYMN

683 xt S.M. Jenks, S
The day is past and gone
Sources. SJ78, Leland, J
Topic. Morning and Evening

684 ft S.M. West, E
Our moments fly apace
Sources. MNAN7/40, WP90
Topic. Time and Eternity

EVENING SHADE

685 ft S.M. Jenks, S
The day is past and gone
Sources. SJ79, Leland, J
Topic. Morning and Evening

EXETER

686 xt C.M. Billings, W
My thoughts on awful subjects roll
Sources. WB2/152, WH2/2
Topic. Death and Resurrection

687 xt L.M. Jenks, S
From pleasant trees which shade the brink
Sources. SJ80, WP104
Topic. Creation and Providence

688   ft P.M. Kimball, J
       Think, mighty God, on feeble man
       Sources. MNAN12/161, WP89
       Topic. Death and Resurrection

EXHORTATION

689   ft L.M. Doolittle, E
       Now in the heat of youthful blood
       Sources. MNAN15/25, WH1/91
       Topic. Youth and Old Age

690   ft L.M. French, J
       Ye nations round the earth, rejoice
       Sources. MNAN9/115, WP100/1
       Topic. Universal Praise

EXULTATION

691   ft C.M. Holden, O
       He spake, and heav'n's high arches rung
       Sources. MNAN13/67, Stennett, S
       Topic. Exaltation of Christ

FADING NATURE

692   pt L.M. Jenks, S
       So fades the lovely blooming flow'r
       Sources. SJ81, Steele, A
       Topic. Faith

693   xt L.M. Jenks, S
       Thousands of journeys night and day
       Sources. SJ82, Anon.
       Topic. Death and Resurrection

FAIRFIELD

694   xt C.M. Benham, A
       The glorious armies of the sky
       Sources. MNAN8/28, Anon.
       Topic. Universal Praise

695   pt S.M. Billings, W
       From lowest depths of woe
       Sources. WB1/86, NV130
       Topic. Pardon

FAIRFORD

696   xt P.M. Kimball, J
       Jesus, who dy'd a world to save
       Sources. MNAN12/163, Hammond, W
       Topic. Resurrection of Christ

FAIR-HAVEN

697   ft S.M. Jenks, S
       Come, sound his praise abroad
       Sources. SJ83, WP95
       Topic. Worship

FAIRHAVEN

698   ft L.M. French, J
       There was an hour when Christ rejoic'd
       Sources. MNAN9/117, WH1/11
       Topic. Election

FAIRLEE

699   pt L.M. Holden, O
       Jesus shall reign where'er the sun
       Sources. MNAN13/68, WP72/2
       Topic. The Christian Church

FAIRVIEW

700   xt S.M. Jenks, S
       Come we that love the Lord
       Sources. SJ293, WH2/30
       Topic. Joy and Rejoicing

FALL OF BABYLON, THE

701   an French, J
       Now after these things I saw another angel
       Sources. MNAN9/118, Bible
       Topic. Day of Judgment

FALMOUTH

702   xt C.M. Bull, A
       This is the day the Lord hath made
       Sources. MNAN1/60, WP118/4
       Topic. Lord's Day

FAMILY BIBLE, THE

703   xt P.M. Jenks, S
       How painfully pleasing the fond recollection
       Sources. SJ295, Anon.
       Topic. Scripture

FAREWELL

704   pt P.M. Jenks, S
       When shall I see the day
       Sources. SJ297, Anon.
       Topic. Death and Resurrection

FAREWELL ANTHEM

705   an French, J
       My friends, I am going a long and tedious journey
       Sources. MNAN9/127, Anon.
       Topic. Funeral

FARMINGTON

706   ft L.M. Belcher, S
       Come, my beloved, haste away
       Sources. MNAN5/43, WH1/78
       Topic. Solomon's Song

707   pt L.M. French, J
       Black, heavy thoughts like mountains roll
       Sources. MNAN9/132, WHor
       Topic. Pardon

708   ft P.M. Gillet, A
       Think, mighty God, on feeble man
       Sources. MNAN2/87, WP89
       Topic. Death and Resurrection

FARNHAM

709   ft P.M. Doolittle, E
       Ye that delight to serve the Lord
       Sources. MNAN15/27, WP113
       Topic. Perfections of God

FARNUM

710 ft C.M. French, J
Sing to the Lord a new-made song
Sources. MNAN9/133, NV98
Topic. Birth of Christ

FEAR OF THE LORD, THE

711 pt P.M. Wood, A
The fear of the Lord, Our days will prolong
Sources. MNAN6/37, Hart, J
Topic. Fear and Hope

FELICITY

712 pt L.M. Benham, A
This life's a dream, an empty show
Sources. MNAN8/29, WP17
Topic. Saints and Sinners

713 ft C.M. Doolittle, E
Joy to the world, the Lord is come
Sources. MNAN15/29, WP98/2
Topic. Birth of Christ

FELLOWSHIP

714 pt S.M. Doolittle, E
Blest be the tie that binds
Sources. MNAN15/31, Fawcett, J
Topic. Love

FERNAY

715 xt C.M. Holyoke, S
Blest is the nation where the Lord
Sources. MNAN12/64, WP33/2
Topic. Perfections of God

FIDELITY

716 ft C.M. Read, D
Then in the Lord let Israel trust
Sources. DR67, WP130
Topic. Pardon

FIRMAMENT

717 xt P.M. Read, D
Great God, the heav'n's well order'd frame
Sources. DR70, WP19
Topic. Scripture

FITCHBURGH

718 pt L.M. Billings, W
Deep in our hearts, let us record
Sources. WB2/274, WP69/1
Topic. Sufferings and Death of Christ

719 xt S.M. Jenks, S
My God, permit my tongue
Sources. SJ84, WP63
Topic. Lord's Day

720 ft C.M. Wood, A
With rev'rence let the saints appear
Sources. MNAN6/39, WP89/2
Topic. Perfections of God

FLANDERS

721 xt C.M. Babcock, S
Since I have plac'd my trust in God
Sources. MNAN11/54, NV11
Topic. Saints and Sinners

722 xt L.M. Swan, T
The saints shall flourish in his days
Sources. TS103, WP72/1
Topic. The Christian Church

FLORENCE

723 xt P.M. Babcock, S
Immense compassion reigns
Sources. MNAN11/55, WH1/148
Topic. Characters and Offices of Christ

724 xt C.M. Bull, A
Behold the glories of the lamb
Sources. MNAN1/61, WH1/1
Topic. Addresses to Christ

725 pt P.M. Swan, T
Rejoice, the Lord is king
Sources. TS105, Wesley, C
Topic. Dominion of Christ

726 xt L.M. Woodruff, M
Sweet is the work, my God, my king
Sources. MNAN8/85, WP92/1
Topic. Lord's Day

FLUVANNA

727 ft C.M. Woodruff, M
The Lord descended from above
Sources. MNAN8/87, OV18
Topic. Perfections of God

FLY

728 xt P.M. French, J
Busy, curious, thirsty fly
Sources. MNAN9/135, Oldys, W
Topic. Resignation

FLYCREEK

729 ft C.M. Billings, N
When all thy mercies, O my God
Sources. MNAN3/98, Addison, J
Topic. Creation and Providence

FORMATION

730 xt C.M. French, J
When I with pleasing wonder stand
Sources. MNAN9/137, WP139/2
Topic. Perfections of God

FRAGILITY

731 xt P.M. Billings, N
Think, mighty God, on feeble man
Sources. MNAN3/101, WP89
Topic. Death and Resurrection

FRAMINGHAM

732   xt L.M. Belknap, D
He dies! the friend of sinners dies
Sources. MNAN14/46, WHor
Topic. Sufferings and Death of Christ

733   pt S.M. Billings, W
Shall wisdom cry aloud
Sources. WB2/272, WH1/92
Topic. Invitations and Promises

734   ft S.M. Billings, W
Shall wisdom cry aloud
Sources. WB3/9, WH1/92
Topic. Invitations and Promises

FRANCONIA

735   xt P.M. Holyoke, S
Not to our names, thou only just and true
Sources. MNAN12/66, WP115
Topic. Perfections of God

FRANKLIN

736   pt L.M. Billings, W
Lord, how secure and blest are they
Sources. WB2/292, WH2/57
Topic. Joy and Rejoicing

737   ft L.M. Jenks, S
Sweet is the work, my God, my king
Sources. SJ86, WP92/1
Topic. Lord's Day

738   xt P.M. Swan, T
Hosanna to Jesus on high
Sources. TS107, Anon.
Topic. Hosannas to Christ

FREEDOM

739   pt S.M. Billings, W
To God with mournful voice
Sources. WB1/206, NV142
Topic. Perfections of God

740.   xt P.M. Edson, L J
Tune your loud harps, ye Nine, to strains celestial
Sources. MNAN3/58, Townsend, W
Topic. Patriotic

741   ft P.M. Gillet, A
The Lord of glory reigns, he reigns on high
Sources. MNAN2/89, WP93/1
Topic. Perfections of God

742   ft P.M. West, E
The Lord hath eyes to give the blind
Sources. MNAN7/42, WP146
Topic. Perfections of God

FREETOWN

743   ft P.M. Read, D
Join all the glorious names
Sources. DR72, WH1/150
Topic. Characters and Offices of Christ

744   ft P.M. Read, D
Join all the glorious names
Sources. DR262, WH1/150
Topic. Characters and Offices of Christ

FRIENDSHIP

745   xt P.M. Belcher, S
How pleasant 'tis to see
Sources. MNAN5/45, WP133
Topic. Public Worship

746   pt S.M. Billings, W
My saviour and my king
Sources. WB1/217, WP45
Topic. Beauty of the Church

747   sp Brownson, O
He dies! the friend of sinners dies
Sources. MNAN2/17, WHor
Topic. Sufferings and Death of Christ

748   xt L.M. Edson, L Jr
From low pursuits exalt my mind
Sources. MNAN3/60, Anon.
Topic. Humility

749   xt P.M. Read, D
How pleasant 'tis to see
Sources. DR75, WP133
Topic. Public Worship

FUNERAL ANTHEM

750   an Belcher, S
Farewell, farewell, a sad and long farewell
Sources. MNAN5/46, Kneeland, A
Topic. Funeral

751   an Billings, W
Samuel the priest gave up the ghost
Sources. WB3/214, Bible
Topic. Funeral

752   an Holden, O
Man that is born of a woman is of few days
Sources. MNAN13/70, Bible
Topic. Funeral

753   an Holt, B
Man that is born of a woman
Sources. AA2/70, Bible/Watts
Topic. Funeral

754   an Kimball, J
I heard a great voice from heav'n, saying unto me
Sources. MNAN12/164, Bible
Topic. Funeral

FUNERAL ANTHEM, A

755   an Billings, W
I heard a great voice from heav'n saying unto me
Sources. WB2/175, Bible
Topic. Funeral

756   an Billings, W
       I heard a great voice from heav'n saying unto me
       Sources. AA2/59, Bible
       Topic. Funeral

757   an Camp, S
       Put not your trust in princes
       Sources. AA2/61, BP146
       Topic. Funeral

758   an Goff, E
       I heard a voice from heav'n
       Sources. AA2/67, Bible
       Topic. Funeral

759   an Holden, O
       The sound of the harp ceaseth: the voice of mirth
       Sources. MNAN13/163, Bible
       Topic. Funeral

FUNERAL DIRGE

760   sp Holyoke, S
       Farewell, a sad, a long farewell
       Sources. MNAN12/68, Anon.
       Topic. Death and Resurrection

FUNERAL DIRGE, A

761   sp Jenks, S
       Muse, breathe the dirge o'er Delia's tomb
       Sources. SJ87, Smith, Mr.
       Topic. Death and Resurrection

FUNERAL ELEGY, A

762   xt P.M. Jenks, S
       Why starts the tear from grief's uplifted eye
       Sources. SJ93, Messenger, C
       Topic. Death and Resurrection

763   sp Jenks, S
       Hark! hark! what doleful sounds I hear
       Sources. SJ95, Janes, W
       Topic. Death and Resurrection

764   sp Wood, A
       Know ye not that a great man hath fall'n today
       Sources. MNAN6/41, WHor/Hart, J
       Topic. Funeral

FUNERAL HYMN

765   xt C.M. Belcher, S
       Why do we mourn departing friends
       Sources. MNAN5/49, WH2/3
       Topic. Death and Resurrection

766   ft C.M. French, J
       I, in the burying place, may see
       Sources. MNAN9/138, Anon.
       Topic. Death and Resurrection

767   xt C.M. Holden, O
       Why do we mourn departing friends
       Sources. MNAN13/73, WH2/3
       Topic. Death and Resurrection

768   ft S.M. Stone, J
       The spirits of the just
       Sources. MNAN10/25, Hart, J
       Topic. Death and Resurrection

FUNERAL HYMN, A

769   xt C.M. Holden, O
       Up to thy throne, almighty king
       Sources. MNAN13/181, Anon.
       Topic. Trust and Confidence

FUNERAL ODE

770   pt P.M. Belknap, D
       Deep resound the solemn strain
       Sources. MNAN14/48, Lane, J
       Topic. Patriotic

FUNERAL THOUGHT

771   pt C.M. Anon.
       Hark! from the tombs a doleful sound
       Sources. CR56, WH2/63
       Topic. Death and Resurrection

GARDEN

772   xt P.M. Edson, L Jr
       Agonizing in the garden
       Sources. MNAN3/62, Hart, J
       Topic. Exaltation of Christ

773   xt L.M. Jenks, S
       Lord, 'tis a pleasant thing to stand
       Sources. SJ299, WP92/2
       Topic. The Christian Church

GARDINER

774   xt L.M. Read, D
       Come, let our voices join to raise
       Sources. DR77, WP95
       Topic. Worship

775   ft L.M. Stone, J
       On line of life our bodies hang
       Sources. MNAN10/27, Anon.
       Topic. Death and Resurrection

GARDNER

776   xt L.M. Belknap, D
       When I survey the wond'rous cross
       Sources. MNAN14/49, WH3/7
       Topic. The Lord's Supper

777   ft S.M. Billings, N
       To God in whom I trust
       Sources. MNAN3/103, NV25
       Topic. Christian

GARMENT, THE

778   xt L.M. Jenks, S
       Come, O my soul, in sacred lays
       Sources. SJ300, Blacklock
       Topic. Universal Praise

GENIUS

779   xt P.M. Jenks, S
Now be still, ye boist'rous passions
Sources. SJ102, Phelps, Mr.
Topic. Patriotic

GEORGIA

780   pt L.M. Billings, W
Now to the Lord that makes us know
Sources. WB1/274, WH1/61
Topic. Characters and Offices of Christ

781   pt L.M. Billings, W
Shew pity, Lord, O Lord, forgive
Sources. WB2/330, WP51/1
Topic. Christian

GERMANTOWN

782   xt C.M. Billings, W
Why do we mourn departing friends
Sources. WB3/318, WH2/3
Topic. Death and Resurrection

GERRY

783   pt L.M. Stone, J
When God makes up his last account
Sources. MNAN10/28, Anon.
Topic. Redemption

GETHSEMANE

784   pt L.M. Belcher, S
'Twas on that dark, that doleful night
Sources. MNAN5/51, WH3/1
Topic. The Lord's Supper

785   xt P.M. Wood, A
Great high priest, we view thee stooping
Sources. MNAN6/47, Hart, J
Topic. Sufferings and Death of Christ

GIHON

786   xt P.M. Babcock, S
The Lord Jehovah reigns, And royal
Sources. MNAN11/57, WP93/2
Topic. Perfections of God

GILBOA

787   xt S.M. Olmsted, T
And must this body die
Sources. MNAN15/94, WH2/110
Topic. Death and Resurrection

GILEAD

788   ft C.M. Billings, W
Salvation! O the joyful sound
Sources. WB4/122, WH1/88
Topic. Salvation

GLAD TIDINGS

789   pt P.M. Jenks, S
no text
Sources. SJ302

GLAD-TIDINGS

790   ft C.M. Jenks, S
Fear not, said he, for mighty dread
Sources. SJ103, Tate, N
Topic. Birth of Christ

GLOCESTER

791   pt P.M. Billings, W
Jesus, thy name we praise
Sources. WB3/206, RCH68
Topic. Redemption

GLORY

792   pt P.M. Jenks, S
Come, saints and sinners hear me tell
Sources. SJ303, Anon.
Topic. Salvation

GLOUCESTER

793   ft L.M. Kimball, J
Give to the Lord immortal praise
Sources. MNAN12/166, WP136
Topic. Creation and Providence

GOLGOTHA

794   xt C.M. Billings, W
Hark! from the tombs a doleful sound
Sources. WB3/80, WH2/63
Topic. Death and Resurrection

GONE TO REST

795   xt C.M. Jenks, S
Brother, thou art gone to rest
Sources. SJ305, Anon.
Topic. Death and Resurrection

GOOD FRIDAY

796   xt L.M. Jenks, S
Pardon and grace and boundless love
Sources. SJ104, WHor
Topic. Sufferings and Death of Christ

GOSHEN

797   ft C.M. Belknap, D
He comes, the royal conq'ror comes
Sources. MNAN14/50, Doddridge, P
Topic. Day of Judgment

798   ft L.M. Jenks, S
O wash my soul from ev'ry sin
Sources. SJ106, WP51/1
Topic. Christian

GOSPEL ARMOR, THE

799   pt L.M. Jenks, S
        Stand up, my soul, shake off thy fears
        Sources. SJ306, WH2/77
        Topic. Christian

GOSPEL BANNER, THE

800   pt P.M. Jenks, S
        Now be the gospel banner
        Sources. SJ307, Hastings, T
        Topic. Salvation

GOSPEL CALL, THE

801   xt L.M. Jenks, S
        Come, weary souls with sin distrest
        Sources. SJ309, Steele, A
        Topic. Invitations and Promises

GOSPEL MARKET, THE

802   pt P.M. Jenks, S
        Why stand ye here idle, my friends, all the day
        Sources. SJ312, Anon.
        Topic. Pardon

GOVERNMENT

803   xt P.M. Swan, T
        The Lord Jehovah reigns, And royal
        Sources. TS109, WP93/2
        Topic. Perfections of God

GRAFTON

804   ft C.M. Stone, J
        Jesus, the vision of thy face
        Sources. MNAN10/29, WH1/19
        Topic. Death and Resurrection

GRANBY

805   xt S.M. Gillet, A
        Come sound his praise abroad
        Sources. MNAN2/91, WP95
        Topic. Worship

806   xt P.M. Swan, T
        Awake, our drowsy souls
        Sources. TS111, Scott, E
        Topic. Resurrection of Christ

GRANVILLE

807.   xt L.M. Olmsted, T
        The Lord is come; the heav'ns proclaim
        Sources. MNAN15/95, WP97/2
        Topic. Birth of Christ

GRATITUDE

808   ft C.M. Babcock, S
        What shall I render to my God
        Sources. MNAN11/58, WP116/2
        Topic. Public Worship

809   an Billings, W
        I love the Lord because he hath heard
        Sources. WB2/194, BP116
        Topic. Thanksgiving

810   ft C.M. French, J
        What shall I render to my God
        Sources. MNAN9/139, WP116/2
        Topic. Public Worship

811   ft C.M. Gillet, A
        What shall I render to my God
        Sources. MNAN2/93, WP116/2
        Topic. Public Worship

812   pt L.M. Read, D
        Bless, O my soul, the living God
        Sources. DR80, WP103/1
        Topic. Perfections of God

GRAVE

813   xt L.M. Benham, A
        There the dark earth and dismal shade
        Sources. MNAN8/30, WP49
        Topic. Death and Resurrection

GREAT-PLAIN

814   ft L.M. Billings, W
        Ye slumb'ring saints, a heav'nly host
        Sources. WB4/55, WHor
        Topic. Death and Resurrection

GREENFIELD

815   ft P.M. Edson, L
        God is our refuge in distress
        Sources. CR57, NV46
        Topic. The Christian Church

816   ft P.M. Edson, L
        God is our refuge in distress
        Sources. MNAN3/20, NV46
        Topic. The Christian Church

GREENLAND

817   pt S.M. Billings, W
        Have mercy, Lord, on me
        Sources. WB1/116, NV51
        Topic. Christian

GREENSBURG

818   ft C.M. Stone, J
        Salvation, O the joyful sound
        Sources. MNAN10/31, WH2/88
        Topic. Salvation

GREENWICH

819   ft L.M. Read, D
        Lord, what a thoughtless wretch was I
        Sources. CR59, WP73
        Topic. The World

820　ft L.M. Read, D
Lord, what a thoughtless wretch was I
Sources. DR82, WP73
Topic. The World

821　ft L.M. Read, D
Lord, what a thoughtless wretch was I
Sources. DR264, WP73
Topic. The World

GRIEF

822　pt L.M. Jenks, S
On ev'ry side I cast mine eye
Sources. SJ314, Anon.
Topic. Fear and Hope

GUILDFORD

823　pt S.M. Brownson, O
Far as thy name is known
Sources. MNAN2/23, WP48/2
Topic. The Christian Church

HABAKKUK

824　sp Anon.
Away, my unbelieving fears
Sources. CR61, Wesley, C
Topic. Faith

HACKER'S HALL

825　xt C.M. Billings, W
Ye people all, with one accord
Sources. WB3/320, OV47
Topic. Perfections of God

HADLEY

826　ft L.M. Billings, W
Hark! hear you not a cheerful noise
Sources. WB3/322, Billings?
Topic. Birth of Christ

827　pt P.M. Kimball, J
The God of glory sends his summons forth
Sources. MNAN12/169, WP50/2
Topic. Day of Judgment

828　ft C.M. Stone, J
That awful day will surely come
Sources. MNAN10/32, WH2/107
Topic. Day of Judgment

HAGUE

829　pt C.M. Holyoke, S
Up from my youth, may Israel say
Sources. MNAN12/72, WP129
Topic. The Jewish Church

HALIFAX

830　pt P.M. Billings, W
Not to our names, thou only just and true
Sources. WB2/111, WP115
Topic. Perfections of God

831　ft P.M. Swan, T
Zion, thrice happy place
Sources. TS113, WP122
Topic. Public Worship

HALLELUJAH

832　sp Bull, A
Loud hallelujahs to the Lord
Sources. MNAN1/64, WP148
Topic. Universal Praise

HALLELUJAH CHORUS

833　an Taylor, R
Hallelujah, Amen
Sources. AA2/153, Anon.
Topic. Universal Praise

HALLIFAX

834　pt P.M. Billings, W
The God of glory sends his summons forth
Sources. WB3/325, WP50/2
Topic. Day of Judgment

HALLOWELL

835　ft S.M. Belcher, S
O let thy God and king
Sources. MNAN5/52, WP45
Topic. Beauty of the Church

HAMBURG

836　ft L.M. Babcock, S
Rise, saith the prince of mercy, rise
Sources. MNAN11/60, WHor
Topic. Grace

837　xt L.M. Belknap, D
Eternal spirit, we confess
Sources. MNAN14/51, WH2/133
Topic. Addresses to the Holy Spirit

HAMDEN

838　pt P.M. Doolittle, E
To bless the Lord, let ev'ry land combine
Sources. MNAN15/32, DP145
Topic. Perfections of God

HAMILTON

839　xt S.M. Olmsted, T
My saviour and my king
Sources. MNAN15/98, WP45
Topic. Beauty of the Church

840　ft P.M. Read, D
Like fruitful show'rs of rain
Sources. DR84, WP133
Topic. Public Worship

HAMPSHIRE

841　pt L.M. Billings, W
In thine own ways, O God of love
Sources. WB1/46, WH1/30
Topic. Thanksgiving

842.   pt C.M. Billings, W
Return, O God of love, return
Sources. WB2/312, WP90/3
Topic. Christian

843   ft C.M. Stone, J
Shepherds rejoice, lift up your eyes
Sources. MNAN10/34, WHor
Topic. Birth of Christ

HAMPTON
844   xt C.M. Belknap, D
Dearest of all the names above
Sources. MNAN14/53, WH2/148
Topic. Addresses to Christ

845   ft L.M. Doolittle, E
Ye flow'ry plains proclaim his skill
Sources. MNAN15/35, WP148
Topic. Universal Praise

846   xt S.M. Jenks, S
The Lord my shepherd is
Sources. SJ107, WP23
Topic. Communion with God

HAMSHIRE
847   sp Read, D
He dies! the heav'nly lover dies
Sources. DR86, WHor
Topic. Sufferings and Death of Christ

HAMTON
848   pt L.M. Billings, W
Let mortal tongues attempt to sing
Sources. WB1/90, WH1/58
Topic. Safety and Triumph of the Church

HANCOCK
849   ft L.M. Belknap, D
Hark! from the skies a dreadful sound
Sources. MNAN14/55, Anon.
Topic. Day of Judgment

HANDSEL
850   pt L.M. Belcher, S
Jesus shall reign where'er the sun
Sources. MNAN5/54, WP72/2
Topic. The Christian Church

HANLEY
851   xt C.M. Wood, A
Swift as the sun revolves the day
Sources. MNAN6/48, WHor
Topic. Youth and Old Age

HANOVER
852   pt L.M. Billings, W.
Bless'd is the man, supremely bless'd
Sources. WB1/271, Billings?
Topic. Trust and Confidence

HANOVER NEW
853   pt C.M. Billings, W
O praise the Lord and thou my soul
Sources. WB1/272, NV146
Topic. Perfections of God

HAPPINESS [I]
854   an French, J
Sing, O daughter of Zion
Sources. MNAN9/142, Bible
Topic. Thanksgiving

HAPPINESS [II]
855   xt C.M. French, J
Joy to the world, the Lord is come
Sources. MNAN9/144, WP98/2
Topic. Birth of Christ

HAPPY CITY
856   pt L.M. Read, D
Happy the city where their sons
Sources. DR92, WP144
Topic. Thanksgiving

HAPPY-MORN
857   pt P.M. Doolittle, E
All hail, happy day
Sources. MNAN15/37, Wesley, C
Topic. Birth of Christ

HARDWICK
858   xt C.M. Stone, J
Erect your heads, eternal gates
Sources. MNAN10/36, NV24
Topic. Ascension and Exaltation of Christ

HARLEM
859   xt P.M. Edson, L Jr
Not to our names, thou only just and true
Sources. MNAN3/63, WP115
Topic. Perfections of God

860   sp Kimball, J
Ye nations round the earth rejoice
Sources. MNAN12/172, WP100/1
Topic. Universal Praise

HARMONY
861   ft C.M. Belcher, S
Come, let us join our cheerful songs
Sources. MNAN5/55, WH1/62
Topic. Addresses to Christ

862   ft S.M. Jenks, S
How pleasant 'tis to see
Sources. SJ109, WP133
Topic. Public Worship

HARMONY [I]
863   ft P.M. West, E
Say, mighty love, and teach my song
Sources. MNAN7/44, WHor
Topic. Love

HARMONY [II]

864   ft C.M. West, E
       That awful day will surely come
       Sources. MNAN7/47, WH2/107
       Topic. Day of Judgment

HARRISBURGH

865   ft C.M. Stone, J
       Our life contains a thousand springs
       Sources. MNAN10/38, WH2/19
       Topic. Creation and Providence

HARTFORD

866   xt P.M. Billings, W
       Glorious Jesus! glorious Jesus
       Sources. WB3/168, RCH84
       Topic. Addresses to Christ

867   xt P.M. Bull, A
       Hail the day that sees him rise
       Sources. MNAN1/70, Wesley, C
       Topic. Ascension and Exaltation of Christ

868   xt L.M. Carpenter, E
       This spacious earth is all the Lord's
       Sources. CR64, WP24
       Topic. Ascension and Exaltation of Christ

869   pt P.M. Jenks, S
       I'll praise my maker with my breath
       Sources. SJ315, WP146
       Topic. Perfections of God

HARVARD

870   xt P.M. Babcock, S
       Sing to the Lord, exalt him high
       Sources. MNAN11/61, WP147/1
       Topic. Creation and Providence

871   pt C.M. Billings, W
       O Lord, I am not proud of heart
       Sources. WB1/245, NV131
       Topic. Humility

HARVEST HYMN, THE

872   pt P.M. Jenks, S
       The fields are all white and the harvest is near
       Sources. SJ317, Anon.
       Topic. Day of Judgment

HARWICK

873   ft S.M. Holyoke, S
       Exalt the Lord our God
       Sources. MNAN12/73, WP99/2
       Topic. Perfections of God

HASTE O SINNER

874   pt P.M. Jenks, S
       Haste, O sinner; now be wise
       Sources. SJ319, Scott, T
       Topic. Saints and Sinners

HATFIELD

875   xt C.M. Gillet, A
       This is the day the Lord hath made
       Sources. MNAN2/94, WP118/4
       Topic. Lord's Day

HATFIELD [I]

876   xt C.M. Billings, W
       Naked as from the earth we came
       Sources. WB3/282, WH1/5
       Topic. Resignation

HATFIELD [II]

877   xt C.M. Billings, W
       Let others boast how strong they be
       Sources. WB3/284, WH2/19
       Topic. Creation and Providence

HATFIELD [III]

878   pt C.M. Billings, W
       Though beauty grace the comely face
       Sources. WB3/328, Peck, J
       Topic. Death and Resurrection

HAVERHILL

879   ft S.M. West, E
       Alas, the brittle clay
       Sources. MNAN7/49, WP90
       Topic. Time and Eternity

HAVERILL

880   xt C.M. Billings, W
       Through all the changing scenes of life
       Sources. WB1/335, NV34
       Topic. Christian

HEATH

881   ft L.M. Billings, W
       Awake my soul! awake my eyes
       Sources. WB2/69, Flatman, T
       Topic. Morning and Evening

HEAVENLY VISION, THE

882   an French, J
       I beheld and lo, a great multitude
       Sources. MNAN9/146, Bible
       Topic. Day of Judgment

883   an French, J
       I beheld and lo, a great multitude
       Sources. AA2/115, Bible
       Topic. Day of Judgment

HEBRON

884   pt S.M. Billings, W
       My God, my life, my love
       Sources. WB1/246, WH2/93
       Topic. Communion with God

885   pt S.M. Billings, W
       My God, my life, my love
       Sources. WB2/86, WH2/93
       Topic. Communion with God

886   ft P.M. Billings, W
       Behold the splendor, hear the shout
       Sources. WB3/286, Anon.
       Topic. Birth of Christ

HELMSTON

887   pt P.M. Holyoke, S
       Great God! the heav'n's well order'd frame
       Sources. MNAN12/75, WP19
       Topic. Scripture

HEROISM

888   ft P.M. Belcher, S
       Why should vain mortals tremble at the sight of
       Sources. MNAN5/57, Niles, N
       Topic. Patriotic

HERSKILL

889   xt C.M. Edson, L Jr
       Happy the man whose tender care
       Sources. MNAN3/66, NV41
       Topic. Liberality

HESPERUS

890   ft C.M. Woodruff, M
       My thoughts on awful subjects roll
       Sources. MNAN8/90, WH2/2
       Topic. Death and Resurrection

HEXHAM

891   xt P.M. Holyoke, S
       Great God! the heav'n's well order'd frame
       Sources. MNAN12/76, WP19
       Topic. Scripture

HILLSBOROUGH

892   ft C.M. Kimball, J
       Come, saints, adore Jehovah's name
       Sources. MNAN12/176, Anon.
       Topic. Universal Praise

HINGHAM

893   pt S.M. Billings, W
       Shall we go on to sin
       Sources. WB1/62, WH1/106
       Topic. Christian

HINSDALE

894   ft C.M. Holyoke, S
       My saviour God, my sov'reign prince
       Sources. MNAN12/78, WH2/141
       Topic. Baptism

HIRAM ANTHEM

895   an Benham, A
       Behold how good and pleasant it is
       Sources. MNAN8/32, BP133
       Topic. Love

896   an Peck, L
       Behold, how good and how pleasant it is
       Sources. AA2/139, BP133
       Topic. Love

HOLDEN

897   pt P.M. Billings, W
       Ye saints and servants of the Lord
       Sources. WB1/312, NV113
       Topic. Perfections of God

898   xt C.M. Stone, J
       Our term of time is sev'nty years
       Sources. MNAN10/39, NV90
       Topic. Death and Resurrection

HOLLAND

899   xt P.M. Read, D
       Say, mighty love, and teach my song
       Sources. DR93, WHor
       Topic. Love

900   xt P.M. Read, D
       Say, mighty love, and teach my song
       Sources. DR266, WHor
       Topic. Love

901   ft L.M. Swan, T
       Uncertain life, how soon it flies
       Sources. TS116, Steele, A
       Topic. Time and Eternity

HOLLIS

902   pt L.M. Billings, W
       How rich are thy provisions, Lord
       Sources. WB1/306, WH3/12
       Topic. The Lord's Supper

903   ft C.M. Holden, O
       My soul come meditate the day
       Sources. MNAN13/74, WH2/61
       Topic. Death and Resurrection

HOLLIS STREET

904   pt P.M. Billings, W
       Let angels above and saints here below
       Sources. WB1/329, Byles, M
       Topic. Hosannas to Christ

905   pt P.M. Billings, W
       Ye servants of God
       Sources. WB2/88, Wesley, C
       Topic. Exaltation of Christ

HOLLISTON

906   ft S.M. Belknap, D
       Your harps, ye trembling saints
       Sources. MNAN14/57, Toplady, A
       Topic. Christian

907   ft C.M. Jenks, S
       Time, like an ever-rolling stream
       Sources. SJ110, WP90/1
       Topic. Time and Eternity

HOLLOWALL

908   xt P.M. French, J
       And can this mighty king
       Sources. MNAN9/151, WH2/169
       Topic. Perfections of God

HOPKINTON

909   xt C.M. Belknap, D
       Hark, from the tombs a doleful sound
       Sources. MNAN14/58, WH2/63
       Topic. Death and Resurrection

910   ft P.M. Billings, W
       Lo! he cometh, countless trumpets
       Sources. WB4/214, Cennick, J
       Topic. Day of Judgment

911   pt L.M. Wood, A
       Death, like an overflowing stream
       Sources. MNAN6/50, WP90
       Topic. Death and Resurrection

HOREB

912   xt P.M. Babcock, S
       Hearts of stone, relent, relent
       Sources. MNAN11/62, Wesley, C
       Topic. Repentance

HORIZON

913   xt P.M. Doolittle, E
       Great God, the heav'n's well order'd frame
       Sources. MNAN15/38, WP19
       Topic. Scripture

HOTHAM

914   xt P.M. Anon.
       Jesus, lover of my soul
       Sources. CR66, Wesley, C
       Topic. Christian

915   xt L.M. Belknap, D
       There is a glorious world on high
       Sources. MNAN14/60, Steele, A
       Topic. Faith

HOW SWEETLY

916   pt P.M. Holden, O
       How sweetly along the gay mead
       Sources. MNAN13/76, Anon.
       Topic. Thanksgiving

HUDSON

917   xt C.M. Chandler, S
       Time, what an empty vapour 'tis
       Sources. MNAN2/148, WH2/58
       Topic. Time and Eternity

918   pt S.M. Edson, L
       Come, sound his praise abroad
       Sources. MNAN3/22, WP95
       Topic. Worship

919   xt L.M. Olmsted, T
       My refuge is the God of love
       Sources. MNAN15/100, WP11
       Topic. Saints and Sinners

HULL

920   xt P.M. Billings, W
       We celebrate the praise to day
       Sources. WB3/204, RCH58
       Topic. Birth of Christ

HUMAN FRAILTY

921   ft C.M. Read, D
       Thee we adore, eternal name
       Sources. DR95, WH2/55
       Topic. Time and Eternity

HUMILITY

922   xt C.M. Babcock, S
       God of my life, look gently down
       Sources. MNAN11/64, WP39/3
       Topic. Sickness and Recovery

HUNTINGTON

923   ft L.M. Morgan, J
       Lord, what a thoughtless wretch was I
       Sources. MNAN7/123, WP73
       Topic. The World

HURON

924   pt P.M. Doolittle, E
       I love the volumes of thy word
       Sources. MNAN15/40, WP19
       Topic. Scripture

HYMN, A

925   xt P.M. Holden, O
       And is th'illustrious chieftain dead
       Sources. MNAN13/175, Gardner, J
       Topic. Funeral

HYMN 35

926   xt P.M. Belcher, S
       Sinners, turn, why will ye die
       Sources. MNAN5/59, Wesley, C
       Topic. Salvation

HYMN 98

927　xt P.M. Belcher, S
　　　Come, thou almighty king
　　　Sources. MNAN5/61, Anon.
　　　Topic. Universal Praise

HYMN 116

928　xt P.M. Belcher, S
　　　All ye that pass by, to Jesus draw nigh
　　　Sources. MNAN5/62, Wesley, C
　　　Topic. Atonement

HYMN 170

929　pt P.M. Belcher, S
　　　Though troubles assail and dangers affright
　　　Sources. MNAN5/64, Newton, J
　　　Topic. Fear and Hope

HYMN FOR CHRISTMAS, AN

930　xt C.M. Billings, W
　　　While shepherds watch'd their flocks by night
　　　Sources. WB1/92, Tate, N
　　　Topic. Birth of Christ

HYMN ON PEACE, A

931　sp Wood, A
　　　Behold, array'd in light, and by divine command
　　　Sources. MNAN6/51, Anon.
　　　Topic. Thanksgiving

IDUMEA

932　xt C.M. West, E
　　　What mighty man or mighty God
　　　Sources. MNAN7/50, WH1/28
　　　Topic. The Christian Church

I'LL LIFT MY HANDS

933　pt L.M. Swan, T
　　　I'll lift my hands, I'll raise my voice
　　　Sources. TS118, WP63
　　　Topic. Lord's Day

IMMANUEL

934　xt P.M. Babcock, S
　　　Hail, thou once despised Jesus
　　　Sources. MNAN11/65, Bakewell, J
　　　Topic. Atonement

IMMENSITY

935　ft L.M. Doolittle, E
　　　Within thy circling pow'r I stand
　　　Sources. MNAN15/42, WP139/1
　　　Topic. Perfections of God

IMMORTAL BLOOM

936　pt P.M. Jenks, S
　　　Angels, roll the rock away
　　　Sources. SJ320, Scott, T
　　　Topic. Resurrection of Christ

IMMORTALITY

937　xt P.M. Bull, A
　　　I'll praise my maker with my breath
　　　Sources. MNAN1/72, WP146
　　　Topic. Perfections of God

INCENSE

938　xt L.M. Holden, O
　　　Nature with all her pow'rs shall sing
　　　Sources. MNAN13/77, WH2/1
　　　Topic. Thanksgiving

INDEPENDENCE

939　an Billings, W
　　　The states, O Lord, with songs of praise
　　　Sources. WB2/244, WP21
　　　Topic. Patriotic

INDOSTAN

940　sp Holyoke, S
　　　These glorious minds, how bright they shine
　　　Sources. MNAN12/80, WH1/41
　　　Topic. Hell and Heaven

INSTRUMENTAL CONCERT

941　sp West, E
　　　Descend, ye nine, descend and sing
　　　Sources. MNAN7/52, Pope, A
　　　Topic. Music

INTERCESSION

942　sp Babcock, S
　　　Pardon and grace, and boundless love
　　　Sources. MNAN11/67, WHor
　　　Topic. Sufferings and Death of Christ

943　xt P.M. Doolittle, E
　　　Jesus, once for sinners slain
　　　Sources. MNAN15/44, Hart, J
　　　Topic. Resurrection of Christ

944　xt C.M. Jenks, S
　　　Father, he cries, forgive their sins
　　　Sources. SJ111, WH2/12
　　　Topic. Intercession of Christ

INVITATION

945　sp Belcher, S
　　　Child of the summer, charming rose
　　　Sources. MNAN5/66, Anon.
　　　Topic. Secular

946　xt P.M. Brownson, O
　　　Come, ye sinners, poor and wretched
　　　Sources. MNAN2/24, Hart, J
　　　Topic. Invitations and Promises

947　xt C.M. Bull, A
　　　Let ev'ry mortal ear attend
　　　Sources. MNAN1/74, WH1/7
　　　Topic. Invitations and Promises

948 xt P.M. Jenks, S
Come, sinners, attend
Sources. SJ112, Allen, W
Topic. Salvation

949 ft L.M. Kimball, J
Come, my beloved, haste away
Sources. MNAN12/177, WH1/78
Topic. Solomon's Song

950 xt C.M. West, E
Let ev'ry mortal ear attend
Sources. MNAN7/55, WH1/7
Topic. Invitations and Promises

INVITE

951 pt P.M. Jenks, S
Pilgrim, burdened with thy sin
Sources. SJ321, Crabbe, G
Topic. Repentance

INVOCATION

952 ft L.M. Billings, W
Majestic God, our muse inspire
Sources. WB4/76, Billings, W
Topic. Communion with God

953 ft L.M. Jenks, S
O may thy church, thy turtle dove
Sources. SJ113, Anon.
Topic. The Christian Church

INVOCATION TO CHARITY

954 sp Holden, O
Come charity with goodness crown'd
Sources. MNAN13/79, Anon.
Topic. Charity

IPSWICH

955 pt C.M. Billings, W
Lord, hear my cry, regard my pray'r
Sources. WB1/258, NV61
Topic. Christian

IRISH

956 pt C.M. Anon.
Blest morning, whose young dawning rays
Sources. CR68, WH2/72
Topic. Worship

ISLE OF WIGHT

957 pt C.M. Anon.
Great God is this our certain doom
Sources. CR69, WH2/63
Topic. Death and Resurrection

958 pt C.M. Anon.
Infinite grief! amazing woe
Sources. WB3/347, WH2/95
Topic. Christian

ITALY

959 ft P.M. Edson, L Jr
Upward I lift mine eyes
Sources. MNAN3/67, WP121
Topic. Creation and Providence

960 pt L.M. French, J
Teach us, O Lord, how frail is man
Sources. MNAN9/153, WP90
Topic. Death and Resurrection

IXWORTH

961 pt L.M. Doolittle, E
The heav'ns declare thy glory, Lord
Sources. MNAN15/45, WP19
Topic. Scripture

JAMAICA

962 pt L.M. Billings, W
When I survey the wond'rous cross
Sources. WB1/230, WH3/7
Topic. The Lord's Supper

963 pt C.M. Billings, W
Joy to the world, the Lord is come
Sources. WB2/282, WP98/2
Topic. Birth of Christ

964 pt C.M. Stone, J
Must friends and helpers drop and die
Sources. MNAN10/41, Watts
Topic. Death and Resurrection

JARGON

965 pt P.M. Billings, W
Let horrid jargon split the air
Sources. WB2/263, Billings, W
Topic. Secular

JEFFERSON

966 sp Doolittle, E
I'll search the land, and raise the just
Sources. MNAN15/46, WP101
Topic. Magistracy

JEHOVAH SPEAKS

967 sp Holden, O
Jehovah speaks! let Israel hear
Sources. MNAN13/82, WH1/84
Topic. Invitations and Promises

JERUSALEM

968 xt L.M. Benham, A
Go forth, ye heralds, in my name
Sources. MNAN8/34, Maxwell, J
Topic. Gospel

969 pt P.M. Billings, W
All is hush, the battle's o'er
Sources. WB3/196, RCH40
Topic. Salvation

JERUSALEM [I]

970   xt P.M. French, J
God's temple crowns the holy mount
Sources. MNAN9/154, NV87
Topic. The Jewish Church

JERUSALEM [II]

971   an French, J
Awake, put on thy strength, O Zion
Sources. MNAN9/156, Bible
Topic. The Jewish Church

JERUSALEM ANTHEM

972   an West, E
Awake, awake, put on thy strength, O Zion
Sources. MNAN7/57, Bible
Topic. Dedication

JEWRY

973   xt P.M. Belcher, S
Hark! the herald angels sing
Sources. MNAN5/68, Wesley, C
Topic. Birth of Christ

JORDAN

974   xt C.M. Billings, W
There is a land of pure delight
Sources. CR70, WH2/66
Topic. Death and Resurrection

975   xt C.M. Billings, W
There is a land of pure delight
Sources. WB3/180, WH2/66
Topic. Death and Resurrection

JORDAN'S STREAMS

976   xt C.M. Jenks, S
There is a land of pure delight
Sources. SJ323, WH2/66
Topic. Death and Resurrection

JOYFUL SOUND

977   ft C.M. Benham, A
Jesus our God ascends on high
Sources. MNAN8/36, WP47
Topic. Ascension and Exaltation of Christ

978   xt S.M. Jenks, S
Far as thy name is known
Sources. SJ325, WP48/2
Topic. The Christian Church

JUBILANT

979   ft P.M. Belcher, S
Blow ye the trumpet, blow
Sources. MNAN5/70, Wesley, C
Topic. Worship

JUBILEE

980   ft P.M. Brownson, O
Blow ye the trumpet, blow
Sources. MNAN2/25, Wesley, C
Topic. Worship

981   pt P.M. Jenks, S
The chariot! the chariot! its wheels roll in fire
Sources. SJ327, Milman, H
Topic. Day of Judgment

JUDEA

982   xt P.M. Billings, W
A virgin unspotted the prophet foretold
Sources. WB2/52, Anon.
Topic. Birth of Christ

JUDGMENT

983   pt P.M. Brownson, O
I am the saviour, I th'almighty God
Sources. MNAN2/27, WP50/2
Topic. Day of Judgment

984   ft C.M. Gillet, A
That awful day will surely come
Sources. MNAN2/97, WH2/107
Topic. Day of Judgment

985   pt P.M. Jenks, S
Ah, guilty sinner, ruined by transgression
Sources. SJ330, Beecher, C
Topic. Saints and Sinners

986   pt P.M. Read, D
Behold, the judge descends; his guards are nigh
Sources. CR72, WP50/1
Topic. Day of Judgment

987   pt P.M. Read, D
Behold, the judge descends; his guards are nigh
Sources. DR97, WP50/1
Topic. Day of Judgment

988   pt P.M. Read, D
Behold, the judge descends; his guards are nigh
Sources. DR268, WP50/1
Topic. Day of Judgment

989   pt P.M. Read, D
Behold, the judge descends; his guards are nigh
Sources. DR270, WP50/1
Topic. Day of Judgment

990   sp Swan, T
The God of glory sends his summons forth
Sources. TS119, WP50/2
Topic. Day of Judgment

991   sp Swan, T
The God of glory sends his summons forth
Sources. TS340, WP50/2
Topic. Day of Judgment

JUDGMENT ANTHEM

992   an Morgan, J
Hark! ye mortals, hear the trumpet
Sources. MNAN7/125, Watts, &c.
Topic. Day of Judgment

JUSTICE

993   pt P.M. Chandler, S
The God of glory sends his summons forth
Sources. MNAN2/149, WP50/2
Topic. Day of Judgment

JUSTICE ANTHEM

994   an Edson, L Jr
That day I sing, the day of gen'ral doom
Sources. MNAN3/69, Townsend, W
Topic. Day of Judgment

JUSTIFICATION

995   ft S.M. Woodruff, M
I shall behold the face
Sources. MNAN8/92, WP17
Topic. Saints and Sinners

KEENE

996   xt C.M. Belknap, D
Since I have plac'd my trust in God
Sources. MNAN14/61, NV11
Topic. Saints and Sinners

KENSINGTON

997   xt P.M. Woodruff, M
Now begin the heav'nly theme
Sources. MNAN8/93, Langford, J
Topic. Redemption

KILLINGLY

998   xt S.M. Jenks, S
My willing soul would stay
Sources. SJ114, WH2/14
Topic. Worship

KINGSBRIDGE

999   pt L.M. Anon.
Rejoice ye shining worlds on high
Sources. CR74, WP24 & 107
Topic. Ascension and Exaltation of Christ

KINGSTON

1000   xt C.M. Kimball, J
Infinite grief! amazing woe
Sources. MNAN12/179, WH2/95
Topic. Christian

1001   pt P.M. Belknap, D
Along the banks where Babel's current flows
Sources. MNAN14/63, BarP137
Topic. Afflictions of the Church

1002   pt S.M. Read, D
The law by Moses came
Sources. DR100, WH1/118
Topic. Law and Gospel

KINSALE

1003   xt S.M. Swan, T
Raise your triumphant songs
Sources. TS129, WH2/104
Topic. Perfections of God

KITTERY

1004   ft C.M. Billings, W
Our father, who in heaven art
Sources. WB3/152, Tate, N
Topic. Doxology

1005   ft C.M. Billings, W
Our father, who in heaven art
Sources. WB3/288, Tate, N
Topic. Doxology

LAINDON

1006   xt C.M. Holyoke, S
Alas! and did my saviour bleed
Sources. MNAN12/83, WH2/9
Topic. Repentance

LAMENTATION

1007   xt C.M. Belcher, S
No songs of triumph now be sung
Sources. MNAN5/72, Anon.
Topic. Sufferings and Death of Christ

1008   xt C.M. French, J
O, if my soul was form'd for woe
Sources. MNAN9/157, WH2/106
Topic. Repentance

1009   xt L.M. Jenks, S
Spare us, O Lord, aloud we pray
Sources. SJ331, WP102
Topic. Death and Resurrection

LAMENTATION FOR JERUSALEM

1010   an French, J
Why dost thou sit solitary, O Jerusalem
Sources. MNAN9/159, Bible
Topic. Fast Day

LAMENTATION OVER BOSTON

1011   an Billings, W
By the rivers of Watertown we sat down
Sources. WB2/136, Bible/Billings
Topic. Patriotic

LANCASTER

1012   pt L.M. Billings, W
Come hither all ye weary souls
Sources. WB1/324, WH1/127
Topic. Invitations and Promises

1013   sp Wood, A
        Yet, gracious God, yet will I seek thy smiling face
        Sources. MNAN6/59, WHor
        Topic. Faith

LAND OF PLEASURE

1014   xt P.M. Jenks, S
        There is a land of pleasure
        Sources. SJ333, Anon.
        Topic. Salvation

LANDAFF

1015   pt P.M. Anon.
        The God of glory sends his summons forth
        Sources. CR76, WP50/2
        Topic. Day of Judgment

LANESBOROUGH

1016   ft S.M. Edson, L
        And must this body die
        Sources. MNAN3/23, WH2/110
        Topic. Death and Resurrection

LARK

1017   xt L.M. Brownson, O
        From pleasant trees that shade the brink
        Sources. MNAN2/29, WP104
        Topic. Creation and Providence

1018   ft C.M. West, E
        Hov'ring among the leaves there stands
        Sources. MNAN7/60, WH3/8
        Topic. The Lord's Supper

LARK, THE

1019   sp Billings, W
        Look up and see th'unwearied sun
        Sources. WB3/232, Anon.
        Topic. Morning and Evening

LAST DAY

1020   ft P.M. Billings, N
        Be dark! thou sun, in one eternal night
        Sources. MNAN3/105, White, J
        Topic. Day of Judgment

1021   pt P.M. Jenks, S
        The Lord, the sov'reign, sends his summons forth
        Sources. SJ116, WP50/1
        Topic. Day of Judgment

LEBANON

1022   pt C.M. Billings, W
        Lord, what is man, poor feeble man
        Sources. CR78, WP144/2
        Topic. Time and Eternity

1023   pt C.M. Billings, W
        Death, with his warrent in his hand
        Sources. WB1/333, Billings, W
        Topic. Death and Resurrection

1024   pt C.M. Billings, W
        Death, with his warrant in his hand
        Sources. WB2/78, Billings, W
        Topic. Death and Resurrection

1025   pt C.M. Bull, A
        Thou art my portion, O my God
        Sources. MNAN1/75, WP119/3
        Topic. Sincerity

LEEDS

1026   xt C.M. Swan, T
        Dread Sov'reign, let my evening song
        Sources. TS130, WH2/7
        Topic. Morning and Evening

LEGHORN

1027   xt L.M. Swan, T
        Deep in our hearts, let us record
        Sources. TS132, WP69/1
        Topic. Sufferings and Death of Christ

LEICESTER

1028   ft C.M. Kimball, J
        Not from the dust affliction grows
        Sources. MNAN12/181, WH1/83
        Topic. Creation and Providence

1029   pt P.M. Stone, J
        Not to our names, thou only just and true
        Sources. MNAN10/43, WP115
        Topic. Perfections of God

LENA [I]

1030   pt P.M. Belknap, D
        See the Lord of glory dying
        Sources. MNAN14/64, Anon.
        Topic. Ascension and Exaltation of Christ

LENA [II]

1031   pt P.M. Belknap, D
        As lost in lonely grief, I tread
        Sources. MNAN14/66, BarP88
        Topic. Fear and Hope

LENOX

1032   ft P.M. Edson, L
        Ye tribes of Adam join
        Sources. CR79, WP148
        Topic. Universal Praise

1033   ft P.M. Edson, L
        Ye tribes of Adam join
        Sources. MNAN3/24, WP148
        Topic. Universal Praise

LENWICK

1034   pt P.M. Holyoke, S
        O love divine! what hast thou done
        Sources. MNAN12/84, Wesley, C
        Topic. Sufferings and Death of Christ

LEOMINSTER

1035   xt C.M. Belknap, D
        I'm not asham'd to own my Lord
        Sources. MNAN14/68, WH1/103
        Topic. Trust and Confidence

1036   xt C.M. Stone, J
        To vanity and earthly pride
        Sources. MNAN10/45, Anon.
        Topic. Trust and Confidence

LEWIS-TOWN

1037   xt C.M. Billings, W
        How vast must their advantage be
        Sources. WB4/292, NV133
        Topic. Love

LEXINGTON

1038   xt C.M. Babcock, S
        Indulgent God, with pitying eyes
        Sources. MNAN11/68, Doddridge, P
        Topic. Redemption

1039   pt L.M. Billings, W
        Thy mercy, Lord, to me extend
        Sources. WB1/236, NV57
        Topic. Creation and Providence

1040   pt C.M. Doolittle, E
        Sing to the Lord, ye distant lands
        Sources. MNAN15/50, WP96
        Topic. Birth of Christ

1041   xt C.M. Wood, A
        Hold not thy peace, O Lord our God
        Sources. MNAN6/62, NV83
        Topic. Afflictions of the Church

LIBERTY

1042   pt S.M. Billings, W
        God bless our gracious king
        Sources. WB1/75, Billings?
        Topic. Prudence

1043   ft C.M. Jenks, S
        No more beneath th'oppressive hand
        Sources. SJ119, Anon.
        Topic. Patriotic

LIFE

1044   pt P.M. Jenks, S
        Life is like a summer's day
        Sources. SJ335, Jenks?
        Topic. Youth and Old Age

LILLY

1045   xt C.M. Edson, L
        What shall I render to my God
        Sources. MNAN3/26, WP116/2
        Topic. Public Worship

LILLY, THE

1046   pt P.M. Belcher, S
        Peaceful and lowly in their native soil
        Sources. MNAN5/73, Anon.
        Topic. Secular

LIMA

1047   xt S.M. Babcock, S
        To God, the only wise
        Sources. MNAN11/69, WH1/51
        Topic. Perseverance

LINCOLN

1048   ft C.M. Belcher, S
        Let all the just to God, with joy
        Sources. MNAN5/74, NV33
        Topic. Creation and Providence

1049   pt S.M. Billings, W
        See what a living stone
        Sources. WB1/278, WP118
        Topic. Worship

1050   xt P.M. Mann, E
        Lord of the worlds above
        Sources. MNAN4/38, WP84
        Topic. Public Worship

1051   pt P.M. Wood, A
        Join all the glorious names
        Sources. MNAN6/63, WH1/150
        Topic. Characters and Offices of Christ

LINEVILLE

1052   pt L.M. Jenks, S
        Death, like an overflowing stream
        Sources. SJ336, WP90
        Topic. Death and Resurrection

LINNET

1053   xt L.M. Stone, J
        The swelling billows know their bound
        Sources. MNAN10/46, WP104
        Topic. Creation and Providence

LINTON

1054   pt S.M. Doolittle, E
        Within thy churches, Lord
        Sources. MNAN15/51, WP63
        Topic. Lord's Day

LISBON

1055   ft S.M. Read, D
        Welcome, sweet day of rest
        Sources. CR81, WH2/14
        Topic. Worship

1056   ft S.M. Read, D
        Welcome, sweet day of rest
        Sources. DR101, WH2/14
        Topic. Worship

1057   ft S.M. Read, D
        Welcome, sweet day of rest
        Sources. DR272, WH2/14
        Topic. Worship

1058   ft S.M. Read, D
        Welcome, sweet day of rest
        Sources. DR273, WH2/14
        Topic. Worship

1059   xt S.M. Read, D
        Welcome, sweet day of rest
        Sources. DR274, WH2/14
        Topic. Worship

1060   xt S.M. Swan, T
        O let thy God and king
        Sources. TS134, WP45
        Topic. Beauty of the Church

LITCHFIELD

1061   ft L.M. Brownson, O
        'Twas from thy hand, my God, I came
        Sources. MNAN2/32, WP139/2
        Topic. Creation and Providence

1062   xt C.M. Kimball, J
        Our God, our help in ages past
        Sources. MNAN12/183, WP90/1
        Topic. Time and Eternity

LITTLE MARLBOROUGH

1063   pt S.M. Anon.
        Welcome, sweet day of rest
        Sources. CR82, WH2/14
        Topic. Worship

LODI

1064   xt L.M. Holden, O
        Happy the church, thou sacred place
        Sources. MNAN13/85, WH2/64
        Topic. The Christian Church

LONDON

1065   pt L.M. Belknap, D
        Exalted prince of life, we own
        Sources. MNAN14/69, Doddridge, P
        Topic. Exaltation of Christ

1066   ft L.M. French, J
        The wond'ring world inquires to know
        Sources. MNAN9/167, WH1/75
        Topic. Solomon's Song

1067   xt L.M. Swan, T
        Methinks I hear the heav'ns resound
        Sources. TS135, Anon.
        Topic. Birth of Christ

LONDON NEW

1068   pt C.M. Anon.
        Let ev'ry tongue thy goodness speak
        Sources. CR83, WP145/3
        Topic. Perfections of God

LORD APPEARS, THE

1069   sp Swan, T
        The Lord appears my helper now
        Sources. TS139, WP118/1
        Topic. Christian

LORD'S DAY

1070   xt S.M. Holden, O
        This is the glorious day
        Sources. MNAN13/86, WP118
        Topic. Worship

LOUISIANA

1071   xt P.M. West, E
        I'll praise my maker with my breath
        Sources. MNAN7/62, WP146
        Topic. Perfections of God

LOUDON

1072   pt P.M. Holyoke, S
        And can this mighty king
        Sources. MNAN12/86, WH2/169
        Topic. Perfections of God

1073   xt S.M. Olmsted, T
        Come sound his praise abroad
        Sources. MNAN15/102, WP95
        Topic. Worship

LOWER FALLS

1074   xt L.M. Belknap, D
        Now let our mournful songs record
        Sources. MNAN14/70, WP22
        Topic. Ascension and Exaltation of Christ

LUBEC

1075.   ft S.M. Babcock, S
        Let all our tongues be one
        Sources. MNAN11/71, WH3/9
        Topic. The Lord's Supper

LUTESTRING

1076   xt C.M. Swan, T
        O God, my heart is fully bent
        Sources. TS143, NV108
        Topic. Universal Praise

LYDD

1077   pt C.M. French, J
        Give thanks to God, invoke his name
        Sources. MNAN9/168, WP105
        Topic. The Jewish Church

LYME

1078   pt C.M. Read, D
Laugh, ye profane, and swell, and burst
Sources. DR103, WHor
Topic. Death and Resurrection

1079   pt C.M. Read, D
Laugh, ye profane, and swell, and burst
Sources. DR275, WHor
Topic. Death and Resurrection

1080   ft P.M. Swan, T
You tribes of Adam join
Sources. TS148, WP148
Topic. Universal Praise

LYNN

1081   pt P.M. Belknap, D
Loud to the prince of heav'n
Sources. MNAN14/72, Doddridge, P
Topic. Exaltation of Christ

1082   pt C.M. Billings, W
Lord let thy servant now depart
Sources. WB1/252, Tate, N
Topic. Trust and Confidence

LYNNFIELD

1083   sp Holden, O
My God, permit me not to be
Sources. MNAN13/87, WH2/122
Topic. Worship

MADISON

1084   ft L.M. Read, D
Great shepherd of thine Israel
Sources. DR105, WP80
Topic. Afflictions of the Church

MADRID

1085   pt P.M. Billings, W
How charmingly sounds the word of the Lord
Sources. WB2/332, RCH87
Topic. Redemption

MAJESTY

1086   ft C.M. Belcher, S
Behold the glories of the lamb
Sources. MNAN5/76, WH1/1
Topic. Addresses to Christ

1087   xt C.M. Billings, W
The Lord descended from above
Sources. CR84, OV18
Topic. Perfections of God

1088   xt C.M. Billings, W
The Lord descended from above
Sources. WB2/203, OV18
Topic. Perfections of God

1089   ft C.M. Jenks, S
When God, our leader, shines in arms
Sources. SJ120, WP18/1
Topic. Thanksgiving

1090   ft P.M. Swan, T
He framed the globe, he built the sky
Sources. TS151, WP96
Topic. Hell and Heaven

MALDEN

1091   ft C.M. Belknap, D
Now sable clouds from western skies
Sources. MNAN14/74, Anon.
Topic. Seasons of the Year

1092   pt L.M. Billings, W
O render thanks to God above
Sources. WB1/51, NV106
Topic. The Jewish Church

1093   xt C.M. Kimball, J
Now shall my head be lifted high
Sources. MNAN12/184, WP27/1
Topic. Public Worship

MANCHESTER

1094   pt L.M. Billings, W
Let the shrill trumpet's warlike voice
Sources. WB2/286, NV150
Topic. Universal Praise

1095   ft L.M. Billings, W
Let the shrill trumpet's warlike voice
Sources. WB3/12, NV150
Topic. Universal Praise

MANLIUS

1096   xt L.M. Olmsted, T
Bless, O ye western world, your God
Sources. MNAN15/103, DP147/2
Topic. Perfections of God

MANSFIELD

1097   xt C.M. Belknap, D
Thus saith the ruler of the skies
Sources. MNAN14/75, WH2/83
Topic. Ascension and Exaltation of Christ

1098   pt P.M. Billings, W
Think, mighty God, on feeble man
Sources. WB2/322, WP89
Topic. Death and Resurrection

1099   xt L.M. Billings, W
Jehovah! 'tis a glorious word
Sources. WB3/290, WP148
Topic. Universal Praise

MANTUA

1100 ft C.M. Holden, O
A blooming paradise of joy
Sources. MNAN13/90, WH2/59
Topic. Joy and Rejoicing

MARBLEHEAD

1101 pt C.M. Billings, W
How vast must their advantage be
Sources. WB1/256, NV133
Topic. Love

1102 pt C.M. Billings, W
How vast must their advantage be
Sources. WB2/80, NV133
Topic. Love

MARCELLUS

1103 xt S.M. Jenks, S
Then let our songs abound
Sources. SJ122, WH2/30
Topic. Joy and Rejoicing

1104 xt P.M. Olmsted, T
Think, mighty God, on feeble man
Sources. MNAN15/106, WP89
Topic. Death and Resurrection

MARLBOROUGH

1105 ft S.M. French, J
My saviour and my king
Sources. MNAN9/171, WP45
Topic. Beauty of the Church

1106 ft C.M. Wood, A
O for a shout of sacred joy
Sources. MNAN6/65, WP47
Topic. Ascension and Exaltation of Christ

MARSHFIELD

1107 pt L.M. Billings, W
When we, our weary'd limbs to rest
Sources. WB1/276, NV137
Topic. Afflictions of the Church

1108 pt L.M. Billings, W
When we, our weary'd limbs to rest
Sources. WB2/84, NV137
Topic. Afflictions of the Church

MARSHGROVE

1109 xt P.M. Holyoke, S
The God I trust Is true and just
Sources. MNAN12/87, Hart, J
Topic. Adoption

MARYLAND

1110 ft S.M. Billings, W
And must this body die
Sources. CR86, WH2/110
Topic. Death and Resurrection

1111 ft S.M. Billings, W
And must this body die
Sources. WB2/126, WH2/110
Topic. Death and Resurrection

MASONIC DIRGE

1112 sp Holden, O
While ev'ry orator and bard displays
Sources. MNAN13/179, Harris, T
Topic. Masonic

MASONICK ODE

1113 sp Jenks, S
Let there be light! th'almighty spoke
Sources. SJ123, Anon.
Topic. Creation and Providence

MASSACHUSETTS

1114 sp Billings, N
Had not the Lord, may Israel say
Sources. MNAN3/108, WP124
Topic. Thanksgiving

1115 pt P.M. Billings, W
Great is the Lord God, the thunder's his voice
Sources. WB1/153, Morton, P
Topic. Universal Praise

1116 xt L.M. French, J
Had not the Lord, may Israel say
Sources. MNAN9/172, WP124
Topic. Thanksgiving

MEAR

1117 pt C.M. Anon.
Sing to the Lord, ye distant lands
Sources. CR88, WP96
Topic. Birth of Christ

MEDFIELD

1118 pt L.M. Billings, W
When I my various blessings see
Sources. WB1/330, Byles, S
Topic. Intercession of Christ

1119 pt L.M. Billings, W
When I my various blessings see
Sources. WB2/66, Byles, S
Topic. Intercession of Christ

MEDFORD

1120 xt S.M. Babcock, S
Hosanna to the king
Sources. MNAN11/72, WP118
Topic. Worship

1121 pt L.M. Billings, W
With glory clad, with strength array'd
Sources. WB1/304, NV93
Topic. Perfections of God

1122   pt L.M. Stone, J
Black, heavy thoughts like mountains roll
Sources. MNAN10/48, WHor
Topic. Fear and Hope

MEDITATION

1123   xt C.M. Jenks, S
When I with pleasing wonder stand
Sources. SJ128, WP139/2
Topic. Perfections of God

1124   pt P.M. West, E
Come now, O my soul, meditate on that day
Sources. MNAN7/63, Anon.
Topic. Day of Judgment

MEDWAY

1125   ft C.M. Billings, W
Sing to the Lord Jehovah's name
Sources. WB2/94, WP95
Topic. Worship

MELODY

1126   ft C.M. Edson, L
Long as I live I'll bless thy name
Sources. MNAN3/28, WP145/1
Topic. Perfections of God

1127   xt S.M. Jenks, S
Come, sound his praise abroad
Sources. SJ337, WP95
Topic. Worship

MENDOM

1128   xt P.M. Billings, W
My redeemer, let me be
Sources. WB3/170, RCH17
Topic. Redemption

MENDON

1129   xt C.M. Belknap, D
Thee we adore, eternal name
Sources. MNAN14/77, WH2/55
Topic. Time and Eternity

1130   xt P.M. French, J
I'll praise my maker with my breath
Sources. MNAN9/174, WP146
Topic. Perfections of God

MENOTOMY

1131   xt L.M. Babcock, S
To Jesus, our exalted Lord
Sources. MNAN11/74, Steele, A
Topic. Thanksgiving

MENTZ

1132   pt C.M. Holyoke, S
Now from the roaring lion's rage
Sources. MNAN12/88, WP22/2
Topic. Ascension and Exaltation of Christ

MERCY SEAT

1133   pt L.M. Holden, O
Jesus, where'er thy people meet
Sources. MNAN13/92, Cowper, W
Topic. Worship

MEREDITH

1134   ft L.M. Doolittle, E
My spirit looks to God alone
Sources. MNAN15/52, WP62
Topic. Trust and Confidence

MERRIFIELD

1135   xt C.M. French, J
No sleep nor slumber to his eyes
Sources. MNAN9/175, WP132
Topic. The Christian Church

MESSIAH

1136   ft C.M. Bull, A
Joy to the world, the Lord is come
Sources. MNAN1/77, WP98/2
Topic. Birth of Christ

1137   xt L.M. French, J
Sun, moon, and stars convey thy praise
Sources. MNAN9/177, WP19
Topic. Scripture

1138   xt L.M. Gillet, A
Go worship at Immanuel's feet
Sources. MNAN2/99, WH1/146
Topic. Characters and Offices of Christ

1139   sp Holden, O
Ye nymphs of Solima begin the song
Sources. MNAN13/93, Pope, A
Topic. Birth of Christ

METHUEN

1140   pt P.M. Wood, A
The moment a sinner believes
Sources. MNAN6/67, Hart, J
Topic. Grace

MEXICO

1141   xt L.M. Jenks, S
Thus saith the high and lofty one
Sources. SJ339, WH1/87
Topic. Invitations and Promises

MIDDLEBURY

1142   xt L.M. Swan, T
Deep in our hearts, let us record
Sources. TS309, WP69/1
Topic. Sufferings and Death of Christ

MIDDLESEX

1143   pt C.M. Billings, W
Blest be the everlasting God
Sources. WB1/222, WH1/26
Topic. Resurrection of Christ

1144   xt C.M. French, J
Death! 'tis a melancholy day
Sources. MNAN9/178, WH2/52
Topic. Christ

1145   xt P.M. Holden, O
The Lord of glory reigns: he reigns on high
Sources. MNAN13/101, WP93/1
Topic. Perfections of God

MIDDLETON

1146   xt S.M. Kimball, J
When overwhelm'd with grief
Sources. MNAN12/185, WP61
Topic. Christian

MIDDLETOWN

1147   pt S.M. Billings, W
Shall we go on to sin
Sources. WB1/267, WH1/106
Topic. Christian

1148   xt P.M. Bull, A
Hail the day that sees him rise
Sources. CR89, Wesley, C
Topic. Ascension and Exaltation of Christ

1149   xt P.M. Bull, A
Hail the day that sees him rise
Sources. MNAN1/79, Wesley, C
Topic. Ascension and Exaltation of Christ

MIFFLIN

1150   ft C.M. Read, D
Life, like a vain amusement flies
Sources. DR108, WP90/2
Topic. Youth and Old Age

MILFORD

1151   ft C.M. Stephenson, J
If angels sung a saviour's birth
Sources. CR91, Anon.
Topic. Birth of Christ

MILLENIUM

1152   pt P.M. Gillet, A
Let all the earth their voices raise
Sources. MNAN2/102, WP96
Topic. Hell and Heaven

1153   sp Olmsted, T
Jesus shall reign where'er the sun
Sources. MNAN15/108, WP72/2
Topic. The Christian Church

MILLINGTON

1154   ft P.M. Holyoke, S
Immense compassion reigns
Sources. MNAN12/90, WH1/148
Topic. Characters and Offices of Christ

MILTON

1155   sp Babcock, S
My flesh shall slumber in the ground
Sources. MNAN11/75, WP17
Topic. Saints and Sinners

1156   xt C.M. Belknap, D
When verdure clothes the fertile vale
Sources. MNAN14/79, Steele, A
Topic. Times and Seasons

1157   ft C.M. Billings, W
Thee will I laud my God and king
Sources. WB1/167, NV145
Topic. Perfections of God

1158   ft P.M. Edson, L
Ye boundless realms of joy
Sources. MNAN3/29, NV148
Topic. Universal Praise

1159   ft C.M. Olmsted, T
With earnest longings of the mind
Sources. MNAN15/117, WP42
Topic. Fear and Hope

1160   pt C.M. Swan, T
My soul, the awful hour will come
Sources. TS154, Doddridge, P
Topic. Death and Resurrection

1161   ft P.M. West, E
The shining worlds above
Sources. MNAN7/64, WP148
Topic. Universal Praise

MINDEN

1162   ft L.M. French, J
Ye sons of Adam, vain and young
Sources. MNAN9/179, WH1/89
Topic. Youth and Old Age

1163   ft P.M. Olmsted, T
The Lord Jehovah reigns, And royal
Sources. MNAN15/119, WP93/2
Topic. Perfections of God

MINORCA

1164   xt P.M. Babcock, S
Almighty king of heav'n above
Sources. MNAN11/77, Anon.
Topic. Creation and Providence

1165   xt L.M. French, J
Jesus shall reign where'er the sun
Sources. MNAN9/181, WP72/2
Topic. The Christian Church

MODERN MUSIC

1166   sp Billings, W
We are met for a concert of modern invention
Sources. WB3/97, Billings?
Topic. Secular

MONMOUTH

1167   xt C.M. French, J
Why do we mourn departing friends
Sources. MNAN9/182, WH2/3
Topic. Death and Resurrection

1168   ft C.M. Stone, J
When God reveal'd his gracious name
Sources. MNAN10/49, WP126
Topic. Church Meetings

MONSON

1169   xt L.M. Belknap, D
Thus saith the high and lofty one
Sources. MNAN14/80, WH1/87
Topic. Invitations and Promises

MONTAGUE

1170   ft L.M. Swan, T
Ye sons of men with joy record
Sources. CR93, Doddridge, P
Topic. Creation and Providence

1171   ft L.M. Swan, T
You sons of men, with joy record
Sources. TS156, Doddridge, P
Topic. Creation and Providence

1172   ft L.M. Swan, T
You sons of men, with joy record
Sources. TS311, Doddridge, P
Topic. Creation and Providence

1173   ft L.M. Swan, T
Hast thou not planted with thy hands
Sources. TS313, WP80
Topic. Afflictions of the Church

MONTGOMERY

1174   ft C.M. Morgan, J
Early, my God, without delay
Sources. CR95, WP63/1
Topic. Lord's Day

1175   ft C.M. Morgan, J
Early, my God, without delay
Sources. MNAN7/136, WP63/1
Topic. Lord's Day

MONTICELLO

1176   xt L.M. Read, D
The world's foundations, by his hand
Sources. DR110, WP104
Topic. Creation and Providence

MONTVILLE

1177   ft C.M. Woodruff, M
O the sharp pangs of smarting pain
Sources. MNAN8/96, WH2/95
Topic. Christian

MORAVIA

1178   xt P.M. Billings, W
O love! what a secret to mortals thou art
Sources. WB3/212, RCH16
Topic. Love

MOREEN

1179   ft L.M. Swan, T
Oft I am told the muse will prove
Sources. TS158, WHor
Topic. Humility

MORIAH

1180   pt P.M. Billings, W
All over lovely is my Lord and God
Sources. WB3/190, RCH8
Topic. Redemption

MORNING

1181   xt C.M. Holden, O
Once more, my soul, the rising day
Sources. MNAN13/103, WH2/6
Topic. Morning and Evening

1182   pt L.M. Jenks, S
Awake my soul! awake my eyes
Sources. SJ341, Flatman, T
Topic. Morning and Evening

1183   ft C.M. Read, D
Lord, in the morning thou shalt hear
Sources. DR112, WP5
Topic. Lord's Day

MORNING HYMN

1184   pt L.M. Anon.
Awake my soul! awake mine eyes
Sources. CR98, Flatman, T
Topic. Morning and Evening

1185   xt C.M. Babcock, S
Once more, my soul, the rising day
Sources. MNAN11/78, WH2/6
Topic. Morning and Evening

1186   ft C.M. Billings, W
Once more, my soul, the rising day
Sources. WB4/98, WH2/6
Topic. Morning and Evening

1187   pt S.M. Jenks, S
Behold the morning sun
Sources. SJ129, WP19/2
Topic. Lord's Day

1188   xt C.M. West, E
With rev'rence let the saints appear
Sources. MNAN7/67, WP89/2
Topic. Perfections of God

MORNING SONG

1189   sp French, J
        God of the morning, at whose voice
        Sources. MNAN9/184, WH1/79
        Topic. Morning and Evening

MORNING-STAR

1190   ft L.M. Gillet, A
        Ye worlds of light that roll so near
        Sources. MNAN2/103, Beddome, B
        Topic. Hell and Heaven

MORNING VIEW

1191   xt P.M. Billings, N
        Let us all fly to music this morning
        Sources. MNAN3/113, Anon.
        Topic. Thanksgiving

MORPHEUS

1192   pt L.M. Billings, W
        Sleep, downy sleep, come close my eyes
        Sources. WB2/302, Flatman, T
        Topic. Regeneration

1193   ft L.M. Billings, W
        Sleep, downy sleep, come close my eyes
        Sources. WB2/337, Flatman, T
        Topic. Regeneration

MORRIS

1194   ft C.M. Read, D
        Were I in heav'n without my God
        Sources. DR114, WP73/2
        Topic. Communion with God

MORRISTON

1195   pt L.M. Billings, W
        Man has a soul of vast desires
        Sources. WB3/330, WH2/146
        Topic. The World

MORTALITY

119   xt L.M. Belknap, D
        It is the Lord, our maker's hand
        Sources. MNAN14/82, WP102/2
        Topic. Perfections of God

1197   pt P.M. Jenks, S
        Few are our days, those few we dream away
        Sources. SJ342, Anon.
        Topic. Time and Eternity

1198   pt L.M. Read, D
        Death, like an overflowing stream
        Sources. DR116, WP90
        Topic. Death and Resurrection

MORTALITY NEW

1199   ft L.M. Jenks, S
        Death, like an overflowing stream
        Sources. SJ131, WP90
        Topic. Death and Resurrection

MOUNT CALVARY

1200   pt P.M. Jenks, S
        Hearts of stone, relent, relent
        Sources. SJ133, Wesley, C
        Topic. Repentance

1201   xt P.M. Jenks, S
        Hearts of stone, relent, relent
        Sources. SJ134, Wesley, C
        Topic. Repentance

MOUNT CARMEL

1202   pt P.M. Holden, O
        I am the saviour, I th'almighty God
        Sources. MNAN13/104, WP50/2
        Topic. Day of Judgment

MOUNT OLIVET

1203   xt P.M. Jenks, S
        O come let us join
        Sources. SJ136, Wesley, C
        Topic. Redemption

MOUNT PARAN

1204   an West, E
        God came from Timon and the holy one
        Sources. MNAN7/68, Bible
        Topic. Thanksgiving

MOUNT PLEASANT

1205   pt P.M. Jenks, S
        Not to our names, thou only just and true
        Sources. SJ138, WP115
        Topic. Perfections of God

MOUNT VERNON

1206   ft P.M. Benham, A
        Great God, the heav'n's well order'd frame
        Sources. MNAN8/37, WP19
        Topic. Scripture

1207   xt S.M. French, J
        What if a saint must die
        Sources. MNAN9/188, Peck, J
        Topic. Day of Judgment

1208   sp Holden, O
        From Vernon's mount, behold the hero rise
        Sources. MNAN13/171, Anon.
        Topic. Patriotic

MOUNT-VERNON

1209   ft L.M. Jenks, S
        What solemn sounds the ear invade
        Sources. SJ140, Anon.
        Topic. Patriotic

MOUNT ZION

1210   ft L.M. French, J
        Deep in our hearts, let us record
        Sources. MNAN9/191, WP69/1
        Topic. Sufferings and Death of Christ

MOUNTAIN

1211 xt C.M. Holden, O
When some kind shepherd from his fold
Sources. MNAN13/107, Needham, J
Topic. Salvation

MOURNFUL SONG

1212 sp West, E
'Twas on that dark and doleful night
Sources. MNAN7/78, WH3/1
Topic. The Lord's Supper

MUSICAL CAPTIVE

1213 xt P.M. Wood, A
Music descending on a silent cloud
Sources. MNAN6/69, WHor
Topic. Music

NANTASKET

1214 pt L.M. Billings, W
Awake our souls (away our fears
Sources. WB1/158, WH1/48
Topic. Christian

NANTUCKET

1215 pt S.M. Billings, W
How beauteous are their feet
Sources. WB1/44, WH1/10
Topic. Law and Gospel

NAPLES

1216 ft L.M. Read, D
Shall the vile race of flesh and blood
Sources. DR117, WH1/82
Topic. Perfections of God

NATIVITY

1217 xt C.M. Babcock, S
Thus Gabriel sang, and straight around
Sources. MNAN11/79, WHor
Topic. Birth of Christ

NAZARETH

1218 pt C.M. Billings, W
My God, how many are my fears
Sources. WB2/290, WP3
Topic. Fear and Hope

NEEDHAM

1219 xt P.M. Babcock, S
O tell me no more of this world's vain store
Sources. MNAN11/80, Gambold, J
Topic. Grace

NEW BOSTON

1220 pt P.M. Billings, W
Ye boundless realms of joy
Sources. WB1/60, NV148
Topic. Universal Praise

NEW-BRAINTREE

1221 ft L.M. Stone, J
Raise monumental praises high
Sources. MNAN10/51, WH2/1
Topic. Thanksgiving

NEW CANAAN

1222 ft P.M. Holden, O
The Lord Jehovah reigns, And royal
Sources. MNAN13/109, WP93/2
Topic. Perfections of God

NEW-CASTLE

1223 pt C.M. Billings, W
We love thee, Lord, and we adore
Sources. WB2/278, WP18/1
Topic. Thanksgiving

NEW COLCHESTER

1224 pt C.M. Anon.
My soul, how lovely is the place
Sources. WB3/348, WP84
Topic. Public Worship

NEW DEDHAM

1225 ft S.M. Jenks, S
Since God is all my trust
Sources. SJ142, NV11
Topic. Faith

NEW EASTER ANTHEM, A

1226 an Read, D
I know that my redeemer lives
Sources. AA1/163, Bible
Topic. Easter

NEW-ENGLAND

1227 pt C.M. Gillet, A
My thoughts on awful subjects roll
Sources. MNAN2/106, WH2/2
Topic. Death and Resurrection

1228 ft L.M. Read, D
Let tyrants shake their iron rod
Sources. DR120, Billings, W
Topic. Faith

NEW ENGLAND

1229 ft L.M. Read, D
Let tyrants shake their iron rod
Sources. DR276, Billings, W
Topic. Faith

NEW-GREENFIELD

1230 ft C.M. Jenks, S
Hark! from the tombs a doleful sound
Sources. SJ144, WH2/63
Topic. Death and Resurrection

NEW-HARTFORD

1231   xt L.M. Jenks, S
        From all that dwell below the skies
        Sources. SJ146, WP117
        Topic. The Christian Church

NEW HAVEN

1232   pt L.M. Billings, W
        Come now, my soul, my heart, my tongue
        Sources. WB3/332, Anon.
        Topic. Universal Praise

NEW-HAVEN

1233   xt P.M. Jenks, S
        How pleas'd and blest was I
        Sources. SJ148, WP122
        Topic. Public Worship

1234   xt P.M. West, E
        How pleas'd and blest was I
        Sources. MNAN7/81, WP122
        Topic. Public Worship

NEW-HINGHAM

1235   pt S.M. Billings, W
        Death, O! the awful sound
        Sources. WB1/209, Billings, W
        Topic. Death and Resurrection

1236   pt S.M. Billings, W
        Death! O the awful sound
        Sources. WB2/83, Billings, W
        Topic. Death and Resurrection

NEW JERSEY

1237   ft L.M. Read, D
        Who shall the Lord's elect condemn
        Sources. DR277, WH1/14
        Topic. Fear and Hope

NEW JERUSALEM

1238   ft C.M. Ingalls, J
        From the third heav'n where God resides
        Sources. CR99, WH1/21
        Topic. Prayer and Praise for the Church

NEW LISBON

1239   pt P.M. Jenks, S
        Lord of the worlds above
        Sources. SJ343, WP84
        Topic. Public Worship

NEW LONDON

1240   xt C.M. Jenks, S
        While shepherds watch'd their flocks by night
        Sources. SJ150, Tate, N
        Topic. Birth of Christ

NEW NORTH

1241   pt C.M. Billings, W
        O praise the Lord with one consent
        Sources. WB1/248, NV135
        Topic. Perfections of God

1242   pt C.M. Billings, W
        O praise the Lord with one consent
        Sources. WB2/200, NV135
        Topic. Perfections of God

1243   ft C.M. Billings, W
        Let ev'ry mortal ear attend
        Sources. WB2/264, WH1/71
        Topic. Invitations and Promises

NEW-PLYMOUTH

1244   ft C.M. Billings, W
        O Lord, our fathers oft have told
        Sources. WB4/251, NV44
        Topic. Afflictions of the Church

NEW PRESTON

1245   xt C.M. Edson, L
        With songs and honours sounding loud
        Sources. MNAN3/32, WP147
        Topic. Seasons of the Year

NEW SHARON

1246   ft L.M. Belcher, S
        When such as we attempt to sing
        Sources. MNAN5/77, Anon.
        Topic. Humility

NEW SOUTH

1247   pt S.M. Billings, W
        To bless thy chosen race
        Sources. WB1/80, NV67
        Topic. Joy and Rejoicing

1248   pt S.M. Billings, W
        To bless thy chosen race
        Sources. WB2/64, NV67
        Topic. Joy and Rejoicing

NEW-SPRINGFIELD

1249   xt C.M. Billings, N
        Come, let us join our cheerful songs
        Sources. MNAN3/114, WH1/62
        Topic. Addresses to Christ

NEW-STRATFORD

1250   xt C.M. Gillet, A
        Out of the deeps of long distress
        Sources. MNAN2/107, WP130
        Topic. Pardon

NEW SUFFIELD

1251 pt L.M. Edson, L
Great God, attend while Zion sings
Sources. MNAN3/33, WP84/2
Topic. Public Worship

1252 pt S.M. Jenks, S
My sorrows, like a flood
Sources. SJ151, WHor
Topic. Pardon

NEW TOWN

1253 pt L.M. Billings, W
Ye princes that in might excel
Sources. WB1/48, NV29
Topic. Seasons of the Year

NEW UNION

1254 pt P.M. Holden, O
Attend, ye saints, and hear me tell
Sources. MNAN13/110, Anon.
Topic. Trust and Confidence

NEW-YEAR

1255 xt P.M. Jenks, S
Come, let us anew
Sources. SJ153, Wesley, C
Topic. New Year

NEW YEAR'S THOUGHT

1256 sp Woodruff, M
While in revolving course the glowing sun
Sources. MNAN8/97, Anon.
Topic. Death and Resurrection

NEWARK

1257 pt P.M. Read, D
Now begin the heav'nly theme
Sources. DR119, Langford, J
Topic. Redemption

NEWBERN

1258 pt P.M. Kimball, J
Not to our names, thou only just and true
Sources. MNAN12/187, WP115
Topic. Perfections of God

NEWBURN

1259 pt L.M. Billings, W
Thee will I love, O Lord my strength
Sources. WB2/316, WP18/1
Topic. Christian

NEWBURY

1260 ft C.M. Anon.
How awful is thy chast'ning rod
Sources. CR101, WP77/2
Topic. The Jewish Church

NEWBURYPORT

1261 xt L.M. Jenks, S
In ev'ry land begin the song
Sources. SJ154, WP117
Topic. The Christian Church

NEWINGTON

1262 ft P.M. Jenks, S
The God of glory sends his summons forth
Sources. SJ156, WP50/2
Topic. Day of Judgment

NEWMARK

1263 ft C.M. Belknap, D
Thron'd on a cloud, our God shall come
Sources. MNAN14/83, WP50/1
Topic. Day of Judgment

1264 pt C.M. Bull, A
Come, holy spirit, heavn'ly dove
Sources. MNAN1/81, WH2/34
Topic. Addresses to the Holy Spirit

NEWPORT

1265 pt C.M. Belknap, D
Life is a span, a fleeting hour
Sources. MNAN14/85, Steele, A
Topic. Death and Resurrection

1266 pt L.M. Billings, W
Who is this fair one in distress
Sources. WB1/308, WH1/78
Topic. Solomon's Song

1267 ft C.M. Brownson, O
O God, to whom revenge belongs
Sources. MNAN2/33, WP94/1
Topic. Saints and Sinners

1268 xt L.M. Read, D
I send the joys of earth away
Sources. DR122, WH2/11
Topic. Christian

NEWTON

1269 pt S.M. Anon.
Come sound his praise abroad
Sources. CR103, WP95
Topic. Worship

1270 xt C.M. Babcock, S
My saviour God, no voice but thine
Sources. MNAN11/82, Doddridge, P
Topic. Salvation

NEWTOWN

1271 xt L.M. Woodruff, M
People and realms of ev'ry tongue
Sources. MNAN8/103, WP72/2
Topic. The Christian Church

No. Four

1272 ft L.M. Belknap, D
Mankind must all return to dust
Sources. MNAN14/86, Anon.
Topic. Death and Resurrection

No. 1

1273 ft L.M. Mann, E
Majestic God, our muse inspire
Sources. MNAN4/3, Billings, W
Topic. Communion with God

No. 2

1274 sp Mann, E
He reigns, the Lord, the saviour reigns
Sources. MNAN4/5, WP97/1
Topic. Day of Judgment

No. 3 Cooper

1275 pt S.M. Mann, E
From lowest depths of woe
Sources. MNAN4/10, NV130
Topic. Pardon

No. 4

1276 xt P.M. Mann, E
The God of glory sends his summons forth
Sources. MNAN4/20, WP50/2
Topic. Day of Judgment

No. 5 Northampton

1277 xt S.M. Mann, E
Come we who love the Lord
Sources. MNAN4/23, WH2/30
Topic. Joy and Rejoicing

No. 6 Worcester New

1278 sp Mann, E
Now to the Lord a noble song
Sources. MNAN4/25, WH2/47
Topic. Christ

No. 7

1279 sp Mann, E
Now shall my inward joys arise
Sources. MNAN4/30, WH1/39
Topic. Safety and Triumph of the Church

No. 8 Foster

1280 xt S.M. Mann, E
I hear the voice of woe
Sources. MNAN4/35, Enfield, W
Topic. Liberality

No. 9

1281 xt P.M. Mann, E
Let earth and heav'n agree
Sources. MNAN4/36, Wesley, C
Topic. Exaltation of Christ

No. 12 Supplication

1282 sp Mann, E
Eternal God! enthron'd on high
Sources. MNAN4/44, Anon.
Topic. Youth and Old Age

No. 15

1283 sp Mann, E
Begin the high celestial strain
Sources. MNAN4/65, Rowe, E
Topic. Universal Praise

No. 16

1284 sp Mann, E
Before the rosy dawn of day
Sources. MNAN4/71, Rowe, E
Topic. Morning and Evening

No. 17

1285 sp Mann, E
Eternal source of ev'ry joy
Sources. MNAN4/78, Doddridge, P
Topic. Seasons of the Year

No. 18

1286 sp Mann, E
Father supreme! all nature's God
Sources. MNAN4/82, Lathrop, J
Topic. Communion with God

No. 19 Seraph's Lyre

1287 sp Mann, E
Hark, hark! what distant music melts upon the ear
Sources. MNAN4/89, Harris, T
Topic. Universal Praise

No. 21 Stillwater

1288 sp Mann, E
Up to thy throne, almighty king
Sources. MNAN4/93, Anon.
Topic. Trust and Confidence

No. 22 Turner

1289 pt C.M. Mann, E
Once more, my soul, the rising day
Sources. MNAN4/97, WH2/6
Topic. Morning and Evening

No. 24 Verona

1290 pt P.M. Mann, E
I am the saviour, I th'almighty God
Sources. MNAN4/101, WP50/2
Topic. Day of Judgment

No. 25

1291 sp Mann, E
Behold! the bright morning appears
Sources. MNAN4/104, Barnard, J
Topic. Resurrection of Christ

No. 26

1292 sp Mann, E
Now let our songs address the God of peace
Sources. MNAN4/108, Anon.
Topic. Thanksgiving

No. 27 YEOVIL

1293 pt P.M. Mann, E
Almighty king of heav'n above
Sources. MNAN4/111, Anon.
Topic. Creation and Providence

No. 28

1294 sp Mann, E
Hark! from the tombs a doleful sound
Sources. MNAN4/112, WH2/63
Topic. Death and Resurrection

No. 29 ADAMS

1295 xt P.M. Mann, E
The Lord Jehovah reigns, And royal
Sources. MNAN4/115, WP93/2
Topic. Perfections of God

No. 30 BELFAST

1296 pt L.M. Mann, E
Great is the Lord, exalted high
Sources. MNAN4/117, WP135/2
Topic. The Jewish Church

No. 31

1297 xt C.M. Mann, E
When God reveal'd his gracious name
Sources. MNAN4/118, WP126
Topic. Church Meetings

No. 32

1298 pt P.M. Mann, E
How pleasant 'tis to see
Sources. MNAN4/121, WP133
Topic. Public Worship

No. 35

1299 sp Mann, E
Welcome, sweet day of rest
Sources. MNAN4/122, WH2/14
Topic. Worship

No. 36

1300 pt P.M. Mann, E
Why moves to mournful measures slow
Sources. MNAN4/125, Anon.
Topic. Resignation

No. 37

1301 sp Mann, E
Salvation! O the joyful sound
Sources. MNAN4/127, WH2/88
Topic. Salvation

No. 38

1302 pt C.M. Mann, E
Thou, round the heav'nly arch, dost draw
Sources. MNAN4/130, Rowe, E
Topic. Morning and Evening

No. 39 IMMORTALITY

1303 xt P.M. Mann, E
I'll praise my maker with my breath
Sources. MNAN4/131, WP146
Topic. Perfections of God

No. 40 KILBY-STREET

1304 xt P.M. Mann, E
Begin, my soul, th'exalted lay
Sources. MNAN4/138, Ogilvy, J
Topic. Universal Praise

No. 41 LAWRENCE

1305 xt P.M. Mann, E
God of mercy, God of love
Sources. MNAN4/141, Taylor, J
Topic. Repentance

No. 42 MAY-STREET

1306 xt C.M. Mann, E
Come, Lord, and warm each languid heart
Sources. MNAN4/142, Steele, A
Topic. Hell and Heaven

No. 43 SPRING

1307 sp Mann, E
How sweetly along the gay mead
Sources. MNAN4/144, Anon.
Topic. Thanksgiving

No. 44 PEARL-STREET

1308 pt S.M. Mann, E
When overwhelm'd with grief
Sources. MNAN4/147, WP61
Topic. Christian

No. 45

1309 xt P.M. Billings, W
To him that chose us first
Sources. WB1/286, WH3/39
Topic. Doxology

No. 45 OSGOOD

1310 pt S.M. Mann, E
Is this the kind return
Sources. MNAN4/148, WH2/74
Topic. Repentance

NORFOLK

1311 xt L.M. Babcock, S
Now for a tune of lofty praise
Sources. MNAN11/83, WH2/43
Topic. Ascension and Exaltation of Christ

1312   xt L.M. Billings, W
       Let the old heathens tune their song
       Sources. WB4/64, WH2/21
       Topic. Addresses to Christ

1313   ft S.M. Brownson, O
       And must this body die
       Sources. MNAN2/35, WH2/110
       Topic. Death and Resurrection

1314   xt P.M. Gillet, A
       What a mournful life is mine
       Sources. MNAN2/109, Newton, J
       Topic. Perseverance

1315   xt C.M. Holyoke, S
       The God of mercy be ador'd
       Sources. MNAN12/92, WH3/30
       Topic. Doxology

NORTH BOLTON

1316   ft C.M. French, J
       When God reveal'd his gracious name
       Sources. MNAN9/193, WP126
       Topic. Church Meetings

NORTH-HAVEN

1317   xt C.M. Doolittle, E
       'Twas for my sins my dearest Lord
       Sources. MNAN15/53, WH2/106
       Topic. Repentance

NORTH-KINGSTON

1318   xt C.M. Babcock, S
       Sing to the Lord Jehovah's name
       Sources. MNAN11/85, WP95
       Topic. Worship

NORTH PROVIDENCE

1319   ft C.M. Billings, W
       Come, let us join our cheerful songs
       Sources. WB2/210, WH1/62
       Topic. Addresses to Christ

NORTH RIVER

1320   pt C.M. Billings, W
       Whence do our mournful tho'ts arise
       Sources. WB1/96, WH1/32
       Topic. Perfections of God

NORTH SALEM

1321   ft C.M. Jenks, S
       My soul, come meditate the day
       Sources. SJ160, WH2/61
       Topic. Death and Resurrection

1322   ft C.M. Jenks, S
       My soul, come meditate the day
       Sources. SJ161, WH2/61
       Topic. Death and Resurrection

NORTH STAMFORD

1323   xt C.M. Jenks, S
       Sing to the Lord, ye distant lands
       Sources. SJ163, WP96
       Topic. Birth of Christ

NORTHAMPTON

1324   xt L.M. French, J
       Rejoice, ye shining worlds on high
       Sources. MNAN9/195, WP24
       Topic. Ascension and Exaltation of Christ

NORTHBOROUGH

1325   xt C.M. Belknap, D
       Why do we mourn departing friends
       Sources. MNAN14/88, WH2/3
       Topic. Death and Resurrection

1326   ft P.M. Billings, W
       Behold the splendor, hear the shout
       Sources. WB3/157, Anon.
       Topic. Birth of Christ

NORTHBURY

1327   pt L.M. Doolittle, E
       Shew pity, Lord, O Lord, forgive
       Sources. MNAN15/55, WP51/1
       Topic. Christian

NORTHFIELD

1328   sp Mann, E
       Plung'd in a gulf of dark despair
       Sources. MNAN4/40, WH2/79
       Topic. Addresses to Christ

NORTON

1329   ft S.M. Read, D
       Mine eyes and my desire
       Sources. DR124, WP25/3
       Topic. Christian

NORWALK

1330   ft C.M. Jenks, S
       O God, to whom revenge belongs
       Sources. SJ165, WP94/1
       Topic. Saints and Sinners

1331   pt C.M. Read, D
       O all ye nations, praise the Lord
       Sources. DR126, WP117
       Topic. The Christian Church

NORWAY

1332   ft P.M. Woodruff, M
       O praise ye the Lord, prepare your glad voice
       Sources. MNAN8/105, NV149
       Topic. Universal Praise

NORWICH

1333 ft S.M. Hibbard
My sorrows, like a flood
Sources. CR104, WHor
Topic. Pardon

1334 pt L.M. Read, D
Broad is the road that leads to death
Sources. DR279, WH2/158
Topic. Depravity and Fall of Man

NUTFIELD

1335 pt S.M. Billings, W
From lowest depths of woe
Sources. WB1/244, NV130
Topic. Pardon

OAKHAMPTON

1336 pt C.M. French, J
God in the great assembly stands
Sources. MNAN9/196, NV82
Topic. Magistracy

OAKSCREEK

1337 ft L.M. Billings, N
Bless, O my soul, the living God
Sources. MNAN3/116, WP103/1
Topic. Perfections of God

OCCOM

1338 xt P.M. Wood, A
Throughout the saviour's life we trace
Sources. MNAN6/70, Occom, S
Topic. Sufferings and Death of Christ

OCEAN

1339 ft C.M. Anon.
Thy works of glory, mighty Lord
Sources. CR105, WP107/4
Topic. Creation and Providence

1340 ft C.M. Belcher, S
Thy words the raging winds control
Sources. MNAN5/79, WP89/2
Topic. Perfections of God

ODE ON MUSIC

1341 sp Holden, O
Descend, ye nine, descend and sing
Sources. MNAN13/112, Pope, A
Topic. Music

ODE ON MUSICK

1342 sp Mann, E
Descend, ye nine, descend and sing
Sources. MNAN4/13, Pope, A
Topic. Music

ODE ON THE SETTING SUN

1343 sp Jenks, S
Ah, whither rolls thou fair retiring light
Sources. SJ167, Anon.
Topic. Morning and Evening

ODE, AN

1344 xt P.M. Holden, O
Now let your plaintive numbers gently rise
Sources. MNAN13/182, Anon.
Topic. Patriotic

OHIO

1345 ft L.M. French, J
Some trust in horses train'd for war
Sources. MNAN9/198, WP20
Topic. Thanksgiving

1346 ft P.M. Holyoke, S
I'll praise my maker with my breath
Sources. MNAN3/35, WP146
Topic. Perfections of God

1347 ft P.M. Holyoke, S
I'll praise my maker with my breath
Sources. MNAN12/93, WP146
Topic. Perfections of God

1348 xt S.M. Jenks, S
Revive our drooping faith
Sources. SJ173, Hart, J
Topic. Regeneration

1349 ft P.M. West, E
My feet shall never slide
Sources. MNAN7/82, WP121
Topic. Creation and Providence

OLD BRICK

1350 pt L.M. Billings, W
Shall the vile race of flesh and blood
Sources. WB1/110, WH1/82
Topic. Perfections of God

OLD HUNDRED

1351 pt L.M. Anon.
Ye nations round the earth rejoice
Sources. WB3/351, WP100/1
Topic. Universal Praise

OLD NORTH

1352 xt S.M. Billings, W
Awake, my soul, awake
Sources. WB1/118, Billings?
Topic. Morning and Evening

OLD SOUTH

1353 pt C.M. Billings, W
Hark! from the tombs a doleful sound
Sources. WB1/114, WH2/63
Topic. Death and Resurrection

Olney

1354   ft L.M. Holden, O
        Dear fountain of delight unknown
        Sources. MNAN13/115, Cowper, W
        Topic. Humility

Omega

1355   xt P.M. Belcher, S
        Come, thou almighty king
        Sources. MNAN5/81, Anon.
        Topic. Universal Praise

Omicron

1356   xt P.M. Babcock, S
        Let us love, and sing, and wonder
        Sources. MNAN11/87, Newton, J
        Topic. Intercession of Christ

Ontario

1357   xt P.M. Brownson, O
        Ye that delight to serve the Lord
        Sources. MNAN2/36, WP113
        Topic. Perfections of God

1358   xt L.M. Olmsted, T
        This spacious earth is all the Lord's
        Sources. MNAN15/121, WP24
        Topic. Ascension and Exaltation of Christ

Onward Speed

1359   xt P.M. Jenks, S
        Onward speed thy conq'ring flight
        Sources. SJ345, Smith, S
        Topic. Safety and Triumph of the Church

Opening Heavens

1360   xt C.M. Holden, O
        The op'ning heav'ns around me shine
        Sources. MNAN13/117, WH2/54
        Topic. Christian

Orange

1361   xt P.M. Billings, N
        With cheerful voice I sing
        Sources. MNAN3/117, WH1/148
        Topic. Characters and Offices of Christ

1362   xt C.M. Jenks, S
        Early, my God, without delay
        Sources. SJ174, WP63/1
        Topic. Lord's Day

1363   xt S.M. Stone, J
        How free the fountain flows
        Sources. MNAN10/53, Doddridge, P
        Topic. Joy and Rejoicing

1364   ft S.M. Swan, T
        You birds of lofty wing
        Sources. TS161, WP148
        Topic. Universal Praise

1365   ft S.M. Swan, T
        You birds of lofty wing
        Sources. TS315, WP148
        Topic. Universal Praise

1366   ft C.M. West, E
        Sing to the Lord, ye distant lands
        Sources. MNAN7/84, WP96
        Topic. Birth of Christ

Orange Street

1367   pt C.M. Billings, W
        How short and hasty is our life
        Sources. WB1/162, WH2/32
        Topic. Time and Eternity

Ordination Anthem

1368   an Belcher, S
        Hail! hail! hail thou king of saints
        Sources. MNAN5/82, Bible
        Topic. Ordination

1369   an Belcher, S
        Hail! hail! hail thou king of saints
        Sources. AA2/29, Bible
        Topic. Ordination

1370   an Harmon, J
        Hail! hail! thou king of saints
        Sources. AA2/38, Bible
        Topic. Ordination

Ordination Anthem, An

1371   an Holden, O
        Sing, O ye heav'ns, and be joyful, O earth
        Sources. MNAN13/118, Bible
        Topic. Ordination

Orland

1372   xt L.M. Belknap, D
        Shall the vile race of flesh and blood
        Sources. MNAN14/89, WH1/82
        Topic. Perfections of God

Orleans

1373   pt C.M. Billings, W
        Indulgent God, with pitying eyes
        Sources. WB1/281, Doddridge, P
        Topic. Redemption

1374   xt L.M. Holyoke, S
        High in the heav'ns, eternal God
        Sources. MNAN12/95, WP36
        Topic. Creation and Providence

1375   xt P.M. Olmsted, T
        Let all the earth their voices raise
        Sources. MNAN15/123, WP96
        Topic. Hell and Heaven

ORMOND

1376　xt L.M. Bull, A
My God, my king, thy various praise
Sources. MNAN1/82, WP145
Topic. Perfections of God

ORONOKE

1377　xt S.M. Woodruff, M
Our days are as the grass
Sources. MNAN8/107, WP103/2
Topic. Perfections of God

OTSEGO

1378　sp Billings, N
Behold God's pow'r in beauteous forms
Sources. MNAN3/119, Farnsworth
Topic. Creation and Providence

OUSE

1379　ft P.M. Belknap, D
Let all the earth-born race
Sources. MNAN14/91, WP148
Topic. Universal Praise

OXFORD

1380　pt P.M. Billings, W
Ye saints and servants of the Lord
Sources. WB2/308, NV113
Topic. Perfections of God

1381　pt C.M. Holyoke, S
And must I part with all I have
Sources. MNAN12/98, Beddome, B
Topic. Prudence

1382　ft C.M. Stone, J
Hark! the glad sound! the saviour comes
Sources. MNAN10/55, Doddridge, P
Topic. Life and Ministry of Christ

PAINESVILLE

1383　ft P.M. Jenks, S
Ye tribes of Adam join
Sources. SJ347, WP148
Topic. Universal Praise

PALMER

1384　ft L.M. Babcock, S
I'll lift my hands, I'll raise my voice
Sources. MNAN11/88, WP63
Topic. Lord's Day

1385　pt L.M. Stone, J
Eternal are thy mercies, Lord
Sources. MNAN10/57, WP117
Topic. The Christian Church

PALMYRA

1386　sp Babcock, S
When I survey the wond'rous cross
Sources. MNAN11/89, WH3/7
Topic. The Lord's Supper

PARADISE

1387　xt L.M. Holden, O
Now to the shining realms above
Sources. MNAN13/122, WH2/11
Topic. Christian

PARDONING GRACE

1388　xt L.M. Gillet, A
From deep distress and troubled thoughts
Sources. MNAN2/110, WP130
Topic. Pardon

PASTORAL ANTHEM

1389　an Olmsted, T
The Lord is my shepherd, I shall not want
Sources. MNAN15/124, BP23
Topic. Thanksgiving

PATMOS

1390　ft P.M. Swan, T
Think, mighty God, on feeble man
Sources. TS163, WP89
Topic. Death and Resurrection

PARIS

1391　pt L.M. Billings, W
Praise ye the Lord; 'tis good to raise
Sources. WB2/326, WP147/1
Topic. Creation and Providence

PAWTUXET

1392　sp French, J
Our days, alas! our mortal days
Sources. MNAN9/199, WH2/39
Topic. Time and Eternity

PAXTON

1393　pt C.M. Holyoke, S
When in the light of faith divine
Sources. MNAN12/99, WH2/101
Topic. The World

1394　pt L.M. Stone, J
Hail, holy lamb, to slaughter led
Sources. MNAN10/58, Anon.
Topic. Sufferings and Death of Christ

PEACE

1395　an Billings, W
God is the king of all the earth
Sources. WB3/257, Bible
Topic. Universal Praise

1396   xt P.M. Bull, A
How pleasant 'tis to see
Sources. MNAN1/83, WP133
Topic. Public Worship

PEACEFUL REST

1397   xt P.M. Jenks, S
There is an hour of peaceful rest
Sources. SJ349, Tappan, W
Topic. Hell and Heaven

PEMBROKE

1398   pt L.M. Billings, W
Thus saith the high and lofty one
Sources. WB1/56, WH1/87
Topic. Invitations and Promises

1399   sp Read, D
Arise, my gracious God
Sources. DR127, WP17
Topic. Saints and Sinners

PEMBROKE NEW

1400   pt P.M. Billings, W
My God, my gracious God, to thee
Sources. WB1/76, NV63
Topic. Lord's Day

PENNSYLVANIA

1401   sp Kimball, J
Rejoice, ye shining worlds on high
Sources. MNAN12/189, WP24
Topic. Ascension and Exaltation of Christ

PENOBSCOT

1402   ft C.M. Belknap, D
Teach me the measure of my days
Sources. MNAN14/93, WP39/2
Topic. Time and Eternity

PEPPERRELL

1403   ft C.M. Wood, A
As pants the hart for cooling streams
Sources. MNAN6/71, NV42
Topic. Fear and Hope

PERSEPOLIS

1404   xt L.M. French, J
O come, loud anthems let us sing
Sources. MNAN9/202, NV95
Topic. Worship

PERSEVERANCE

1405   pt C.M. Jenks, S
Lord, hast thou made me know thy ways
Sources. SJ350, Anon.
Topic. Perseverance

PERSIA

1406   xt P.M. French, J
How pleasant 'tis to see
Sources. MNAN9/204, WP133
Topic. Public Worship

1407   xt L.M. Holden, O
Now to the Lord who makes us know
Sources. MNAN13/123, WH1/61
Topic. Characters and Offices of Christ

PETERSBURGH

1408   xt L.M. Billings, W
Thus saith the high and lofty one
Sources. WB3/173, WH1/87
Topic. Invitations and Promises

PETERSHAM

1409   sp Mann, E
O God, how endless is thy love
Sources. MNAN4/53, WH1/81
Topic. Morning and Evening

1410   ft P.M. Stone, J
I'll praise my maker with my breath
Sources. MNAN10/59, WP146
Topic. Perfections of God

PHALIA

1411   ft C.M. Woodruff, M
In pleasure's flow'ry path to stray
Sources. MNAN8/108, Anon.
Topic. Death and Resurrection

PHANTOM

1412   pt P.M. Woodruff, M
Rise, my soul, and stretch thy wings
Sources. MNAN8/111, Seagrave, R
Topic. Christian

PHENOMENA

1413   pt P.M. Holden, O
See the noon day cloth'd in darkness
Sources. MNAN13/125, Anon.
Topic. Secular

PHILADELPHIA

1414   ft S.M. Billings, W
Let diff'ring nations join
Sources. WB2/172, NV67
Topic. Universal Praise

PHILADELPHIA NEW

1415   xt S.M. French, J
Let ev'ry creature join
Sources. MNAN9/206, WP148
Topic. Universal Praise

PHOEBUS

1416   xt C.M. Billings, W
        Lord, in the morning thou shalt hear
        Sources. WB2/148, WP5
        Topic. Lord's Day

PHYLANTHROPY

1417   xt P.M. Billings, W
        Jesus, the saviour, from above
        Sources. WB3/186, RCH11
        Topic. Ascension and Exaltation of Christ

PIERMONT

1418   xt L.M. Bull, A
        Rejoice, ye shining worlds on high
        Sources. MNAN1/85, WP24
        Topic. Ascension and Exaltation of Christ

PILGRIM, THE

1419   pt P.M. Jenks, S
        no text
        Sources. SJ352

PILGRIM'S SONG, THE

1420   xt P.M. Bull, A
        Rise, my soul, and stretch thy wings
        Sources. MNAN1/123, Seagrave, R
        Topic. Christian

1421   xt P.M. Jenks, S
        Guide me, O thou great Jehovah
        Sources. SJ353, Williams, W
        Topic. Death and Resurrection

PINE-HILL

1422   xt C.M. Belknap, D
        In the full choir a broken string
        Sources. MNAN14/95, WHor
        Topic. Ascension and Exaltation of Christ

PITSTOWN

1423   pt P.M. Swan, T
        The Lord my pasture shall prepare
        Sources. TS166, Addison, J
        Topic. Creation and Providence

PITT

1424   xt S.M. Billings, W
        Behold what wond'rous grace
        Sources. WB1/204, WH1/64
        Topic. Adoption

PITTSBURGH

1425   xt L.M. Stone, J
        Thou sacred one, almighty three
        Sources. MNAN10/61, Anon.
        Topic. Perfections of God

PITTSFORD

1426   pt L.M. Belknap, D
        God, the eternal, awful name
        Sources. MNAN14/96, WH2/27
        Topic. Universal Praise

PITTSTON

1427   ft C.M. Belcher, S
        Now shall my head be lifted high
        Sources. MNAN5/92, WP27
        Topic. Public Worship

PLACENTIA

1428   xt P.M. Babcock, S
        How tedious and tasteless the hours
        Sources. MNAN11/93, Newton, J
        Topic. Trust and Confidence

PLAINFIELD

1429   pt C.M. Billings, W
        Come, let us join our cheerful songs
        Sources. WB1/326, WH1/62
        Topic. Addresses to Christ

1430   xt L.M. Gillet, A
        Shew pity, Lord, O Lord, forgive
        Sources. MNAN2/112, WP51/1
        Topic. Christian

1431   xt L.M. Jenks, S
        Happy the city where thy sons
        Sources. SJ176, WP144
        Topic. Thanksgiving

1432   xt S.M. Jenks, S
        How beauteous are their feet
        Sources. SJ355, WH1/10
        Topic. Law and Gospel

1433   xt C.M. Kimball, J
        Let him, to whom we now belong
        Sources. MNAN12/192, Wesley, C
        Topic. Trust and Confidence

PLATTSBURG

1434   xt P.M. Olmsted, T
        O Lord our God most high
        Sources. MNAN15/132, DP19
        Topic. Perfections of God

PLEASANT STREET

1435   pt L.M. Billings, W
        No more my God, I boast no more
        Sources. WB1/156, WH1/109
        Topic. Justification

PLEASANT VALLEY

1436   xt P.M. Jenks, S
        Lord of the worlds above
        Sources. SJ178, WP84
        Topic. Public Worship

1437   ft C.M. Morgan, J
        My soul lies cleaving to the dust
        Sources. MNAN7/139, WP119/16
        Topic. Christian

PLEASURE

1438   xt L.M. Jenks, S
        Descend from heav'n, immortal dove
        Sources. SJ180, WH2/23
        Topic. Addresses to the Holy Spirit

PLENITUDE

1439   ft P.M. Belcher, S
        Array'd in beauteous green
        Sources. MNAN5/93, Doddridge, P
        Topic. Gospel

PLYMOUTH

1440   pt C.M. Tans'ur, W
        O God of mercy, hear my call
        Sources. CR107, WP51/2
        Topic. Repentance

PLYMOUTH NEW

1441   xt C.M. Billings, W
        Lift up your heads eternal gates
        Sources. WB3/293, NV24
        Topic. Ascension and Exaltation of Christ

PLYMTON

1442   pt P.M. Billings, W
        In deep distress I oft have cry'd
        Sources. WB1/78, NV120
        Topic. Christian

POLAND

1443.   pt C.M. Swan, T
        God of my life, look gently down
        Sources. TS168, WP39/3
        Topic. Sickness and Recovery

POMERANIA

1444   xt C.M. Olmsted, T
        Now I'm convinc'd the Lord is kind
        Sources. MNAN15/134, WP73/1
        Topic. Creation and Providence

POMFRET

1445   pt L.M. Babcock, S
        Let everlasting glories crown
        Sources. MNAN11/94, WH2/131
        Topic. Law and Gospel

1446   pt C.M. Billings, W
        How good and pleasant must it be
        Sources. WB1/66, NV92
        Topic. Trust and Confidence

1447   xt L.M. Holyoke, S
        'Tis by the faith of joys to come
        Sources. MNAN12/100, WH2/129
        Topic. Faith

1448   ft C.M. Stone, J
        O for an overcoming faith
        Sources. MNAN10/63, WH1/17
        Topic. Death and Resurrection

1449   ft P.M. Woodruff, M
        Think, mighty God, on feeble man
        Sources. MNAN8/112, WP89
        Topic. Death and Resurrection

POND

1450   xt L.M. French, J
        Sing to the Lord with joyful voice
        Sources. MNAN9/208, WP100/2
        Topic. Universal Praise

PORTLAND

1451   ft S.M. Bull, A
        Behold the lofty sky
        Sources. MNAN1/86, WP19/1
        Topic. Lord's Day

1452   ft P.M. French, J
        The God of glory sends his summons forth
        Sources. MNAN9/210, WP50/2
        Topic. Day of Judgment

1453   xt C.M. Holyoke, S
        Sing to the Lord Jehovah's name
        Sources. MNAN12/102, WP95
        Topic. Worship

1454   pt L.M. Swan, T
        Sweet is the work, my God, my king
        Sources. TS170, WP92/1
        Topic. Lord's Day

1455   sp West, E
        Father, how wide thy glory shines
        Sources. MNAN7/85, WHor
        Topic. Law and Gospel

1456   xt P.M. Wood, A
        Jesus, Lord of life and peace
        Sources. MNAN6/73, Hart, J
        Topic. Addresses to Christ

PORTSMOUTH

1457   pt C.M. Anon.
        There the great monarch of the skies
        Sources. CR108, WP84
        Topic. Public Worship

1458   xt P.M. Anon.
Ye boundless realms of joy
Sources. CR109, NV148
Topic. Universal Praise

1459   pt C.M. Anon.
O God, my God, I early seek
Sources. WB3/352, OV63
Topic. Communion with God

PORTUGAL

1460   pt L.M. Thorley, T
How lovely, how divinely sweet
Sources. CR112, Steele, A
Topic. Christian

POTENCY

1461   pt L.M. Belcher, S
'Twas from thy hand, my God, I came
Sources. MNAN5/95, WP139/2
Topic. Creation and Providence

POUGHKEEPSIE

1462   xt C.M. Chandler, S
Since I have plac'd my trust in God
Sources. MNAN2/153, NV11
Topic. Saints and Sinners

POUNDRIDGE

1463   ft C.M. Jenks, S
To our almighty maker, God
Sources. SJ182, WP98/1
Topic. Law and Gospel

POWER OF MUSICK, THE

1464   sp Belcher, S
Hark! some soft swell pants on the ev'ning breeze
Sources. MNAN5/96, Stoddard
Topic. Music

POWNAL

1465   pt S.M. Swan, T
Sure there's a righteous God
Sources. TS172, WP73
Topic. Creation and Providence

1466   pt L.M. Billings, W
To thee, my God and saviour, I
Sources. WB1/240, NV88
Topic. Addresses to Christ

PRECEPT

1467   ft S.M. West, E
The watchmen join their voice
Sources. MNAN7/89, WH1/10
Topic. Law and Gospel

PREPARATION

1468   ft L.M. French, J
My loving friend, as you pass by
Sources. MNAN9/214, Anon.
Topic. Death and Resurrection

PRESERVATION

1469   pt C.M. Bull, A
To heav'n I lift my waiting eyes
Sources. MNAN1/88, WP121
Topic. Creation and Providence

PRESTON

1470   xt P.M. Jenks, S
Ye tribes of Adam join
Sources. SJ183, WP148
Topic. Universal Praise

PRETORIUM

1471   sp Babcock, S
Infinite grief! amazing woe
Sources. MNAN11/95, WH2/95
Topic. Christian

PRINCETOWN

1472   pt C.M. Billings, W
Lord, hear the voice of my complaint
Sources. WB1/172, NV64
Topic. Faith

1473   pt C.M. Billings, W
Lord, hear the voice of my complaint
Sources. WB2/90, NV64
Topic. Faith

PROCLAMATION

1474   xt L.M. French, J
He reigns, the Lord, the saviour reigns
Sources. MNAN9/216, WP97/1
Topic. Day of Judgment

PRODIGAL

1475   pt C.M. French, J
Behold the wretch, whose lust and wine
Sources. MNAN9/218, WH1/123
Topic. Repentance

1476   ft C.M. West, E
A day of feasting I ordain
Sources. MNAN7/91, WH1/123
Topic. Repentance

PROMISE, THE

1477   pt P.M. Jenks, S
Though troubles assail, and dangers affright
Sources. SJ357, Newton, J
Topic. Fear and Hope

PROSPECT

1478　pt P.M. Bull, A
Think, mighty God, on feeble man
Sources. MNAN1/89, WP89
Topic. Death and Resurrection

PROTECTION

1479　ft P.M. Belcher, S
God is our refuge in distress
Sources. MNAN5/101, NV46
Topic. The Christian Church

1480　xt P.M. Billings, N
Hush, my dear, lie still and slumber
Sources. MNAN3/123, WDMS
Topic. Trust and Confidence

1481　xt P.M. Bull, A
Upward I lift my eyes
Sources. MNAN1/90, WP121
Topic. Creation and Providence

1482　ft P.M. Jenks, S
Hast thou not giv'n thy word
Sources. SJ185, WP121
Topic. Creation and Providence

1483　pt L.M. Jenks, S
My shepherd is the living Lord
Sources. SJ359, WP23
Topic. Communion with God

PROVIDENCE

1484　pt L.M. Billings, W
Who shall the Lord's elect condemn
Sources. WB1/282, WH1/14
Topic. Fear and Hope

1485　xt C.M. Bull, A
'Tis by thy strength the mountains stand
Sources. MNAN1/92, WP65/2
Topic. Seasons of the Year

1486　ft P.M. French, J
Give thanks aloud to God
Sources. MNAN9/219, WP136
Topic. The Jewish Church

1487　ft L.M. Read, D
Deep in our hearts, let us record
Sources. DR130, WP69/1
Topic. Sufferings and Death of Christ

PRUSSIA

1488　xt C.M. Edson, L
Rejoice, ye righteous in the Lord
Sources. MNAN3/37, WP33/1
Topic. Creation and Providence

1489　xt S.M. Jenks, S
Let ev'ry creature join
Sources. SJ186, WP148
Topic. Universal Praise

5TH PSALM, THE

1490　ft C.M. Read, D
Lord, in the morning thou shalt hear
Sources. DR260, WP5
Topic. Lord's Day

PSALM 8

1491　xt S.M. Bull, A
O Lord, our heav'nly king
Sources. MNAN1/94, WP8
Topic. Perfections of God

1492　ft C.M. Stone, J
O thou, to whom all creatures bow
Sources. MNAN10/65, NV8
Topic. Perfections of God

18TH PSALM, THE

1493　xt C.M. Billings, W
To thine almighty arm we owe
Sources. WB1/288, WP18/2
Topic. Thanksgiving

PSALM 19 [I]

1494　xt P.M. Chandler, S
Great God, the heav'n's well-order'd frame
Sources. MNAN2/155, WP19
Topic. Scripture

PSALM 19 [II]

1495　xt P.M. Chandler, S
Great God, the heav'ns' well-order'd frame
Sources. MNAN2/157, WP19
Topic. Scripture

PSALM 21

1496　ft C.M. Bull, A
The states, O Lord, with songs of praise
Sources. MNAN1/95, WP21
Topic. Magistracy

PSALM 23

1497　pt L.M. Bull, A
My shepherd is the living Lord
Sources. MNAN1/98, WP23
Topic. Communion with God

1498　xt S.M. Jenks, S
The Lord my shepherd is
Sources. SJ360, WP23
Topic. Communion with God

PSALM 25

1499　xt S.M. Gillet, A
I lift my soul to God
Sources. CR113, WP25/1
Topic. Christian

1500　xt S.M. Gillet, A
I lift my soul to God
Sources. MNAN2/115, WP25/1
Topic. Christian

PSALM 29

1501   pt L.M. Bull, A
        Give to the Lord, ye sons of fame
        Sources. MNAN1/99, WP29
        Topic. Seasons of the Year

PSALM 33

1502   xt C.M. Tuckey, W
        Rejoice, ye righteous, in the Lord
        Sources. CR114, WP33/1
        Topic. Creation and Providence

PSALM 34

1503   ft C.M. Stephenson, J
        Through all the changing scenes of life
        Sources. CR116, NV34
        Topic. Christian

PSALM 45

1504   pt S.M. Bull, A
        Strike through thy stubborn foes
        Sources. MNAN1/101, WP45
        Topic. Beauty of the Church

PSALM 46

1505   pt P.M. Bull, A
        I'll praise my maker with my breath
        Sources. CR118, WP146
        Topic. Perfections of God

1506   pt P.M. Bull, A
        I'll praise my maker with my breath
        Sources. MNAN1/102, WP146
        Topic. Perfections of God

1507   ft P.M. Chandler, S
        The Lord hath eyes to give the blind
        Sources. MNAN2/160, WP146
        Topic. Perfections of God

PSALM 50

1508   pt P.M. Belcher, S
        The God of glory sends his summons forth
        Sources. MNAN5/102, WP50/2
        Topic. Day of Judgment

1509   xt P.M. Olmsted, T
        The God of glory sends his summons forth
        Sources. MNAN15/136, WP50/2
        Topic. Day of Judgment

PSALM 63

1510   xt S.M. Bull, A
        My God, permit my tongue
        Sources. MNAN1/103, WP63
        Topic. Lord's Day

1511   xt S.M. Olmsted, T
        My God, permit my tongue
        Sources. MNAN15/140, WP63
        Topic. Lord's Day

PSALM 73

1512   xt C.M. Bull, A
        God, my supporter and my hope
        Sources. MNAN1/105, WP73/2
        Topic. Communion with God

PSALM 84

1513   xt P.M. Olmsted, T
        Lord of the worlds above
        Sources. MNAN15/141, WP84
        Topic. Public Worship

PSALM 90

1514   pt L.M. Olmsted, T
        Through ev'ry age, eternal God
        Sources. MNAN15/144, WP90
        Topic. Death and Resurrection

PSALM 95

1515   pt L.M. Brownson, O
        Come, let our voices join to raise
        Sources. MNAN2/39, WP95
        Topic. Worship

1516   xt S.M. Bull, A
        Come sound his praise abroad
        Sources. MNAN1/107, WP95
        Topic. Worship

PSALM 100 [NEW]

1517   pt L.M. Anon.
        Death, like an overflowing stream
        Sources. CR121, WP90
        Topic. Death and Resurrection

PSALM 100 [OLD]

1518   pt L.M. Anon.
        Be thou, O God, exalted high
        Sources. CR119, NV57
        Topic. Creation and Providence

PSALM 119

1519   ft C.M. Holden, O
        My soul lies cleaving to the dust
        Sources. MNAN13/125, WP119/16
        Topic. Christian

PSALM 122

1520   ft P.M. Bull, A
        How pleas'd and blest was I
        Sources. MNAN1/108, WP122
        Topic. Public Worship

122 PSALM TUNE, THE

1521   ft C.M. Read, D
        How did my heart rejoice to hear
        Sources. DR280, WP122
        Topic. Public Worship

PSALM 133

1522   ft P.M. Olmsted, T
        How pleasant 'tis to see
        Sources. MNAN15/145, WP133
        Topic. Public Worship

PSALM 136

1523   ft P.M. Deaolph
        Hast thou not giv'n thy word
        Sources. CR122, WP121
        Topic. Creation and Providence

PSALM 148

1524   pt P.M. Anon.
        From heav'n O praise the Lord
        Sources. CR124, BPB148
        Topic. Universal Praise

PSALM 149

1525   pt P.M. Anon.
        O praise ye the Lord, prepare your glad voice
        Sources. CR125, NV149
        Topic. Universal Praise

PUMPILY

1526   xt P.M. Billings, W
        Ye boundless realms of joy
        Sources. WB1/212, NV148
        Topic. Universal Praise

1527   xt P.M. Billings, W
        Ye boundless realms of joy
        Sources. WB2/114, NV148
        Topic. Universal Praise

PURCHASE STREET

1528.   pt S.M. Billings, W
        To God the only wise
        Sources. WB1/264, WH1/51
        Topic. Perseverance

1529.   pt L.M. Billings, W
        Thus far the Lord has led me on
        Sources. WB2/296, WH1/80
        Topic. Morning and Evening

PUTNEY

1530   pt L.M. Williams, A
        Man has a soul of vast desires
        Sources. CR126, WH2/146
        Topic. The World

1531   pt L.M. Williams, A
        Man has a soul of vast desires
        Sources. WB3/354, WH2/146
        Topic. The World

QUAKENBERG

1532   ft L.M. Holyoke, S
        Jesus, our soul's delightful choice
        Sources. MNAN12/104, Doddridge, P
        Topic. Fear and Hope

QUEEN MARY'S PRAYER

1533   xt P.M. Swan, T
        In this last solemn and tremendous hour
        Sources. TS174, Anon.
        Topic. Death and Resurrection

QUEEN STREET

1534   xt C.M. Billings, W
        O clap your hands and shout for joy
        Sources. WB1/188, Morton, P
        Topic. Thanksgiving

QUEENBOROUGH

1535   pt P.M. French, J
        Not to our names, thou only just and true
        Sources. MNAN9/220, WP115
        Topic. Perfections of God

QUINCY

1536   xt P.M. Babcock, S
        The God of glory sends his summons forth
        Sources. MNAN11/98, WP50/2
        Topic. Day of Judgment

1537   pt C.M. Swan, T
        Awake, my soul, to sound his praise
        Sources. TS176, BarP108
        Topic. Universal Praise

RAINBOW

1538   ft C.M. Swan, T
        'Tis by thy strength the mountains stand
        Sources. CR128, WP65/2
        Topic. Seasons of the Year

1539   ft C.M. Swan, T
        'Tis by thy strength the mountains stand
        Sources. TS178, WP65/2
        Topic. Seasons of the Year

1540   ft C.M. Swan, T
        'Tis by thy strength the mountains stand
        Sources. TS317, WP65/2
        Topic. Seasons of the Year

RALEIGH

1541   pt L.M. Billings, W
        My flesh shall slumber in the ground
        Sources. WB3/333, WP17
        Topic. Saints and Sinners

RAMA

1542   xt L.M. Babcock, S
        Dost thou my earthly comforts slay
        Sources. MNAN11/102, Anon.
        Topic. Trust and Confidence

RANDOLPH

1543   xt P.M. Babcock, S
        Loud hallelujahs to the Lord
        Sources. MNAN11/103, WP148
        Topic. Universal Praise

1544　xt C.M. Belknap, D
Thou refuge of my weary soul
Sources. MNAN14/98, Steele, A
Topic. Fear and Hope

RANSOM

1545　ft C.M. Jenks, S
'Tis done! the precious ransom's paid
Sources. SJ189, Wesley, S
Topic. Sufferings and Death of Christ

RAPTURE

1546　ft L.M. Belcher, S
Then jointly all the harpers round
Sources. MNAN5/106, Anon.
Topic. Thanksgiving

RAYNHAM

1547　ft S.M. Belknap, D
The spirits of the just
Sources. MNAN14/100, Hart, J
Topic. Death and Resurrection

1548　ft S.M. Holyoke, S
From winter's barren clods
Sources. MNAN12/105, Anon.
Topic. Seasons of the Year

READING

1549　ft L.M. Kimball, J
Sweet is the work, my God, my king
Sources. MNAN12/194, WP92/1
Topic. Lord's Day

REBELLION

1550　an French, J
Hear, O heav'ns, and give ear, O earth
Sources. MNAN9/222, Bible
Topic. Fast Day

RECEPTION

1551　sp French, J
Well, the redeemer's gone
Sources. MNAN9/231, WH2/36
Topic. Intercession of Christ

RECOVERY

1552　ft L.M. Billings, N
My groans and tears and forms of woe
Sources. MNAN3/124, WP30/2
Topic. Sickness and Recovery

1553　pt C.M. Brownson, O
Lord, thou hast heard thy servant's cry
Sources. MNAN2/40, WP118/2
Topic. Sickness and Recovery

1554　pt C.M. Bull, A
I love the Lord: he heard my cries
Sources. MNAN1/110, WP116/1
Topic. Sickness and Recovery

REDEMPTION

1555　ft L.M. Belknap, D
O thou, whose hand the kingdom sways
Sources. MNAN14/101, DP70
Topic. Addresses to Christ

1556　sp Benham, A
Hark, hark, glad tidings charm our ears
Sources. MNAN8/40, Anon.
Topic. Life and Ministry of Christ

1557　xt P.M. Billings, W
Th'eternal speaks; all heav'n attends
Sources. WB3/32, Anon.
Topic. Redemption

1558　xt C.M. Bull, A
My saviour, my almighty friend
Sources. MNAN1/111, WP71/2
Topic. Justification

1559　xt S.M. Jenks, S
Alas, the cruel spear
Sources. SJ190, WH2/84
Topic. Ascension and Exaltation of Christ

1560　xt P.M. Wood, A
Come raise your thankful voice
Sources. MNAN6/75, Hart, J
Topic. Redemption

REEDFIELD

1561　pt S.M. Belcher, S
Hosanna to the king
Sources. MNAN5/108, WP118
Topic. Worship

REFLECTION

1562　xt L.M. Belcher, S
Lord, what a thoughtless wretch was I
Sources. MNAN5/110, WP73
Topic. The World

REFUGE

1563　xt C.M. Edson, L Jr
Since I have plac'd my trust in God
Sources. MNAN3/75, NV11
Topic. Saints and Sinners

1564　ft L.M. Read, D
My refuge is the God of love
Sources. DR132, WP11
Topic. Saints and Sinners

RELIANCE

1565　xt C.M. Bull, A
My shepherd will supply my need
Sources. MNAN1/112, WP23
Topic. Communion with God

RELIGION

1566   ft C.M. Jenks, S
Some walk in honour's gaudy show
Sources. SJ191, WP39/2
Topic. Time and Eternity

1567   ft S.M. Read, D
My God, permit my tongue
Sources. DR134, WP63
Topic. Lord's Day

RELLEY

1568   xt C.M. French, J
Against thy zealous people, Lord
Sources. MNAN9/236, NV83
Topic. Afflictions of the Church

REPENTANCE

1569   pt L.M. Benham, A
Behold and see as you pass by
Sources. MNAN8/44, Anon.
Topic. Death and Resurrection

REPOSE

1570   xt C.M. Jenks, S
Our sins, alas, how strong they be
Sources. SJ193, WH2/86
Topic. Hell and Heaven

REQUEST

1571   xt C.M. Billings, N
Judge me, O God, and plead my cause
Sources. MNAN3/126, Anon.
Topic. Trust and Confidence

1572   pt P.M. Jenks, S
no text
Sources. SJ362

REQUEST, THE

1573   sp Belcher, S
Give me, O Lord, a soul so high
Sources. MNAN5/111, Anon.
Topic. Liberality

RESIGNATION

1574   xt C.M. Babcock, S
Behold the saviour of mankind
Sources. MNAN11/104, Wesley, S
Topic. Sufferings and Death of Christ

1575   xt C.M. Billings, W
Thus saith the ruler of the skies
Sources. WB3/82, WH2/83
Topic. Ascension and Exaltation of Christ

1576   xt L.M. Jenks, S
But man, poor man, was born to die
Sources. SJ195, WP90
Topic. Death and Resurrection

RESOLUTION

1577   ft S.M. Babcock, S
Let sinners take their course
Sources. MNAN11/106, WP55
Topic. Worship

1578   ft C.M. French, J
I'll lift my banner, saith the Lord
Sources. MNAN9/238, WH1/29
Topic. The Christian Church

1579   ft C.M. Holden, O
Great king of Zion, Lord of all
Sources. MNAN13/127, Anon.
Topic. Fear and Hope

1580   pt P.M. Jenks, S
Ye children of Zion, who're aiming for glory
Sources. SJ363, Anon.
Topic. Salvation

REST

1581   pt P.M. Holden, O
Descend, holy spirit, the dove
Sources. MNAN13/128, Doddridge, P
Topic. Addresses to the Holy Spirit

RESTORATION

1582   xt P.M. Billings, W
Greatly belov'd, Of God approv'd
Sources. WB3/183, RCH5
Topic. Sufferings and Death of Christ

1583   ft L.M. Edson, L Jr
My groans, and tears, and forms of woe
Sources. MNAN3/76, WP30/2
Topic. Sickness and Recovery

1584   xt L.M. Stone, J
When God restor'd our captive state
Sources. MNAN10/66, WP126
Topic. Church Meetings

RESURRECTION

1585   xt P.M. Billings, W
Jesus Christ is ris'n to day, Hallelujah
Sources. WB3/234, Anon.
Topic. Resurrection of Christ

1586   sp Bull, A
Blest morning, whose young dawning rays
Sources. MNAN1/114, WH2/72
Topic. Worship

1587   xt C.M. French, J
The joyful day is coming on
Sources. MNAN9/240, Anon.
Topic. Death and Resurrection

1588   an Gram, H
The first man was of the earth, earthy
Sources. AA1/150, Bible
Topic. Easter

1589　xt P.M. Read, D
The God of glory sends his summons forth
Sources. DR136, WP50/2
Topic. Day of Judgment

RETIREMENT

1590　pt C.M. Holden, O
Far from the world, O Lord, I flee
Sources. MNAN13/129, Cowper, W
Topic. Christian

RETRIBUTION

1591　ft P.M. French, J
The God of glory sends his summons forth
Sources. MNAN9/241, WP50/2
Topic. Day of Judgment

RETROSPECT

1592　an Billings, W
Was not the day dark and gloomy
Sources. WB2/231, Bible/Billings
Topic. Patriotic

REVELATION

1593　pt C.M. Billings, W
Let all the heathen writers join
Sources. WB2/320, WP119/7
Topic. Scripture

1594　ft C.M. Billings, W
Let all the heathen writers join
Sources. WB4/87, WP119/7
Topic. Scripture

REVIVING HOPE

1595　ft C.M. Holden, O
The saviour calls; let ev'ry ear
Sources. MNAN13/130, Steele, A
Topic. Invitations and Promises

REVOLUTION

1596　ft P.M. Olmsted, T
To bless the Lord, our god, in strains divine
Sources. MNAN15/148, DP18
Topic. Universal Praise

RICHFIELD

1597　ft L.M. Edson, L Jr
Bless, O my soul, the living god
Sources. MNAN3/78, WP103/1
Topic. Perfections of God

RICHMOND

1598　xt C.M. Belknap, D
Sing to the Lord, ye distant lands
Sources. MNAN14/103, WP96
Topic. Birth of Christ

1599　xt P.M. Billings, W
My beloved! haste away
Sources. WB2/170, RCH55
Topic. Addresses to Christ

1600　pt P.M. Gillet, A
Ere God had built the mountains
Sources. MNAN2/116, Cowper, W
Topic. Atonement

RIDGEFIELD

1601　pt P.M. Jenks, S
Guide me, O thou great Jehovah
Sources. SJ365, Williams, W
Topic. Death and Resurrection

RIDGFIELD

1602　xt C.M. Jenks, S
Who can command the rolling tide
Sources. SJ197, Anon.
Topic. Time and Eternity

RINDGE

1603　xt C.M. Holyoke, S
My thoughts surmount these lower skies
Sources. MNAN12/106, WH2/162
Topic. Faith

RINGE

1604　xt L.M. Belknap, D
Jehovah reigns, his throne is high
Sources. MNAN14/104, WH2/168
Topic. Perfections of God

RIPTON

1605　xt L.M. Gillet, A
Shew pity, Lord, O Lord, forgive
Sources. MNAN2/118, WP51/1
Topic. Christian

1606　pt P.M. Read, D
That man is blest who stands in awe
Sources. DR139, WP112
Topic. Liberality

RISING DAWN

1607　xt C.M. Holden, O
Behold the rising dawn appears
Sources. MNAN13/132, BelP122
Topic. Prayer and Praise for the Church

ROCHESTER

1608　xt P.M. Billings, W
Ye servants of God
Sources. WB4/120, Wesley, C
Topic. Exaltation of Christ

1609　pt C.M. Holdroyd, I
God, my supporter and my hope
Sources. CR130, WP73/2
Topic. Communion with God

ROCK OF AGES

1610　pt L.M. Jenks, S
We found the rock, the trav'ler cried
Sources. SJ366, Anon.
Topic. Invitations and Promises

ROCKY-NOOK

1611   ft C.M. Billings, W
        Those glorious minds, how bright they shine
        Sources. WB4/58, WH1/41
        Topic. Hell and Heaven

ROME

1612   pt L.M. Jenks, S
        Sweet is the day of sacred rest
        Sources. SJ198, WP92/1
        Topic. Lord's Day

1613   xt P.M. Stone, J
        Farewell, honour's empty pride
        Sources. MNAN10/68, Anon.
        Topic. The World

1614   xt P.M. Swan, T
        Wand'ring pilgrims, mourning Christians
        Sources. TS180, Leland, J
        Topic. Invitations and Promises

RONDA

1615   xt C.M. Swan, T
        Return, O God of love, return
        Sources. TS182, WP90/3
        Topic. Christian

RONDEAU

1616   sp Olmsted, T
        My God, my king, thy various praise
        Sources. MNAN15/152, WP145
        Topic. Perfections of God

ROSS

1617   xt C.M. Swan, T
        As pants the hart for cooling streams
        Sources. TS184, NV42
        Topic. Fear and Hope

ROWLAND

1618   ft C.M. Woodruff, M
        Lord, we have heard thy works of old
        Sources. MNAN8/114, WP44
        Topic. The Christian Church

ROWLEY

1619   ft C.M. Belknap, D
        How long wilt thou forget me, Lord
        Sources. MNAN14/105, NV13
        Topic. Christian

1620   ft L.M. Kimball, J
        The saints shall flourish in his days
        Sources. MNAN12/196, WP72/1
        Topic. The Christian Church

ROXBURY

1621   xt P.M. Babcock, S
        The Lord, he reigns above
        Sources. MNAN11/107, Anon.
        Topic. Perfections of God

1622   xt S.M. Belknap, D
        My sorrows, like a flood
        Sources. MNAN14/107, WHor
        Topic. Pardon

1623   pt L.M. Billings, W
        O Lord, to my relief draw near
        Sources. WB1/112, NV70
        Topic. Faith

1624   pt P.M. Billings, W
        O praise ye the Lord, prepare your glad voice
        Sources. WB2/162, NV149
        Topic. Universal Praise

ROYALSTON

1625   pt P.M. Wood, A
        Ye tribes of Adam join
        Sources. MNAN6/77, WP148
        Topic. Universal Praise

ROYALTON

1626   pt C.M. Doolittle, E
        Jesus is worthy to receive
        Sources. MNAN15/56, WH1/62
        Topic. Addresses to Christ

RUEPORT

1627   pt S.M. Jenks, S
        Ah! wither shall I go
        Sources. SJ199, Wesley, C
        Topic. Saints and Sinners

RUSSELL

1628   ft C.M. French, J
        My lot is fall'n in that bless'd land
        Sources. MNAN9/245, NV16
        Topic. Faith

1629   ft S.M. Swan, T
        Our days are as the grass
        Sources. TS186, WP103/2
        Topic. Perfections of God

RUSSIA

1630   ft L.M. Read, D
        False are the men of high degree
        Sources. CR131, WP62
        Topic. Trust and Confidence

1631   ft L.M. Read, D
        False are the men of high degree
        Sources. DR141, WP62
        Topic. Trust and Confidence

RUTLAND

1632   sp Billings, W
My flesh shall slumber in the ground
Sources. WB3/62, WP17
Topic. Saints and Sinners

SABBATH

1633   xt L.M. Babcock, S
Lord of the Sabbath, hear our vows
Sources. MNAN11/108, Doddridge, P
Topic. Lord's Day

1634   ft C.M. French, J
Blest morning, whose young dawning rays
Sources. MNAN9/246, WH2/72
Topic. Worship

1635   pt L.M. Read, D
Sweet is the work, my God, my king
Sources. DR143, WP92/1
Topic. Lord's Day

SABBATH MORN

1636   xt L.M. Holden, O
Another six days work is done
Sources. MNAN13/133, Stennett, S
Topic. Lord's Day

SABBATH, THE

1637   xt S.M. French, J
Welcome, sweet day of rest
Sources. MNAN9/248, WH2/14
Topic. Worship

SABBATIC YEAR

1638   xt P.M. Jenks, S
When shall I see the day
Sources. SJ368, Anon.
Topic. Death and Resurrection

SACO

1639   xt P.M. Belknap, D
The Lord hath eyes to give the blind
Sources. MNAN14/108, WP146
Topic. Perfections of God

SAINT'S EXIT

1640   pt P.M. Jenks, S
no text
Sources. SJ369

SAINT'S EXIT, THE

1641   sp Jenks, S
Vital spark of heav'nly flame
Sources. SJ201, Pope, A
Topic. Death and Resurrection

SAINT'S HARP, THE

1642   sp Jenks, S
Back from the tomb, O ask her not
Sources. SJ370, Anon.
Topic. Death and Resurrection

SAINT'S INHERITANCE, THE

1643   pt P.M. Wood, A
Perfect holiness of spirit
Sources. MNAN6/79, Hart, J
Topic. Regeneration

SALEM

1644   xt C.M. Belknap, D
Dear Lord! behold our sore distress
Sources. MNAN14/109, WH2/163
Topic. Christian

1645   pt S.M. Bull, A
Far as thy name is known
Sources. MNAN1/117, WP48/2
Topic. The Christian Church

1646   pt P.M. Holden, O
King of Salem, bless my soul
Sources. MNAN13/136, Anon.
Topic. Repentance

1647   ft S.M. Jenks, S
Let ev'ry creature join
Sources. SJ205, WP148
Topic. Universal Praise

1648   pt S.M. Kimball, J
And must this body die
Sources. MNAN12/198, WH2/110
Topic. Death and Resurrection

SALISBURY

1649   xt P.M. Brownson, O
God of my salvation, hear
Sources. MNAN2/42, Wesley, C
Topic. Humility

SALVATION

1650   sp Bull, A
Salvation, O the joyful sound
Sources. MNAN1/118, WH2/88
Topic. Salvation

1651   sp West, E
Shepherds rejoice, lift up your eyes
Sources. MNAN7/92, WHor
Topic. Birth of Christ

SANBORNTOWN

1652   ft L.M. French, J
Now in the heat of youthful blood
Sources. MNAN9/250, WH1/91
Topic. Youth and Old Age

SANDUSKY

1653   sp Holyoke, S
        Lo! he comes, in clouds descending
        Sources. MNAN12/108, Wesley, C
        Topic. Day of Judgment

SANDY RIVER

1654   xt L.M. Belknap, D
        Descend, ye hosts of angels bright
        Sources. MNAN14/111, Anon.
        Topic. Faith

SAPPHICK ODE

1655   sp Billings, W
        When the fierce north wind with his airy forces
        Sources. WB1/355, WHor
        Topic. Day of Judgment

SAPPHO

1656   xt P.M. Billings, W
        When the fierce north wind with his airy forces
        Sources. WB2/105, WHor
        Topic. Day of Judgment

SAREPTA

1657   pt S.M. Holden, O
        I hear the voice of woe
        Sources. MNAN13/137, Enfield, W
        Topic. Liberality

SAVANNAH

1658   pt P.M. Billings, W
        Ah! lovely appearance of death
        Sources. WB2/44, Wesley, C
        Topic. Death and Resurrection

SAYBROOK

1659   ft C.M. Belknap, D
        There is a house not made by hands
        Sources. MNAN14/112, WH1/110
        Topic. Death and Resurrection

1660   pt L.M. Billings, W
        My God, what inward grief I feel
        Sources. WB2/324, WP139/3
        Topic. Trust and Confidence

SCHUYLKILL

1661   ft L.M. Stone, J
        Jehovah, 'tis a glorious word
        Sources. MNAN10/69, WP148
        Topic. Universal Praise

SCIPIO

1662   xt L.M. French, J
        Theron, among his travels, found
        Sources. MNAN9/252, WHor
        Topic. Secular

SCITUATE

1663   pt L.M. Billings, W
        Thus saith the first, the great command
        Sources. WB1/72, WH1/116
        Topic. Law and Gospel

1664   xt C.M. Stone, J
        All ye who faithful servants are
        Sources. MNAN10/71, Tate, N
        Topic. Christian

SCOTLAND

1665   ft S.M. Swan, T
        The Lord my shepherd is
        Sources. TS187, WP23
        Topic. Communion with God

SEASONS, THE

1666   xt L.M. Bull, A
        Eternal source of ev'ry joy
        Sources. MNAN1/125, Doddridge, P
        Topic. Seasons of the Year

1667   sp Swan, T
        Eternal source of every joy
        Sources. TS189, Doddridge, P
        Topic. Seasons of the Year

SEE HE RISES

1668   xt P.M. Holden, O
        Angels, roll the rock away
        Sources. MNAN13/138, Scott, T
        Topic. Resurrection of Christ

SEPARATION

1669   ft C.M. Jenks, S
        Death will dissolve the tend'rest ties
        Sources. SJ208, Anon.
        Topic. Death and Resurrection

SEVERN

1670   sp Kimball, J
        Is this the kind return
        Sources. MNAN12/199, WH2/74
        Topic. Repentance

SHARON

1671   pt P.M. Belknap, D
        Though not with mortal eyes we see
        Sources. MNAN14/114, Anon.
        Topic. Repentance

1672   xt C.M. Billings, W
        How glorious is our heav'nly king
        Sources. WB2/133, WDMS
        Topic. Universal Praise

1673   xt S.M. Brownson, O
        My saviour and my king
        Sources. MNAN2/44, WP45
        Topic. Beauty of the Church

1674   pt L.M. French, J
        Look down in pity, Lord, and see
        Sources. MNAN9/253, Anon.
        Topic. Resignation

1675   ft P.M. West, E
        How pleasant 'tis to see
        Sources. MNAN7/95, WP133
        Topic. Public Worship

SHED NOT A TEAR

1676   xt P.M. Jenks, S
        Shed not a tear o'er your friend's early bier
        Sources. SJ372, Dana, M
        Topic. Death and Resurrection

SHEFFIELD

1677   ft C.M. Billings, W
        Joy to the world, the Lord is come
        Sources. WB3/301, WP98/2
        Topic. Birth of Christ

1678   ft L.M. Woodruff, M
        Stand up, my soul, shake off thy fears
        Sources. MNAN8/117, WH2/77
        Topic. Christian

SHELBURNE

1679   ft C.M. Gillet, A
        Salvation! O the joyful sound
        Sources. MNAN2/121, WH2/88
        Topic. Salvation

1680   ft S.M. Holyoke, S
        My soul with joy attend
        Sources. MNAN12/110, Doddridge, P
        Topic. Characters and Offices of Christ

SHERBURNE

1681   pt P.M. Billings, W
        How pleasant 'tis to see
        Sources. WB2/156, WP133
        Topic. Public Worship

1682   ft C.M. Read, D
        While shepherds watch their flocks by night
        Sources. CR141, Tate, N
        Topic. Birth of Christ

1683   ft C.M. Read, D
        While shepherds watch'd their flocks by night
        Sources. DR145, Tate, N
        Topic. Birth of Christ

SHILOH

1684   xt C.M. Billings, W
        Methinks I see an heav'nly host
        Sources. WB3/138, Billings, W
        Topic. Birth of Christ

SHIRLEY

1685   pt S.M. Belknap, D
        Our moments fly apace
        Sources. MNAN14/115, WP90
        Topic. Time and Eternity

1686   pt L.M. Billings, W
        That man is blest who stands in awe
        Sources. WB1/268, NV112
        Topic. Liberality

SHOREHAM

1687   xt C.M. Belknap, D
        There is a land of pure delight
        Sources. MNAN14/116, WH2/66
        Topic. Death and Resurrection

1688   ft C.M. Stone, J
        In the full choir a broken string
        Sources. MNAN10/72, WHor
        Topic. Ascension and Exaltation of Christ

SHREWSBURY

1689   pt P.M. Belknap, D
        Sav'd from the ocean and tempest'ous skies
        Sources. MNAN14/117, Anon.
        Topic. Death and Resurrection

1690   pt L.M. Wood, A
        Now in the heat of youthful blood
        Sources. MNAN6/80, WH1/91
        Topic. Youth and Old Age

SICILY

1691   pt C.M. Holyoke, S
        Behold the bleeding lamb of God
        Sources. MNAN12/111, Anon.
        Topic. Sufferings and Death of Christ

SILVER-SPRING

1692   xt C.M. Benham, A
        Were I in heav'n without my God
        Sources. MNAN8/45, WP73/2
        Topic. Communion with God

SINAI

1693   xt P.M. Billings, W
        All you, who make the law your choice
        Sources. WB3/200, RCH69
        Topic. Moral Law

1694   ft L.M. Woodruff, M
        Lord, when thou didst ascend on high
        Sources. MNAN8/120, WP68/2
        Topic. Ascension and Exaltation of Christ

SINCERITY

1695   pt L.M. Billings, N
        My God, what inward grief I feel
        Sources. MNAN3/127, WP139/3
        Topic. Trust and Confidence

1696   pt C.M. Woodruff, M
        My never ceasing songs shall show
        Sources. MNAN8/123, WP89/1
        Topic. Perfections of God

SMITHFIELD
1697   xt C.M. Billings, W
        Lord, who's the happy man, that may
        Sources. WB1/322, NV15
        Topic. The Christian Church

1698   ft L.M. Read, D
        This life's a dream, an empty show
        Sources. DR147, WP17
        Topic. Saints and Sinners

SMYRNA
1699   sp Babcock, S
        Now let the Lord, my saviour, smile
        Sources. MNAN11/110, WH2/50
        Topic. Christian

1700   xt C.M. Holden, O
        Why should the children of a king
        Sources. MNAN13/139, WH1/144
        Topic. Addresses to the Holy Spirit

SOLEMN SONG
1701   ft C.M. West, E
        Here is a song which doth belong
        Sources. MNAN7/97, Peck, J
        Topic. Death and Resurrection

SOLEMNITY
1702   xt C.M. Doolittle, E
        Stoop down, my thoughts, that used to rise
        Sources. MNAN15/60, WH2/28
        Topic. Death and Resurrection

1703   ft L.M. Jenks, S
        Mourn, mourn, ye saints, who once did see
        Sources. SJ209, Anon.
        Topic. Sufferings and Death of Christ

SOLID PLEASURES
1704   xt L.M. Holden, O
        Descend from heav'n, immortal dove
        Sources. MNAN13/141, WH2/23
        Topic. Addresses to the Holy Spirit

SOLITUDE
1705   pt L.M. Babcock, L
        See where he languish'd on the cross
        Sources. MNAN11/136, WHor
        Topic. Repentance

1706   ft C.M. Edson, L Jr
        As on some lonely building's top
        Sources. MNAN3/79, WP102/1
        Topic. Sickness and Recovery

1707   pt P.M. Jenks, S
        Seek my soul, the narrow gate
        Sources. SJ374, Onderdonk, H
        Topic. Depravity and Fall of Man

1708   ft C.M. Mann, E
        Oft have I sat in secret sighs
        Sources. MNAN4/11, WHor
        Topic. Faith

1709   sp West, E
        My refuge is the God of love
        Sources. MNAN7/99, WP11/NV11
        Topic. Saints and Sinners

SOLOMON'S SONG
1710   sp Swan, T
        The voice of my beloved sounds
        Sources. TS196, Bible
        Topic. Solomon's Song

SOLON
1711   xt C.M. Belknap, D
        Indulgent God, with pitying eyes
        Sources. MNAN14/119, Doddridge, P
        Topic. Redemption

1712   pt S.M. Jenks, S
        Arise and bless the Lord
        Sources. SJ375, Montgomery, J
        Topic. Universal Praise

1713   xt S.M. Olmsted, T
        Firm and unmov'd are they
        Sources. MNAN15/160, WP125
        Topic. Perseverance

SOMERS
1714   ft S.M. Jenks, S
        Our moments fly apace
        Sources. SJ211, WP90
        Topic. Time and Eternity

1715   pt C.M. Jenks, S
        My God, the spring of all my joys
        Sources. SJ376, WH2/54
        Topic. Christian

SOMERSET
1716   xt S.M. Belknap, D
        Almighty maker, God
        Sources. MNAN14/120, WHor
        Topic. Worship

SOMERSETT
1717   xt L.M. Holyoke, S
        The king of glory sends his son
        Sources. MNAN12/112, WH2/136
        Topic. Birth of Christ

SONG . . . FOR ST. JOHN

1718   xt P.M. Babcock, S
Begin now the song the occasion requires
Sources. MNAN11/112, Harris, T
Topic. Masonic

SONG OF PRAISE

1719   pt P.M. Jenks, S
O Jesus, our Lord, thy name be ador'd
Sources. SJ377, Anon.
Topic. Universal Praise

1720   ft C.M. West, E
He sends his word and melts the snow
Sources. MNAN7/101, WP147
Topic. Seasons of the Year

SONG OF SONGS

1721   an French, J
The song of songs is Solomon's
Sources. MNAN9/254, Bible
Topic. Solomon's Song

SONNET, THE

1722   xt P.M. Jenks, S
When for eternal worlds we steer
Sources. SJ379, Anon.
Topic. Trust and Confidence

SORROW'S TEAR

1723   xt L.M. Jenks, S
Sweet spirit, if thy airy sleep
Sources. SJ212, Moore, T
Topic. Perseverance

SOUNDING-JOY

1724   ft S.M. Morgan, J
Come, sound his praise abroad
Sources. MNAN7/141, WP95
Topic. Worship

SOUTH-BOSTON

1725   xt P.M. Billings, W
Join all the glorious names
Sources. WB4/124, WH1/150
Topic. Characters and Offices of Christ

SOUTH THOMPSON

1726   xt S.M. Jenks, S
The hill of Sion yields
Sources. SJ381, WH2/30
Topic. Joy and Rejoicing

SOUTHBOROUGH

1727   ft L.M. Belknap, D
See where he languish'd on the cross
Sources. MNAN14/122, WHor
Topic. Repentance

1728   ft C.M. Wood, A
Now let our lips with holy fear
Sources. MNAN6/81, WP69/2
Topic. Sufferings and Death of Christ

SOUTHWELL

1729   pt S.M. Anon.
When man grows bold in sin
Sources. CR143, WP36
Topic. Perfections of God

SOVEREIGNTY

1730   pt P.M. Belcher, S
All things from nothing, to their sov'reign Lord
Sources. MNAN5/123, Anon.
Topic. Creation and Providence

SPAIN

1731   pt P.M. Billings, W
How pleas'd and blest was I
Sources. WB2/154, WP122
Topic. Public Worship

1732   pt P.M. Edson, L Jr
Rivers to the ocean run
Sources. MNAN3/81, Seagrave, R
Topic. Christian

SPARROW, THE

1733   xt C.M. Jenks, S
As on some lonely building's top
Sources. SJ382, WP102/1
Topic. Sickness and Recovery

SPARTA

1734   pt P.M. Holden, O
Sing to the Lord a new-made song
Sources. MNAN13/142, NV96
Topic. Birth of Christ

SPENCER

1735   pt C.M. Billings, W
Rejoice, ye righteous, in the Lord
Sources. WB3/334, WP33/1
Topic. Creation and Providence

1736   xt P.M. Holyoke, S
How pleas'd and blest was I
Sources. MNAN12/113, WP122
Topic. Public Worship

SPREAD THY WINGS

1737   pt P.M. Jenks, S
What is life, 'tis but a vapor
Sources. SJ383, Kelly, T
Topic. Trust and Confidence

SPRING

1738 xt P.M. Babcock, S
How sweetly along the gay mead
Sources. MNAN11/114, Anon.
Topic. Thanksgiving

1739 xt P.M. Belcher, S
The scatter'd clouds are fled at last
Sources. MNAN5/124, Anon.
Topic. Secular

1740 ft C.M. Belknap, D
He sends his word and melts the snow
Sources. MNAN14/124, WP147
Topic. Seasons of the Year

1741 xt C.M. Bull, A
Good is the Lord, the heav'nly king
Sources. MNAN1/121, WP65/3
Topic. Seasons of the Year

1742 xt L.M. Doolittle, E
The flow'ry spring at thy command
Sources. MNAN15/62, Doddridge, P
Topic. Seasons of the Year

1743 pt P.M. French, J
Mark how it snows! how fast the valley fills
Sources. MNAN9/264, WHor
Topic. Youth and Old Age

1744 ft C.M. Stone, J
He sends his word and melts the snow
Sources. MNAN10/74, WP147
Topic. Seasons of the Year

1745 pt S.M. Swan, T
Behold the morning sun
Sources. TS201, WP19/2
Topic. Lord's Day

SPRING STREET

1746 xt L.M. Belknap, D
Not to condemn the sons of men
Sources. MNAN14/125, WH1/100
Topic. Faith

SPRING, THE

1747 pt P.M. Jenks, S
From whence does this union arise
Sources. SJ384, Anon.
Topic. Faith

SPRINGFIELD

1748 xt L.M. Belknap, D
Lord, I am vile, conceiv'd in sin
Sources. MNAN14/127, WP51/2
Topic. Depravity and Fall of Man

1749 xt S.M. Jenks, S
Come, sound his praise abroad
Sources. SJ385, WP95
Topic. Worship

SPRINGFIELD [I]

1750 xt P.M. Babcock, L?
Jesus drinks the bitter cup
Sources. MNAN11/137, Wesley, C
Topic. Sufferings and Death of Christ

SPRINGFIELD [II]

1751 xt P.M. Babcock, L?
Jesus drinks the bitter cup
Sources. MNAN11/139, Wesley, C
Topic. Sufferings and Death of Christ

ST. ANDREWS

1752 pt S.M. Belcher, S
Behold the hosts of hell
Sources. MNAN5/113, WP25/3
Topic. Christian

ST. ANDREW'S

1753 ft C.M. Billings, W
Behold the glories of the lamb
Sources. WB4/274, WH1/1
Topic. Addresses to Christ

ST. ANNE

1754 pt C.M. Croft, W
My God, my portion and my love
Sources. CR132, WH2/94
Topic. Communion with God

ST. ANN'S

1755 pt C.M. Croft, W
My God, my portion, and my love
Sources. WB3/356, WH2/94
Topic. Communion with God

ST. DAVID'S

1756 pt C.M. Anon.
Whom should I fear, since God to me
Sources. CR133, NV27
Topic. Worship

ST. DAVID'S NEW

1757 ft P.M. Belcher, S
I'll praise my maker with my breath
Sources. MNAN5/115, WP146
Topic. Perfections of God

ST. ELISHA'S

1758 pt L.M. Billings, W
Thou whom my soul admires above
Sources. WB1/68, WH1/67
Topic. Solomon's Song

ST. ENOCH

1759 ft C.M. Billings, W
Sing to the Lord a new-made song
Sources. WB4/96, NV98
Topic. Birth of Christ

ST. GEORGE'S

1760　xt C.M. Anon.
Awake my heart, arise my tongue
Sources. CR134, WH1/20
Topic. Pardon

ST. HELEN'S

1761　pt P.M. Anon.
Ye that delight to serve the Lord
Sources. CR136, WP113
Topic. Perfections of God

ST. HELLEN'S

1762　pt P.M. Anon.
I'll praise my maker with my breath
Sources. WB3/358, WP146
Topic. Perfections of God

ST. JAMES

1763　pt C.M. Courtville, R
O thou, to whom all creatures bow
Sources. CR137, NV8
Topic. Perfections of God

ST. JOHN'S

1764　pt C.M. Belcher, S
With cheerful notes let all the earth
Sources. MNAN5/117, NV117
Topic. Universal Praise

1765　pt L.M. Billings, W
Where are the mourners, saith the Lord
Sources. WB4/72, WH2/154
Topic. Justification

ST. JOHNS

1766　xt L.M. Doolittle, E
Thrice happy man, who fears the Lord
Sources. MNAN15/58, WP112
Topic. Liberality

ST. LAWRENCE

1767　ft L.M. Olmsted, T
Descend from heav'n, immortal dove
Sources. MNAN15/155, WH2/23
Topic. Addresses to the Holy Spirit

ST. LUKE'S

1768　pt C.M. Belcher, S
Return, O God of love, return
Sources. MNAN5/118, WP90/3
Topic. Christian

ST. MARC

1769　pt L.M. Holden, O
Come, dearest Lord, descend and dwell
Sources. MNAN13/135, WH1/135
Topic. Worship

ST. MARK'S

1770　ft S.M. Belcher, S
And must this body die
Sources. MNAN5/119, WH2/110
Topic. Death and Resurrection

ST. MARTIN'S

1771　pt C.M. Tans'ur, W
Behold the glories of the lamb
Sources. CR138, WH1/1
Topic. Addresses to Christ

1772　pt C.M. Tans'ur, W
Behold the glories of the lamb
Sources. WB3/360, WH1/1
Topic. Addresses to Christ

ST. PAUL'S

1773　ft S.M. Belcher, S
How beauteous are their feet
Sources. MNAN5/120, WH1/10
Topic. Law and Gospel

ST. PETER'S

1774　xt P.M. Billings, W
How shall a lost sinner in pain
Sources. WB3/296, Wesley, C
Topic. Salvation

ST. THOMAS

1775　xt C.M. Billings, W
Methinks I see my saviour dear
Sources. WB4/187, Watts?
Topic. Sufferings and Death of Christ

1776　pt S.M. Williams, A
Let ev'ry creature join
Sources. CR140, WP148
Topic. Universal Praise

ST. VINCENT'S

1777　pt C.M. Billings, W
In vain we lavish out our lives
Sources. WB3/298, WH1/9
Topic. Invitations and Promises

1778　sp Olmsted, T
Salvation, O the joyful sound
Sources. MNAN15/157, WH2/88
Topic. Salvation

STAFFORD

1779　pt C.M. Brownson, O
Return, O God of love, return
Sources. MNAN2/45, WP90/3
Topic. Christian

1780　ft S.M. Read, D
See what a living stone
Sources. CR144, WP118
Topic. Worship

1781   ft S.M. Read, D
        See what a living stone
        Sources. DR149, WP118
        Topic. Worship

1782   ft S.M. Read, D
        See what a living stone
        Sources. DR282, WP118
        Topic. Worship

STANDISH

1783   pt C.M. Anon.
        How shall the young secure their hearts
        Sources. CR146, WP119/4
        Topic. Scripture

STERLING

1784   ft L.M. Doolittle, E
        Lord, what was man, when made at first
        Sources. MNAN15/63, WP8/2
        Topic. Depravity and Fall of Man

1785   xt S.M. Stone, J
        My soul repeat his praise
        Sources. MNAN10/76, WP103/2
        Topic. Perfections of God

STILL-RIVER

1786   ft C.M. Wood, A
        From my youth up, may Isr'el say
        Sources. MNAN6/83, NV129
        Topic. The Jewish Church

STOCKBRIDGE

1787   xt L.M. Billings, W
        From all that dwell below the skies
        Sources. WB2/159, WP117/NV95
        Topic. The Christian Church

1788   pt P.M. Gillet, A
        The birds without barn or storehouse are fed
        Sources. MNAN2/123, Newton, J
        Topic. Trust and Confidence

STONEHAM

1789   xt L.M. Belknap, D
        Now to the Lord a noble song
        Sources. MNAN14/129, WH2/47
        Topic. Christ

1790   ft L.M. Kimball, J
        Thy praise, O God, in Zion waits
        Sources. MNAN12/202, Kimball, J
        Topic. Lord's Day

1791   pt P.M. Wood, A
        The God I trust Is true and just
        Sources. MNAN6/85, Hart, J
        Topic. Adoption

STONINGTON

1792   xt C.M. Read, D
        Let a broad stream with golden sands
        Sources. DR151, WHor
        Topic. Depravity and Fall of Man

STORMY BANKS

1793   xt C.M. Jenks, S
        On Jordan's stormy banks I stand
        Sources. SJ387, Stennett, S
        Topic. Hell and Heaven

STOUGHTON

1794   pt C.M. Billings, W
        My saviour, my almighty friend
        Sources. WB1/160, WP71/2
        Topic. Justification

1795   pt P.M. French, J
        Not to our names, thou only just and true
        Sources. MNAN9/266, WP115
        Topic. Perfections of God

STOW

1796   xt P.M. Babcock, S
        The birds without barn or storehouse are fed
        Sources. MNAN11/115, Newton, J
        Topic. Trust and Confidence

STRATFORD

1797   ft L.M. Read, D
        The Lord, the judge, his churches warns
        Sources. DR152, WP50/3
        Topic. Day of Judgment

STRATTON

1798   xt C.M. Babcock, S
        O! magnify the Lord with me
        Sources. MNAN11/116, NV34
        Topic. Church Meetings

1799   xt P.M. French, J
        Thou sun, with dazzling rays
        Sources. MNAN9/269, WP148
        Topic. Universal Praise

STRONG HOPE

1800   xt L.M. Jenks, S
        Jesus, my all, to heav'n is gone
        Sources. SJ213, Cennick, J
        Topic. Characters and Offices of Christ

STURBRIDGE

1801   pt L.M. Billings, W
        The Lord, how wond'rous are his ways
        Sources. WB2/288, WP103/2
        Topic. Perfections of God

1802 xt C.M. Holyoke, S
To God I made my sorrows known
Sources. MNAN12/115, WP142
Topic. Perfections of God

1803 ft L.M. Stone, J
My flesh shall slumber in the ground
Sources. MNAN10/78, WP17
Topic. Saints and Sinners

SUBLIMITY

1804 pt S.M. Belcher, S
Behold the lofty sky
Sources. MNAN5/126, WP19/1
Topic. Lord's Day

1805 an Billings, W
The heavens declare the glory of God
Sources. WB4/257, BCPP19
Topic. Thanksgiving

SUBMISSION

1806 ft C.M. Woodruff, M
Vain are the hopes the sons of men
Sources. MNAN8/124, WH1/94
Topic. Justification

SUDBURY

1807 pt C.M. Billings, W
Blest be the everlasting God
Sources. WB1/82, WH1/26
Topic. Resurrection of Christ

1808 xt S.M. Billings, W
What if a saint must die
Sources. WB4/100, Peck, J
Topic. Day of Judgment

1809 pt P.M. Read, D
Think, mighty God, on feeble man
Sources. DR154, WP89
Topic. Death and Resurrection

SUFFERING SAVIOUR

1810 sp Jenks, S
When I survey'd the wond'rous cross
Sources. SJ215, WH3/7
Topic. The Lord's Supper

1811 xt C.M. Gillet, A
Save me, O God, the swelling floods
Sources. MNAN2/125, WP69/1
Topic. Sufferings and Death of Christ

SUFFIELD

1812 xt C.M. King, O
Teach me the measure of my days
Sources. CR147, WP39/2
Topic. Time and Eternity

SUFFOLK

1813 pt L.M. Billings, W
Bright king of glory, dreadful God
Sources. WB1/100, WH2/51
Topic. Christ

1814 pt L.M. Billings, W
Bright king of glory, dreadful God
Sources. WB2/92, WH2/51
Topic. Christ

SULLIVAN

1815 pt L.M. Billings, W
Let mortal tongues attempt to sing
Sources. WB2/62, WH1/58
Topic. Safety and Triumph of the Church

SUMMER

1816 pt P.M. Belknap, D
How soon, alas! must summer's sweets decay
Sources. MNAN14/131, Anon.
Topic. Time and Eternity

1817 xt C.M. Billings, N
With songs and honours sounding loud
Sources. MNAN3/128, WP147
Topic. Seasons of the Year

SUMMER STREET

1818 pt C.M. Billings, W
Speak, O ye judges of the earth
Sources. WB1/238, NV58
Topic. Magistracy

SUMMONS

1819 pt P.M. Jenks, S
Day of judgment, day of wonders
Sources. SJ389, Newton, J
Topic. Day of Judgment

SUNDAY

1820 ft C.M. Babcock, S
This day is God's; let all the land
Sources. MNAN11/118, NV118
Topic. Lord's Day

1821 pt C.M. Belcher, S
Arise, arise! the Lord arose
Sources. MNAN5/127, Anon.
Topic. Lord's Day

1822 xt L.M. Billings, W
Majestic God, when I descry
Sources. WB2/178, Billings, W
Topic. Creation and Providence

1823 pt P.M. Brownson, O
Hail, thou happy morn, so glorious
Sources. MNAN2/47, Anon.
Topic. Lord's Day

1824 ft P.M. West, E
The God of glory sends his summons forth
Sources. MNAN7/103, WP50/2
Topic. Day of Judgment

SUNDAY MORNING

1825 xt C.M. Woodruff, M
Early, my God, without delay
Sources. MNAN8/126, WP63/1
Topic. Lord's Day

SUNDERLAND

1826 ft L.M. French, J
Jesus is gone above the skies
Sources. MNAN9/271, WH3/6
Topic. The Lord's Supper

1827 pt P.M. Holyoke, S
Lord of the worlds above
Sources. MNAN12/116, WP84
Topic. Public Worship

1828 ft S.M. Jenks, S
Let ev'ry creature join
Sources. SJ219, WP148
Topic. Universal Praise

1829 xt L.M. Stone, J
The Lord is come, the heav'ns proclaim
Sources. MNAN10/79, WP97/2
Topic. Birth of Christ

SUPPLICATION

1830 ft S.M. Billings, N
When overwhelm'd with grief
Sources. MNAN3/130, WP61
Topic. Christian

1831 sp French, J
Shew pity, Lord, O Lord, forgive
Sources. MNAN9/273, WP51/1
Topic. Christian

1832 pt P.M. Jenks, S
O tell me no more of this world's vain store
Sources. SJ391, Gambold, J
Topic. Grace

1833 ft L.M. Read, D
O wash my soul from ev'ry sin
Sources. DR156, WP51/1
Topic. Christian

SUSPENSION

1834 xt L.M. Holden, O
My harp untun'd and laid aside
Sources. MNAN13/144, Newton, J
Topic. Afflictions of the Church

SUTTON

1835 pt S.M. Anon.
Behold the lofty sky
Sources. CR148, WP19/1
Topic. Lord's Day

1836 ft S.M. Brownson, O
Come sound his praise abroad
Sources. MNAN2/48, WP95
Topic. Worship

1837 ft C.M. Goff, E
Save me, O God, the swelling floods
Sources. CR149, WP69/1
Topic. Sufferings and Death of Christ

1838 xt C.M. Stone, J
Behold the man three score and ten
Sources. MNAN10/81, Robinson, R
Topic. Youth and Old Age

SWABIA

1839 xt P.M. Woodruff, M
Far above the glorious ceiling
Sources. MNAN8/129, Anon.
Topic. Characters and Offices of Christ

SWANZEY

1840 pt C.M. Billings, W
God in the great assembly stands
Sources. WB1/260, NV82
Topic. Magistracy

SWEET FAREWELL

1841 xt P.M. Jenks, S
Lord, dismiss us with thy blessing
Sources. SJ221, Anon.
Topic. The Lord's Supper

SWEET PROSPECT

1842 xt P.M. Jenks, S
How tedious and tasteless the hours
Sources. SJ222, Newton, J
Topic. Trust and Confidence

SWEET REST

1843 pt S.M. Jenks, S
Welcome, sweet day of rest
Sources. SJ223, WH2/14
Topic. Worship

SWEET SURPRISE

1844 xt C.M. Holden, O
Angels are lost in sweet surprise
Sources. MNAN13/145, WHor
Topic. Perfections of God

SYENA

1845 pt P.M. French, J
O Jesus, my hope, for me offer'd up
Sources. MNAN9/278, Wesley, C
Topic. Redemption

SYMPHONY

1846 xt P.M. Morgan, J
Behold, the judge descends; his guards are nigh
Sources. MNAN7/142, WP50/1
Topic. Day of Judgment

SYRIA

1847 xt L.M. Belknap, D
The swelling billows know their bound
Sources. MNAN14/133, WP104
Topic. Creation and Providence

TAUNTON

1848 ft C.M. Billings, W
As pants the hart for cooling streams
Sources. WB1/185, NV42
Topic. Fear and Hope

TE DEUM LAUDAMUS

1849 an Carr, B
We praise thee, O God
Sources. AA2/100, BCP
Topic. Universal Praise

TEMPEST

1850 pt P.M. Doolittle, E
Silent I waited with long-suff'ring love
Sources. MNAN15/65, WP50/1
Topic. Day of Judgment

TEMPLE

1851 ft L.M. Holden, O
Send comforts down from thy right hand
Sources. MNAN13/146, WH2/16
Topic. Communion with God

TEMPLETON

1852 xt C.M. Wood, A
Not from the dust affliction grows
Sources. MNAN6/86, WH1/83
Topic. Creation and Providence

TENDER THOUGHTS

1853 pt L.M. Holden, O
Arise, my tend'rest thoughts, arise
Sources. MNAN13/148, Doddridge, P
Topic. Depravity and Fall of Man

TERROR

1854 ft P.M. French, J
Silent I waited, with long-suff'ring love
Sources. MNAN9/280, WP50/1
Topic. Day of Judgment

TEWKSBURY

1855 xt P.M. Wood, A
I'm tir'd with visits, modes, and forms
Sources. MNAN6/87, WHor
Topic. Christian

THANKSGIVING

1856 sp Swan, T
Meet and right it is to sing
Sources. TS203, Anon.
Topic. Universal Praise

THANKSGIVING ANTHEM

1857 an Capen, S
Sing, sing unto the Lord a new song
Sources. AA1/3, Bible
Topic. Thanksgiving

1858 an French, J
O sing unto the Lord and praise his glor'ous name
Sources. MNAN9/282, BP96
Topic. Thanksgiving

1859 an Shaw, O
O give thanks unto the Lord
Sources. AA1/103, Bible
Topic. Thanksgiving

THANKSGIVING ANTHEM, A

1860 an Hardy, D
O come, let us sing unto the Lord
Sources. AA1/31, Bible
Topic. Thanksgiving

1861 an Holden, O
The Lord reigneth, let the people tremble
Sources. AA1/59, Bible
Topic. Thanksgiving

THESSALY

1862 sp Woodruff, M
Now let the Lord, my saviour, smile
Sources. MNAN8/130, WH2/50
Topic. Christian

THOMAS-TOWN

1863 xt C.M. Billings, W
Great God, how frail a thing is man
Sources. WB4/94, Byles, M
Topic. Faith

THOMPSON

1864 xt L.M. Jenks, S
Bless, O my soul, the living God
Sources. SJ392, WP103/1
Topic. Perfections of God

TIME'S MOTION

1865 xt C.M. Jenks, S
Time, like an ever-rolling stream
Sources. SJ394, WH2/58
Topic. Time and Eternity

TOLLAND

1866 ft C.M. French, J
May peace within this sacred house
Sources. MNAN9/287, Anon.
Topic. Safety and Triumph of the Church

1867 ft P.M. Jenks, S
I'll praise my maker with my breath
Sources. SJ224, WP146
Topic. Perfections of God

1868 xt C.M. Woodruff, M
Teach me the measure of my days
Sources. MNAN8/133, WP39/2
Topic. Time and Eternity

TOPSFIELD

1869 xt L.M. Gillet, A
Sweet is the work, my God, my king
Sources. MNAN2/128, WP92/1
Topic. Lord's Day

1870 ft C.M. Kimball, J
Lo! what an entertaining sight
Sources. MNAN12/203, WP133
Topic. Love

TOPSHAM

1871 ft C.M. Belcher, S
Dearest of all the names above
Sources. MNAN5/127, WH2/148
Topic. Addresses to Christ

TORRINGFORD

1872 xt C.M. Gillet, A
Joy to the world, the Lord is come
Sources. MNAN2/131, WP98/2
Topic. Birth of Christ

1873 ft C.M. Jenks, S
There is a house not made with hands
Sources. SJ226, WH1/110
Topic. Death and Resurrection

TORRINGTON

1874 pt C.M. Gillet, A
Must friends and kindred droop and die
Sources. MNAN2/133, Watts
Topic. Death and Resurrection

TOWER HILL

1875 pt C.M. Billings, W
How many, Lord, of late are grown
Sources. WB1/208, NV3
Topic. Fear and Hope

TOWNSHEND

1876 xt C.M. Wood, A
If why I love my Jesus so
Sources. MNAN6/89, Anon.
Topic. Solomon's Song

TRANSITION

1877 ft C.M. Belcher, S
When snows descend and robe the fields
Sources. MNAN5/129, Anon.
Topic. Seasons of the Year

TRANSMIGRATION

1878 sp Belcher, S
Come, let us renew
Sources. MNAN5/130, Wesley, C
Topic. New Year

TREASURE

1879 xt C.M. Holden, O
How doth thy word my heart engage
Sources. MNAN13/149, WP119/5
Topic. Scripture

TRENTON

1880 pt C.M. Belknap, D
Save me, O God, the swelling floods
Sources. MNAN14/134, WP69/1
Topic. Sufferings and Death of Christ

1881 xt C.M. Doolittle, E
Rejoice ye righteous in the Lord
Sources. MNAN15/67, WP33/1
Topic. Creation and Providence

TRIBULATION

1882 pt P.M. Doolittle, E
Along the banks where Babel's current flows
Sources. MNAN15/68, BarP137
Topic. Afflictions of the Church

TRIBUNAL

1883 xt P.M. Doolittle, E
The God of glory sends his summons forth
Sources. MNAN15/70, WP50/2
Topic. Day of Judgment

TRINITY

1884 xt P.M. Jenks, S
Come, thou almighty king
Sources. SJ228, Wesley, C
Topic. Universal Praise

1885 xt P.M. Swan, T
Come, thou almighty king
Sources. TS213, Wesley, C
Topic. Universal Praise

TRINITY-NEW

1886 pt C.M. Billings, W
O all ye nations, praise the Lord
Sources. WB2/334, WP117
Topic. The Christian Church

TRIUMPH

1887 xt P.M. Babcock, S
All hail! triumphant Lord
Sources. MNAN11/120, Scott, E
Topic. Exaltation of Christ

1888 ft P.M. Jenks, S
Behold, the judge descends; his guards are nigh
Sources. SJ229, WP50/1
Topic. Day of Judgment

1889 xt L.M. Read, D
Who shall the Lord's elect condemn
Sources. DR158, WH1/14
Topic. Fear and Hope

TRIUMPH, THE

1890   sp Bull, A
Stand up, my soul, shake off thy fears
Sources. MNAN1/127, WH2/77
Topic. Christian

TROY

1891   xt C.M. Chandler, S
Sing to the Lord, ye distant lands
Sources. MNAN2/162, WP96
Topic. Birth of Christ

1892   ft C.M. Edson, L
Come, let us join our cheerful songs
Sources. MNAN3/38, WH1/62
Topic. Addresses to Christ

1893   ft S.M. West, E
My saviour and my king
Sources. MNAN7/106, WP45
Topic. Beauty of the Church

TRUMBULL

1894   ft C.M. Benham, A
Lord, what is man, poor feeble man
Sources. MNAN8/46, WP144/2
Topic. Time and Eternity

TRUMPET

1895   pt L.M. Brownson, O
My flesh shall slumber in the ground
Sources. MNAN2/50, WP17
Topic. Saints and Sinners

TRURO

1896   xt P.M. Babcock, S
O praise ye the Lord, prepare your glad voice
Sources. MNAN11/121, NV149
Topic. Universal Praise

TUNBRIDGE

1897   xt C.M. Kimball, J
Our sins, alas! how strong they be
Sources. MNAN12/206, WH2/86
Topic. Hell and Heaven

TUNEFUL HARP

1898   xt C.M. Jenks, S
Before the rosy dawn of day
Sources. SJ232, Rowe, E
Topic. Morning and Evening

TURNER

1899   pt L.M. Belcher, S
Thy mercies, Lord, shall be my song
Sources. MNAN5/133, NV89
Topic. Grace

TYOT

1900   xt L.M. Belknap, D
Aurora veils her lovely face
Sources. MNAN14/136, Erskine, R
Topic. Death and Resurrection

1901   ft L.M. French, J
Beneath this stone death's pris'ner lies
Sources. MNAN9/289, Anon.
Topic. Death and Resurrection

UFFINDELL

1902   xt P.M. Holyoke, S
Mighty God, while angels bless thee
Sources. MNAN12/118, Robinson, R
Topic. Universal Praise

ULSTER

1903   sp Holyoke, S
Now to the Lord a noble song
Sources. MNAN12/120, WH2/47
Topic. Christ

UNION

1904   ft C.M. Belcher, S
Our states, O Lord, with songs of praise
Sources. MNAN5/135, NV21
Topic. Magistracy

1905   pt S.M. Billings, W
To God in whom I trust
Sources. WB1/54, NV25
Topic. Christian

1906   an Billings, W
Behold how good and joyful a thing
Sources. WB3/141, BCPP133
Topic. Love

1907   xt L.M. Billings, W
Loud hallelujahs to the Lord
Sources. WB3/304, WP148
Topic. Universal Praise

1908   pt P.M. Chandler, S
He fram'd the globe, he built the sky
Sources. MNAN2/164, WP96
Topic. Hell and Heaven

1909   pt C.M. Gillet, A
Lo! what an entertaining sight
Sources. MNAN2/134, WP133
Topic. Love

UNITY

1910   xt P.M. Belcher, S
'Twas my beloved spoke
Sources. MNAN5/137, Anon.
Topic. Solomon's Song

1911   pt L.M. Billings, W
Almighty ruler of the skies
Sources. WB1/104, WP8/1
Topic. Times and Seasons

1912   xt P.M. Doolittle, E
How pleasant 'tis to see
Sources. MNAN15/74, WP133
Topic. Public Worship

1913   ft P.M. Edson, L Jr
        How pleasant 'tis to see
        Sources. MNAN3/82, WP133
        Topic. Public Worship

1914   xt C.M. Read, D
        Lo! what an entertaining sight
        Sources. DR161, WP133
        Topic. Love

1915   xt P.M. Wood, A
        How pleasant 'tis to see
        Sources. MNAN6/91, WP133
        Topic. Public Worship

UNIVERSAL PRAISE

1916   an Billings, W
        O praise God, praise him in his holiness
        Sources. WB4/145, BP150/Billings
        Topic. Thanksgiving

1917   xt S.M. French, J
        Let diff'rent nation join
        Sources. MNAN9/290, NV67
        Topic. Universal Praise

UPTON

1918   pt P.M. Swan, T
        'Tis finished, 'tis done
        Sources. TS215, Anon.
        Topic. Death and Resurrection

UR

1919   ft L.M. Holden, O
        I love thy habitation, Lord
        Sources. MNAN13/150, WP26
        Topic. Public Worship

UXBRIDGE

1920   pt C.M. Billings, W
        Our father, who in heaven art
        Sources. WB1/228, Tate, N
        Topic. Doxology

1921   pt C.M. Billings, W
        Our father, who in heaven art
        Sources. WB3/308, Tate, N
        Topic. Doxology

1922   xt C.M. Stone, J
        Happy the heart where graces reign
        Sources. MNAN10/82, WH2/38
        Topic. Love

VALEDICTION

1923   xt L.M. Belknap, D
        Farewell, my friends, I must be gone
        Sources. MNAN14/138, Crossman, S
        Topic. Death and Resurrection

VANITY [I]

1924   xt P.M. French, J
        Well, what a busy world is this
        Sources. MNAN9/292, Anon.
        Topic. The World

VANITY [II]

1925   xt C.M. French, J
        Some walk in honour's gaudy show
        Sources. MNAN9/293, WP39/2
        Topic. Time and Eternity

VARIETY

1926   ft C.M. Jenks, S
        Save me, O God, the swelling floods
        Sources. SJ234, WP69/1
        Topic. Sufferings and Death of Christ

VARIETY, WITHOUT METHOD

1927   an Billings, W
        O God, thou hast been displeased
        Sources. WB4/206, BCPP60
        Topic. Fast Day

VENICE

1928   pt L.M. French, J
        Often I seek my Lord by night
        Sources. MNAN9/294, WH1/71
        Topic. Solomon's Song

VENUS

1929   xt S.M. Jenks, S
        Behold the morning sun
        Sources. SJ395, WP19/2
        Topic. Lord's Day

1930   ft S.M. West, E
        Behold the lofty sky
        Sources. MNAN7/108, WP19
        Topic. Scripture

VERGENNES

1931   xt C.M. Holden, O
        My heart and flesh cry out to thee
        Sources. MNAN13/151, WP84
        Topic. Public Worship

VERMONT

1932   xt C.M. Billings, W
        In vain we lavish out our lives
        Sources. WB2/180, WH1/9
        Topic. Invitations and Promises

1933   pt L.M. Doolittle, E
        Sweet is the work, my God, my king
        Sources. MNAN15/75, WP92/1
        Topic. Lord's Day

1934   xt C.M. Kimball, J
I'm not asham'd to own my Lord
Sources. MNAN12/207, WH1/103
Topic. Trust and Confidence

1935   ft C.M. Swan, T
Come, let us join our cheerful songs
Sources. TS217, WH1/62
Topic. Addresses to Christ

VERNAL DAY

1936   xt C.M. Holden, O
When verdure clothes the fertile vale
Sources. MNAN13/153, Steele, A
Topic. Times and Seasons

VERNON

1937   xt L.M. Babcock, S
Now be my heart inspir'd to sing
Sources. MNAN11/122, WP45/1
Topic. The Christian Church

1938   ft C.M. Olmsted, T
Ye mourning saints whose streaming tears
Sources. MNAN15/161, Doddridge, P
Topic. Death and Resurrection

VERONA

1939   xt L.M. Swan, T
From all that dwell below the skies
Sources. TS219, WP117
Topic. The Christian Church

VESPERS

1940   ft C.M. Read, D
Lord, thou wilt hear me when I pray
Sources. DR163, WP4
Topic. Morning and Evening

VICTORY

1941   pt P.M. Belcher, S
The welcome news
Sources. MNAN5/138, Anon.
Topic. Day of Judgment

1942   xt C.M. Billings, W
To thine almighty arm we owe
Sources. WB4/254, WP18/2
Topic. Thanksgiving

1943   ft C.M. Brownson, O
Hosanna to the prince of light
Sources. MNAN2/51, WH2/76
Topic. Resurrection of Christ

1944   ft C.M. Read, D
Now shall my head be lifted high
Sources. DR165, WP27/1
Topic. Public Worship

1945   ft C.M. Read, D
Now shall my head be lifted high
Sources. DR283, WP27/1
Topic. Public Worship

VIENNA

1946   ft P.M. Babcock, S
Ye boundless realms of joy
Sources. MNAN11/124, NV148
Topic. Universal Praise

1947   ft C.M. Read, D
My soul lies cleaving to the dust
Sources. DR166, WP119/16
Topic. Christian

1948   xt S.M. West, E
Welcome, sweet day of rest
Sources. MNAN7/110, WH2/14
Topic. Worship

VIEW OF THE TEMPLE, A

1949   sp Belknap, D
Sacred to heav'n, behold the dome appears
Sources. MNAN14/139, Anon.
Topic. Masonic

VIRGINIA

1950   xt C.M. Brownson, O
Thy words the raging winds control
Sources. CR151, WP89/2
Topic. Perfections of God

1951   xt C.M. Brownson, O
Thy words the raging winds control
Sources. MNAN2/52, WP89/2
Topic. Perfections of God

VOICE OF MY BELOVED, THE

1952   sp Swan, T
The voice of my beloved sounds
Sources. TS319, Anon.
Topic. Solomon's Song

VOLTA

1953   xt S.M. Swan, T
Your harps, you trembling saints
Sources. TS221, Toplady, A
Topic. Christian

WAKEFIELD

1954   xt S.M. Benham, A
Let ev'ry creature join
Sources. MNAN8/48, WP148
Topic. Universal Praise

WALLINGFORD

1955 ft P.M. Benham, A
O praise ye the Lord, prepare your glad voice
Sources. MNAN8/50, NV149
Topic. Universal Praise

WALPOLE

1956 ft C.M. Wood, A
O, if my soul was form'd for woe
Sources. MNAN6/92, WH2/106
Topic. Repentance

WALPOLE NEW

1957 xt C.M. Jenks, S
Awake, awake, each tuneful heart
Sources. SJ236, WP71/2
Topic. Justification

WALSAL

1958 pt C.M. Woodruff, M
Come, holy spirit, heav'nly dove
Sources. MNAN8/135, WH2/34
Topic. Addresses to the Holy Spirit

WALSALL

1959 pt C.M. Anon.
Lord, in the morning thou shalt hear
Sources. CR152, WP5
Topic. Lord's Day

WALTHAM

1960 xt L.M. Babcock, S
Now to the pow'r of God supreme
Sources. MNAN11/126, WH1/137
Topic. Salvation

1961 pt S.M. Billings, W
To thee I made my cry
Sources. WB1/332, Morton, P
Topic. Faith

1962 pt S.M. Billings, W
My saviour and my king
Sources. WB2/100, WP45
Topic. Beauty of the Church

WANTAGE

1963 pt C.M. Anon.
With rev'rence let the saints appear
Sources. CR153, WP89/2
Topic. Perfections of God

WARD

1964 ft C.M. Stone, J
In all my vast concerns with thee
Sources. MNAN10/85, WP139/1
Topic. Perfections of God

WAREHAM

1965 pt S.M. Billings, W
My God, my life, my love
Sources. WB2/328, WH2/93
Topic. Communion with God

1966 ft S.M. Billings, W
My God, my life, my love
Sources. WB3/67, WH2/93
Topic. Communion with God

WARREN

1967 ft L.M. Babcock, L?
Sleep, downy sleep, come close my eyes
Sources. MNAN11/140, Flatman, T
Topic. Regeneration

1968 xt P.M. Billings, W
Children of the heav'nly king
Sources. WB2/193, Cennick, J
Topic. Christian

1969 pt S.M. Edson, L
Let diff'ring nations join
Sources. MNAN3/39, NV67
Topic. Universal Praise

1970 ft S.M. Edson, L Jr
Our moments fly apace
Sources. MNAN3/83, WP90
Topic. Time and Eternity

1971 xt C.M. Read, D
Stoop down my thoughts that use to rise
Sources. DR168, WH2/28
Topic. Death and Resurrection

1972 sp Wood, A
Descend, immortal muse, inspire my song
Sources. MNAN6/94, Anon.
Topic. Patriotic

WARSAW

1973 xt C.M. Read, D
O that the Lord would guide my ways
Sources. DR284, WP119/11
Topic. Sanctification

WARWICK

1974 xt P.M. Stone, J
Think, mighty God, on feeble man
Sources. MNAN10/87, WP89
Topic. Death and Resurrection

WASHINGTON

1975 ft L.M. Billings, W
Lord, when thou did'st ascend on high
Sources. WB2/227, WP68/2
Topic. Ascension and Exaltation of Christ

1976 ft C.M. Jenks, S
Behold the love, the gen'rous love
Sources. SJ237, WP36
Topic. Perfections of God

1977 xt L.M. Olmsted, T
Shall man, O God of light and life
Sources. MNAN15/164, DP88/2
Topic. Trust and Confidence

1978 ft L.M. Swan, T
O, may the mem'ry of thy name
Sources. TS222, WP20
Topic. Thanksgiving

1979 ft C.M. West, E
Now shall my head be lifted high
Sources. MNAN7/112, WP27/1
Topic. Public Worship

WASHINGTON-STREET

1980 ft C.M. Billings, W
Now shall my inward joys arise
Sources. WB4/91, WH1/39
Topic. Safety and Triumph of the Church

WATER TOWN

1981 pt L.M. Billings, W
O all ye people, clap your hands
Sources. WB1/84, NV47
Topic. The Christian Church

WATERBURY

1982 xt L.M. Doolittle, E
Descend from heav'n, immortal dove
Sources. MNAN15/77, WH2/23
Topic. Addresses to the Holy Spirit

WATERFORD

1983 ft P.M. Edson, L
How pleas'd and blest was I
Sources. MNAN3/41, WP122
Topic. Public Worship

1984 xt S.M. Kimball, J
To bless thy chosen race
Sources. MNAN12/209, NV67
Topic. Joy and Rejoicing

1985 pt P.M. Wood, A
Holy Ghost, inspire our praises
Sources. MNAN6/97, Hart, J
Topic. Addresses to the Holy Spirit

WATERLOO

1986 pt L.M. Belcher, S
Let mortal tongues attempt to sing
Sources. MNAN5/139, WH1/58
Topic. Safety and Triumph of the Church

WATERTOWN

1987 sp Babcock, S
Jesus! my shepherd and my friend
Sources. MNAN11/127, Newton, J
Topic. Exaltation of Christ

1988 ft C.M. Stone, J
Begin the high celestial strain
Sources. MNAN10/89, Rowe, E
Topic. Universal Praise

1989 xt S.M. Woodruff, M
Let earth and ocean know
Sources. MNAN8/137, WP149
Topic. Universal Praise

WAYN

1990 ft P.M. Woodruff, M
Upward I lift my eyes
Sources. MNAN8/139, WP121
Topic. Creation and Providence

WEARY PILGRIM

1991 pt P.M. Holden, O
Come, said Jesus' sacred voice
Sources. MNAN13/155, Barbauld, A
Topic. Invitations and Promises

WEATHERSFIELD

1992 ft C.M. Billings, N
My soul is cleaving to the dust
Sources. MNAN3/132, WP119/16
Topic. Christian

1993 ft P.M. Morgan, J
Ye tribes of Adam join
Sources. MNAN7/145, WP148
Topic. Universal Praise

1994 ft L.M. Olmsted, T
Give to our God immortal praise
Sources. MNAN15/166, WP136
Topic. Creation and Providence

WEEPING NATURE

1995 xt L.M. Jenks, S
Nature, she shows her weeping eyes
Sources. SJ239, Stennett, S
Topic. Death and Resurrection

WELCOME

1996 pt P.M. Holden, O
Come, ye sinners, poor and wretched
Sources. MNAN13/156, Hart, J
Topic. Invitations and Promises

WELCOME MORN

1997 xt C.M. Holden, O
Again the Lord of life and light
Sources. MNAN13/157, Barbauld, A
Topic. Worship

WELLFLEET

1998 pt S.M. Billings, W
Who has believ'd thy word
Sources. WB1/218, WH1/141
Topic. Ascension and Exaltation of Christ

WELLS

1999 pt L.M. Holdroyd, I
Life is the time to serve the Lord
Sources. CR154, WH1/88
Topic. Time and Eternity

WERTER

2000 xt P.M. Edson, L Jr
Say, mighty love, and teach my song
Sources. MNAN3/85, WHor
Topic. Love

WEST

2001 xt C.M. West, E
Hark! from the tombs a mournful sound
Sources. MNAN7/113, WH2/63
Topic. Death and Resurrection

WEST BOSTON

2002 xt P.M. Billings, W
Come, ye lovers of the lamb
Sources. WB3/194, RCH28
Topic. Salvation

WEST SIMSBURY

2003 xt S.M. Jenks, S
Ye birds of lofty wing
Sources. SJ240, WP148
Topic. Universal Praise

WEST-SUDBURY

2004 xt C.M. Billings, W
Here is a song which doth belong
Sources. WB4/61, Peck, J
Topic. Death and Resurrection

WESTBORO'

2005 xt C.M. Wood, A
Behold the man three-score and ten
Sources. MNAN6/99, Robinson, R
Topic. Youth and Old Age

WESTBOROUGH

2006 ft C.M. Babcock, L?
Sing to the Lord, ye heav'nly hosts
Sources. MNAN11/142, WH2/62
Topic. Seasons of the Year

2007 xt C.M. Belknap, D
A span is all that we can boast
Sources. MNAN14/142, WP39/2
Topic. Time and Eternity

WESTERLOW

2008 pt S.M. Edson, L
Lord, I will not repine
Sources. MNAN3/42, Anon.
Topic. Resignation

WESTERN

2009 xt P.M. Stone, J
Christ's fountain, though rich
Sources. MNAN10/91, Hart, J
Topic. Salvation

WESTERN STAR ANTHEM

2010 an Wetmore, T
Let there be light! the almighty spoke
Sources. AA2/161, Anon.
Topic. Creation and Providence

WESTFIELD

2011 pt L.M. Billings, W
Not to condemn the sons of men
Sources. WB1/254, WH1/100
Topic. Faith

2012 xt P.M. Stone, J
The Lord Jehovah reigns, His throne
Sources. MNAN10/92, WH2/169
Topic. Perfections of God

WESTFIELD [I]

2013 ft S.M. Brownson, O
Mine eyes and my desire
Sources. MNAN2/54, WP25/3
Topic. Christian

WESTFIELD [II]

2014 xt C.M. Brownson, O
Awake, my soul, to sound his praise
Sources. MNAN2/55, BarP108
Topic. Universal Praise

WESTFORD

2015 xt P.M. Holyoke, S
I give immortal praise
Sources. MNAN12/122, WH3/38
Topic. Doxology

2016 xt L.M. Read, D
Far from my thoughts, vain world be gone
Sources. DR170, WH2/15
Topic. Communion with God

2017 xt L.M. Read, D
Far from my thoughts, vain world be gone
Sources. DR286, WH2/15
Topic. Communion with God

WESTMINSTER

2018   ft L.M. Stone, J
Behold on flying clouds he comes
Sources. MNAN10/94, WH1/61
Topic. Characters and Offices of Christ

WESTMORELAND

2019   xt C.M. Olmsted, T
Return, O God of love, return
Sources. MNAN15/169, WP90/3
Topic. Christian

WESTON

2020   xt S.M. Babcock, S
Jesus, the saviour, stands
Sources. MNAN11/129, WHor
Topic. Addresses to Christ

WESTON FAVEL

2021   xt C.M. Knapp, W
Come, let us join our cheerful songs
Sources. CR156, WH1/62
Topic. Addresses to Christ

WESTPOINT

2022   ft S.M. Chandler, S
Come sound his praise abroad
Sources. MNAN2/165, WP95
Topic. Worship

WEYMOUTH

2023   ft S.M. Billings, W
Shall we go on to sin
Sources. WB4/109, WH1/106
Topic. Christian

2024   xt P.M. Woodruff, M
Lo! he comes, in clouds descending
Sources. MNAN8/141, Wesley, C
Topic. Day of Judgment

WHALE ROCK

2025   xt C.M. Belknap, D
Death, 'tis a melancholy day
Sources. MNAN14/143, WH2/52
Topic. Christ

WHEELERS POINT

2026   pt L.M. Billings, W
On thee who dwell'st above the skies
Sources. WB1/102, NV123
Topic. Resignation

WHEELER'S POINT

2027   ft C.M. Billings, W
When Sion's God her sons recall'd
Sources. WB3/165, NV126
Topic. The Jewish Church

WHITESTOWN

2028   sp Olmsted, T
He reigns, the Lord, the saviour reigns
Sources. MNAN15/171, WP97/1
Topic. Day of Judgment

WHITFIELD

2029   ft P.M. Woodruff, M
Come, thou almighty king
Sources. MNAN8/143, Cennick, J
Topic. Universal Praise

WHITNEY

2030   xt P.M. Doolittle, E
Lord of the worlds above
Sources. MNAN15/79, WP84
Topic. Public Worship

WHY WEEPEST THOU

2031   xt C.M. Holden, O
Why, O my soul, why weepest thou
Sources. MNAN13/159, Beddome, B
Topic. Repentance

WHY WILL YE DIE

2032   pt P.M. Jenks, S
Sinners, turn, why will ye die
Sources. SJ397, Wesley, C
Topic. Salvation

WILBRAHAM

2033   pt S.M. Jenks, S
O that I could repent
Sources. SJ400, Wesley, C
Topic. Humility

WILKS

2034   pt L.M. Billings, W
Almighty God, eternal king
Sources. WB1/290, Morton, P
Topic. Universal Praise

WILL YOU GO

2035   xt P.M. Jenks, S
We're trav'ling home to heav'n above
Sources. SJ401, Anon.
Topic. Invitations and Promises

WILLIAMSBURGH

2036   xt C.M. Billings, W
Almighty God whose boundless sway
Sources. WB1/311, Billings?
Topic. Fear and Hope

2037   xt L.M. Jenks, S
With pow'r he vindicates the just
Sources. SJ242, WP72/1
Topic. Missionary Meetings

WILLIAMSTOWN

2038　pt P.M. Belknap, D
Almighty king of heav'n above
Sources. MNAN14/145, Anon.
Topic. Creation and Providence

2039　ft L.M. Edson, L
Life is the time to serve the Lord
Sources. MNAN3/43, WH1/88
Topic. Time and Eternity

WILMINGTON

2040　xt C.M. Babcock, S
'Tis God that lifts our comforts high
Sources. MNAN11/131, WH1/5
Topic. Resignation

WILTON

2041　ft S.M. Jenks, S
He form'd the deeps unknown
Sources. SJ244, WP95
Topic. Worship

2042　xt S.M. Kimball, J
Arise, my gracious God
Sources. MNAN12/210, WP17
Topic. Saints and Sinners

2043　ft C.M. Wood, A
Our days, alas! our mortal days
Sources. MNAN6/101, WH2/39
Topic. Time and Eternity

WINCHESTER

2044　pt L.M. Anon.
My God, accept my early vows
Sources. CR157, WP141
Topic. Morning and Evening

WINDHAM

2045　pt C.M. Brownson, O
Death! 'tis a melancholy day
Sources. MNAN2/58, WH2/52
Topic. Christ

2046　pt L.M. Read, D
Broad is the road that leads to death
Sources. CR158, WH2/158
Topic. Depravity and Fall of Man

2047　pt L.M. Read, D
Broad is the road that leads to death
Sources. DR173, WH2/158
Topic. Depravity and Fall of Man

2048　pt L.M. Read, D
Broad is the road that leads to death
Sources. DR288, WH2/158
Topic. Depravity and Fall of Man

2049　pt L.M. Read, D
Broad is the road that leads to death
Sources. DR289, WH2/158
Topic. Depravity and Fall of Man

WINDSOR

2050　pt C.M. Anon.
That awful day will surely come
Sources. CR160, WH2/107
Topic. Day of Judgment

2051　xt C.M. Read, D
He gives the grazing ox his meat
Sources. DR174, WP147
Topic. Seasons of the Year

WINDSOR NEW

2052　xt P.M. Jenks, S
How pleas'd and blest was I
Sources. SJ246, WP122
Topic. Public Worship

2053　xt P.M. Jenks, S
How pleas'd and blest was I
Sources. SJ247, WP122
Topic. Public Worship

WINSOR

2054　ft C.M. Read, D
Sing to the Lord, ye distant lands
Sources. DR176, WP96
Topic. Birth of Christ

WINTER

2055　xt L.M. Belknap, D
Now clouds the wintry skies deform
Sources. MNAN14/146, Anon.
Topic. Seasons of the Year

2056　pt C.M. Read, D
His hoary frost, his fleecy snow
Sources. CR161, WP147
Topic. Seasons of the Year

2057　pt C.M. Read, D
His hoary frost, his fleecy snow
Sources. DR178, WP147
Topic. Seasons of the Year

2058　pt C.M. Read, D
His hoary frost, his fleecy snow
Sources. DR290, WP147
Topic. Seasons of the Year

2059　pt C.M. Read, D
His hoary frost, his fleecy snow
Sources. DR291, WP147
Topic. Seasons of the Year

WINTHROP

2060　ft C.M. Belcher, S
Sing to the Lord, ye distant lands
Sources. MNAN5/140, WP96
Topic. Birth of Christ

2061　ft L.M. French, J
Whom then in heav'n but thee alone
Sources. MNAN9/296, NV73
Topic. Trust and Confidence

2062 xt L.M. West, E
Sweet is the work, my God, my king
Sources. MNAN7/115, WP92/1
Topic. Lord's Day

WINTONBURY

2063 ft S.M. Jenks, S
Alas, the brittle clay
Sources. SJ249, WP90
Topic. Time and Eternity

WISDOM

2064 sp French, J
How shall I praise th'eternal mind
Sources. MNAN9/298, WH2/166
Topic. Perfections of God

2065 xt S.M. Jenks, S
Wisdom, celestial sage
Sources. SJ250, Mann, H
Topic. Knowledge

WOBURN

2066 ft L.M. Kimball, J
Firm was my health, my day was bright
Sources. MNAN12/212, WP30/2
Topic. Sickness and Recovery

WOODBRIDGE

2067 ft C.M. Jenks, S
My soul lies cleaving to the dust
Sources. SJ251, WP119/16
Topic. Christian

WOODBURY

2068 xt L.M. Wood, A
Happy the city where their sons
Sources. MNAN6/102, WP144
Topic. Thanksgiving

WOODROW

2069 xt L.M. Holyoke, S
When God restor'd our captive state
Sources. MNAN12/123, WP126
Topic. Church Meetings

WORCESTER

2070 xt C.M. Billings, W
How short and hasty are our lives
Sources. WB2/166, WH2/32
Topic. Time and Eternity

2071 ft S.M. Wood, A
How beauteous are their feet
Sources. CR162, WH1/10
Topic. Law and Gospel

2072 ft S.M. Wood, A
How beauteous are their feet
Sources. MNAN6/104, WH1/10
Topic. Law and Gospel

WORSHIP

2073 ft S.M. Woodruff, M
Let Israel bless the Lord
Sources. MNAN8/145, WP106
Topic. The Jewish Church

WRENTHAM

2074 ft L.M. Babcock, L?
Methinks I hear the heav'ns resound
Sources. MNAN11/145, Anon.
Topic. Birth of Christ

2075 pt P.M. Billings, W
The God of glory sends his summons forth
Sources. WB2/122, WP50/2
Topic. Day of Judgment

YARMOUTH

2076 xt C.M. Benham, A
As on some lonely building's top
Sources. MNAN8/53, WP102/1
Topic. Sickness and Recovery

2077 ft S.M. Kimball, J
My soul repeat his praise
Sources. MNAN12/213, WP103/2
Topic. Perfections of God

YORK

2078 pt C.M. Anon.
Not all the outward forms on earth
Sources. CR165, WH1/95
Topic. Regeneration

2079 pt L.M. Belcher, S
So let our lips and lives express
Sources. MNAN5/142, WH1/132
Topic. Sanctification

2080 pt P.M. Brownson, O
The God of glory sends his summons forth
Sources. MNAN2/59, WP50/2
Topic. Day of Judgment

YOUTH

2081 xt L.M. Woodruff, M
Now in the heat of youthful blood
Sources. MNAN8/146, WH1/91
Topic. Youth and Old Age

ZENITH

2082 ft L.M. Woodruff, M
Awake my soul in joyful lays
Sources. MNAN8/147, Medley, S
Topic. Joy and Rejoicing

ZION

2083 ft P.M. Bull, A
How pleas'd and blest was I
Sources. MNAN1/129, WP122
Topic. Public Worship

2084   ft C.M. Read, D
        How did my heart rejoice to hear
        Sources. DR179, WP122
        Topic. Public Worship

2085   ft S.M. West, E
        How beauteous are their feet
        Sources. MNAN7/116, WH1/10
        Topic. Law and Gospel

Zion's Fall

2086   xt P.M. Jenks, S
        Give us room that we may dwell
        Sources. SJ402, Anon.
        Topic. The Christian Church

Zoar

2087   pt S.M. Read, D
        Far as thy name is known
        Sources. DR182, WP48/2
        Topic. The Christian Church

Composer

Anonymous

54, 213, 240, 274, 327, 339, 340, 343, 383, 453, 531, 771, 824, 914, 956, 957, 958, 999, 1015, 1063, 1068, 1117, 1184, 1224, 1260, 1269, 1339, 1351, 1457, 1458, 1459, 1517, 1518, 1524, 1525, 1729, 1756, 1760, 1761, 1762, 1783, 1835, 1959, 1963, 2044, 2050, 2078

Babcock, Lemuel or Lemuel?

12, 1705, 1750, 1751, 1967, 2006, 2074

Babcock, Samuel

55, 63, 64, 65, 66, 185, 209, 214, 356, 364, 371, 403, 419, 429, 430, 487, 515, 520, 562, 593, 607, 618, 663, 664, 674, 721, 723, 786, 808, 836, 870, 912, 922, 934, 942, 1038, 1047, 1075, 1120, 1131, 1155, 1164, 1185, 1217, 1219, 1270, 1311, 1318, 1356, 1384, 1386, 1428, 1445, 1471, 1536, 1542, 1543, 1574, 1577, 1621, 1633, 1699, 1718, 1738, 1796, 1798, 1820, 1887, 1896, 1937, 1946, 1960, 1987, 2020, 2040

Belcher, Supply

13, 20, 21, 35, 146, 167, 172, 241, 283, 384, 388, 396, 412, 494, 498, 510, 524, 543, 649, 666, 706, 745, 750, 765, 784, 835, 850, 861, 888, 926, 927, 928, 929, 945, 973, 979, 1007, 1046, 1048, 1086, 1246, 1340, 1355, 1368, 1369, 1427, 1439, 1461, 1464, 1479, 1508, 1546, 1561, 1562, 1573, 1730, 1739, 1752, 1757, 1764, 1768, 1770, 1773, 1804, 1821, 1871, 1877, 1878, 1899, 1904, 1910, 1941, 1986, 2060, 2079

Belknap, Daniel

4, 47, 60, 147, 186, 212, 245, 251, 265, 281, 285, 296, 299, 350, 385, 393, 441, 475, 493, 538, 594, 614, 632, 641, 670, 732, 770, 776, 797, 837, 844, 849, 906, 909, 915, 996, 1001, 1030, 1031, 1035, 1065, 1074, 1081, 1091, 1097, 1129, 1156, 1169, 1196, 1263, 1265, 1272, 1325, 1372, 1379, 1402, 1422, 1426, 1544, 1547, 1555, 1598, 1604, 1619, 1622, 1639, 1644, 1654, 1659, 1671, 1685, 1687, 1689, 1711, 1716, 1727, 1740, 1746, 1748, 1789, 1816, 1847, 1880, 1900, 1923, 1949, 2007, 2025, 2038, 2055

Benham, Asahel

16, 67, 200, 218, 305, 408, 467, 492, 521, 525, 544, 694, 712,

813, 895, 968, 977, 1206, 1556, 1569, 1692, 1894, 1954, 1955, 2076

Billings, Nathaniel

282, 297, 499, 501, 729, 731, 777, 1020, 1114, 1191, 1249, 1337, 1361, 1378, 1480, 1552, 1571, 1695, 1817, 1830, 1992

Billings, William

6, 17, 24, 25, 27, 43, 44, 48, 49, 50, 56, 57, 68, 69, 70, 71, 72, 73, 74, 75, 76, 77, 78, 79, 80, 81, 82, 83, 84, 85, 86, 87, 88, 89, 90, 91, 92, 93, 94, 95, 96, 97, 145, 148, 149, 150, 151, 187, 189, 190, 191, 192, 197, 204, 207, 227, 231, 235, 239, 246, 253, 255, 257, 261, 266, 276, 279, 287, 290, 291, 300, 303, 306, 307, 308, 311, 316, 326, 328, 329, 330, 333, 334, 337, 344, 358, 365, 366, 368, 379, 380, 381, 382, 409, 410, 413, 414, 415, 416, 422, 444, 447, 449, 454, 476, 484, 485, 486, 488, 491, 504, 511, 512, 517, 519, 522, 526, 533, 542, 551, 552, 563, 565, 585, 587, 608, 609, 623, 625, 627, 628, 635, 636, 638, 639, 642, 646, 648, 650, 658, 661, 667, 668, 678, 680, 681, 682, 686, 695, 718, 733, 734, 736, 739, 746, 751, 755, 756, 780, 781, 782, 788, 791, 794, 809, 814, 817, 825, 826, 830, 834, 841, 842, 848, 852, 853, 866, 871, 876, 877, 878, 880, 881, 884, 885, 886, 893, 897, 902, 904, 905, 910, 920, 930, 939, 952, 955, 962, 963, 965, 969, 974, 975, 982, 1004, 1005, 1011, 1012, 1019, 1022, 1023, 1024, 1037, 1039, 1042, 1049, 1082, 1085, 1087, 1088, 1092, 1094, 1095, 1098, 1099, 1101, 1102, 1107, 1108, 1110, 1111, 1115, 1118, 1119, 1121, 1125, 1128, 1143, 1147, 1157, 1166, 1178, 1180, 1186, 1192, 1193, 1195, 1214, 1215, 1218, 1220, 1223, 1232, 1235, 1236, 1241, 1242, 1243, 1244, 1247, 1248, 1253, 1259, 1266, 1309, 1312, 1319, 1320, 1326, 1335, 1350, 1352, 1353, 1367, 1373, 1380, 1391, 1395, 1398, 1400, 1408, 1414, 1416, 1417, 1424, 1429, 1435, 1441, 1442, 1446, 1466, 1472, 1473, 1484, 1493, 1526, 1527, 1528, 1529, 1534, 1541, 1557, 1575, 1582, 1585, 1592, 1593, 1594, 1599, 1608, 1611, 1623, 1624, 1632, 1655, 1656, 1658, 1660, 1663, 1672, 1677, 1681, 1684, 1686, 1693, 1697, 1725, 1731, 1735, 1753, 1758, 1759, 1765, 1774, 1775, 1777, 1787, 1794, 1801, 1805, 1807, 1808, 1813, 1814, 1815, 1818, 1822, 1840, 1848, 1863, 1875, 1886, 1905, 1906, 1907, 1911, 1916, 1920, 1921, 1927, 1932, 1942, 1961, 1962, 1965, 1966, 1968, 1975, 1980, 1981, 1998, 2002, 2004, 2011, 2023, 2026, 2027, 2034, 2036, 2070, 2075

Brown, Bartholomew

170

Brownson, Oliver

228, 247, 288, 341, 354, 367, 450, 621, 633, 747, 823, 946, 980, 983, 1017, 1061, 1267, 1313, 1357, 1515, 1553, 1649, 1673, 1779, 1823, 1836, 1895, 1943, 1950, 1951, 2013, 2014, 2045, 2080

Bull, Amos

18, 19, 125, 126, 127, 128, 129, 130, 131, 132, 133, 134, 135, 136, 137, 270, 495, 561, 601, 702, 724, 832, 867, 937, 947, 1025, 1136, 1148, 1149, 1264, 1376, 1396, 1418, 1420, 1451, 1469, 1478, 1481, 1485, 1491, 1496, 1497, 1501, 1504, 1505, 1506, 1510, 1512, 1516, 1520, 1554, 1558, 1565, 1586, 1645, 1650, 1666, 1741, 1890, 2083

Camp, Samuel

757

Capen, Samuel

1857

Carpenter, Elihu

98, 868

Carr, Benjamin

1849

Chandler, Solomon

42, 99, 331, 671, 672, 917, 993, 1462, 1494, 1495, 1507, 1891, 1908, 2022

Cole, John

100

Cooper, William

161

Courtville, Raphael

1763

Croft, William

1754, 1755

Deaolph

1523

Doolittle, Eliakim

101, 176, 188, 199, 201, 208, 313, 363, 376, 407, 434, 438, 532, 644, 689, 709, 713, 714, 838, 845, 857, 913, 924, 935, 943, 961, 966, 1040, 1054, 1134, 1317, 1327, 1626, 1702, 1742, 1766, 1784, 1850, 1881, 1882, 1883, 1912, 1933, 1982, 2030

Edson, Lewis

23, 28, 292, 314, 315, 325, 372, 418, 534, 541, 602, 815, 816, 918, 1016, 1032, 1033, 1045, 1126, 1158, 1245, 1251, 1488, 1892, 1969, 1983, 2008, 2039

Edson, Lewis Jr

14, 119, 226, 248, 389, 395, 740, 748, 772, 859, 889, 959, 994, 1563, 1583, 1597, 1706, 1732, 1913, 1970, 2000

Forbush, Abijah

102

French, Jacob

2, 120, 163, 181, 194, 196, 198, 202, 215, 219, 223, 243, 252, 254, 271, 272, 324, 351, 378, 397, 399, 400, 405, 420, 428, 448, 451, 462, 463, 468, 483, 496, 500, 505, 513, 540, 549, 554, 568, 582, 583, 597, 598, 611, 613, 631, 645, 690, 698, 701, 705, 707, 710, 728, 730, 766, 810, 854, 855, 882, 883, 908, 960, 970, 971, 1008, 1010, 1066, 1077, 1105, 1116, 1130, 1135, 1137, 1144, 1162, 1165, 1167, 1189, 1207, 1210, 1316, 1324, 1336, 1345, 1392, 1404, 1406, 1415, 1450, 1452, 1468, 1474, 1475, 1486, 1535, 1550, 1551, 1568, 1578, 1587, 1591, 1628, 1634, 1637, 1652, 1662, 1674, 1721, 1743, 1795, 1799, 1826, 1831, 1845, 1854, 1858, 1866, 1901, 1917, 1924, 1925, 1928, 2061, 2064

Frost

171

Frost, Rufus

154

Gibbons, Orlando

59

Gillet, Alexander

8, 31, 33, 37, 175, 206, 221, 222, 263, 264, 708, 741, 805, 811, 875, 984, 1138, 1152, 1190, 1227, 1250, 1314, 1388, 1430, 1499, 1500, 1600, 1605, 1679, 1788, 1811, 1869, 1872, 1874, 1909

Goff, Ezra

758, 1837

Gram, Hans

162, 1588

Hardy, Daniel

1860

Harmon, Joel

1370

Harwood, Edward

637

Herrick, Joseph

166

Hibbard

1333

Holden, Oliver

3, 9, 32, 36, 41, 51, 62, 152, 210, 256, 278, 318, 369, 386, 424, 431, 458, 464, 474, 477, 482, 502, 503, 508, 516, 557, 558, 559, 566, 577, 588, 589, 591, 595, 600, 677, 691, 699, 752, 759, 767, 769, 903, 916, 925, 938, 954, 967, 1064, 1070, 1083, 1100, 1112, 1133, 1139, 1145, 1181, 1202, 1208, 1211, 1222, 1254, 1341, 1344, 1354, 1360, 1371, 1387, 1407, 1413, 1519, 1579, 1581, 1590, 1595, 1607, 1636, 1646, 1657, 1668, 1700, 1704, 1734, 1769, 1834, 1844, 1851, 1853, 1861, 1879, 1919, 1931, 1936, 1991, 1996, 1997, 2031

Holdroyd, Israel

1609, 1999

Holt, Benjamin

753

Holyoke, Samuel

53, 140, 155, 179, 211, 273, 286, 304, 309, 338, 345, 352, 359, 392, 398, 402, 411, 529, 572, 626, 629, 652, 653, 654, 660, 665, 675, 715, 735, 760, 829, 873, 887, 891, 894, 940, 1006, 1034, 1072, 1109, 1132, 1154, 1315, 1346, 1347, 1374, 1381, 1393, 1447, 1453, 1532, 1548, 1603, 1653, 1680, 1691, 1717, 1736, 1802, 1827, 1902, 1903, 2015, 2069

Ingalls, Jeremiah

1238

Janes, Walter

158

Jenks, Stephen

11, 26, 45, 103, 104, 142, 159, 177, 178, 203, 216, 217, 244, 249, 280, 284, 317, 319, 336, 355, 373, 390, 417, 423, 425, 427, 439, 442, 455, 459, 461, 465, 466, 469, 470, 481, 489, 497, 518, 527, 537, 539, 547, 548, 550, 560, 564, 573, 576, 578, 580, 581, 590, 599, 603, 606, 612, 640, 643, 656, 683, 685, 687, 692, 693, 697, 700, 703, 704, 719, 737, 761, 762, 763, 773, 778, 779, 789, 790, 792, 795, 796, 798, 799, 800, 801, 802, 822, 846, 862, 869, 872, 874, 907, 936, 944, 948, 951, 953, 976, 978, 981, 985, 998, 1009, 1014, 1021, 1043, 1044, 1052, 1089, 1103, 1113, 1123, 1127, 1141, 1182, 1187, 1197, 1199, 1200, 1201, 1203, 1205, 1209, 1225, 1230, 1231, 1233, 1239, 1240, 1252, 1255, 1261, 1262, 1321, 1322, 1323, 1330, 1343, 1348, 1359, 1362, 1383, 1397, 1405, 1419, 1421, 1431, 1432, 1436, 1438, 1463, 1470, 1477, 1482, 1483, 1489, 1498, 1545, 1559, 1566, 1570, 1572, 1576, 1580, 1601, 1602, 1610, 1612, 1627, 1638, 1640, 1641, 1642, 1647, 1669, 1676, 1703, 1707, 1712, 1714, 1715, 1719, 1722, 1723, 1726, 1733, 1737, 1747, 1749, 1793, 1800, 1810, 1819, 1828, 1832, 1841, 1842, 1843, 1864, 1865, 1867, 1873, 1884, 1888, 1898, 1929, 1926, 1957, 1976, 1995, 2003, 2032, 2033, 2035, 2037, 2041, 2052, 2053, 2063, 2065, 2067, 2086

Kimball, Jacob

105, 106, 139, 183, 184, 262, 294, 301, 310, 346, 353, 357, 478, 634, 655, 688, 696, 754, 793, 827, 860, 892, 949, 1000, 1028, 1062, 1093, 1146, 1258, 1401, 1433, 1549, 1620, 1648, 1670, 1790, 1870, 1897, 1934, 1984, 2042, 2066, 2077

King, Oliver

1812

Knapp, William

34, 2021

Lane, Isaac

144, 433

Lee, Thomas

107

Lyon, James

121

Madan, Martin

432, 570, 630

Madan, Martin/Mann, Elias

571

Thorley, Thomas

1460

Tuckey, William

118, 1502

Wade, John

10

West, Elisha

46, 168, 220, 268, 275, 277, 348, 401, 457, 514, 545, 546, 567, 596, 657, 684, 742, 863, 864, 879, 932, 941, 950, 972, 1018, 1071, 1124, 1161, 1188, 1204, 1212, 1234, 1349, 1366, 1455, 1467, 1476, 1651, 1675, 1701, 1709, 1720, 1824, 1893, 1930, 1948, 1979, 2001, 2062, 2085

Wetmore, Truman

2010

Wheall, William

250

Williams, Aaron

1530, 1531, 1776

Wood, Abraham

5, 58, 174, 182, 195, 293, 302, 312, 342, 377, 446, 553, 605, 662, 711, 720, 764, 785, 851, 911, 931, 1013, 1041, 1051, 1106, 1140, 1213, 1338, 1403, 1456, 1560, 1625, 1643, 1690, 1728, 1786, 1791, 1852, 1855, 1876, 1915, 1956, 1971, 1985, 2005, 2043, 2068, 2071, 2072

Woodruff, Merit

40, 242, 391, 445, 460, 479, 490, 509, 530, 536, 676, 679, 726, 727, 890, 995, 997, 1177, 1256, 1271, 1332, 1377, 1411, 1412, 1449, 1618, 1678, 1694, 1696, 1806, 1825, 1839, 1862, 1868, 1958, 1989, 1990, 2024, 2029, 2073, 2081, 2082

Tune Type

Anthem

22, 63, 64, 65, 66, 67, 68, 69, 70, 71, 72, 73, 74, 75, 76, 77, 78, 79, 80, 81, 82, 83, 84, 85, 86, 87, 88, 89, 90, 91, 92, 93, 94, 95, 96, 97, 98, 99, 100, 101, 102, 103, 104, 105, 106, 107, 108, 109, 110, 111, 112, 113, 114, 115, 116, 117, 118, 119, 120, 121, 122, 123, 124, 125, 126, 127, 128, 129, 130, 131, 132, 133, 134, 135, 136, 137, 138, 139, 140, 141, 142, 143, 144, 145, 146, 147, 148, 149, 150, 151, 152, 153, 154, 155, 156, 157, 158, 159, 160, 161, 162, 163, 164, 165, 166, 167, 168, 169, 170, 171, 433, 474, 491, 542, 553, 554, 555, 556, 557, 565, 567, 638, 639, 680, 701, 705, 750, 751, 752, 753, 754, 755, 756, 757, 758, 759, 809, 833, 854, 882, 883, 895, 896, 939, 971, 972, 992, 994, 1010, 1011, 1204, 1226, 1368, 1369, 1370, 1371, 1389, 1395, 1550, 1588, 1592, 1721, 1805, 1849, 1857, 1858, 1859, 1860, 1861, 1906, 1916, 1927, 2010

Canon L.M.

379, 380, 381

Canon P.M.

378, 382

Extended Tune C.M.

3, 9, 11, 36, 174, 177, 180, 187, 205, 209, 216, 217, 228, 252, 253, 262, 267, 281, 290, 291, 299, 300, 301, 305, 337, 342, 346, 350, 351, 357, 370, 374, 375, 401, 441, 447, 467, 473, 478, 488, 502, 503, 504, 528, 545, 562, 574, 592, 593, 594, 595, 622, 647, 650, 659, 669, 671, 672, 674, 676, 686, 694, 702, 715, 721, 724, 730, 765, 767, 769, 782, 794, 795, 825, 844, 851, 855, 858, 875, 876, 877, 880, 889, 898, 909, 917, 922, 930, 932, 944, 947, 950, 974, 975, 976, 996, 1000, 1006, 1007, 1008, 1026, 1035, 1036, 1037, 1038, 1041, 1045, 1062, 1076, 1087, 1088, 1093, 1097, 1123, 1129, 1135, 1144, 1156, 1167, 1181, 1185, 1188, 1211, 1217, 1240, 1245, 1249, 1250, 1270, 1297, 1306, 1315, 1317, 1318, 1323, 1325, 1360, 1362, 1416, 1422, 1433, 1441, 1444, 1453, 1462, 1485, 1488, 1493, 1502, 1512, 1534, 1544, 1558, 1563, 1565, 1568, 1570, 1571, 1574, 1575, 1587, 1598, 1602, 1603, 1607, 1615, 1617, 1644, 1664, 1672, 1684, 1687, 1692, 1697, 1700, 1702, 1711, 1733, 1741, 1760, 1775, 1792, 1793, 1798, 1802, 1811, 1812, 1817, 1825, 1838, 1844, 1852, 1863, 1865, 1868, 1872, 1876, 1879, 1881, 1891, 1897, 1898, 1914, 1922, 1925, 1931, 1932, 1934, 1936, 1942, 1950, 1951, 1957, 1971, 1973, 1997, 2001, 2004, 2005, 2007, 2014, 2019, 2021, 2025, 2031, 2036, 2040, 2051, 2070, 2076

Extended Tune L.M.

4, 10, 31, 33, 38, 40, 173, 186, 212, 224, 225, 238, 255, 266, 268, 273, 307, 318, 348, 349, 368, 376, 388, 411, 418, 419, 438, 440, 475, 480, 482, 505, 516, 520, 538, 543, 544, 558, 580, 582, 616, 617, 630, 631, 645, 654, 670, 687, 693, 722, 726, 732, 748, 773, 774, 776, 778, 796, 801, 807, 813, 837, 868, 915, 919, 938, 968, 1009, 1017, 1027, 1053, 1064, 1067, 1074, 1096, 1099, 1116, 1131, 1137, 1138, 1141, 1142, 1165, 1169, 1176, 1196, 1231, 1261, 1268, 1271, 1311, 1312, 1324, 1358, 1372, 1374, 1376, 1387, 1388, 1404, 1407, 1408, 1418, 1425, 1430, 1431, 1438, 1447, 1450, 1474, 1542, 1562, 1576, 1584, 1604, 1605, 1633, 1636, 1654, 1662, 1666, 1704, 1717, 1723, 1742, 1746, 1748, 1766, 1787, 1789, 1800, 1822, 1829, 1834, 1847, 1864, 1869, 1889, 1900, 1907, 1923, 1937, 1939, 1960, 1977, 1982, 1995, 2016, 2017, 2037, 2055, 2062, 2068, 2069, 2081

Extended Tune P.M.

2, 6, 48, 49, 50, 54, 55, 176, 178, 181, 196, 210, 214, 218, 222, 227, 231, 233, 234, 256, 263, 264, 275, 296, 317, 341, 344, 369, 371, 384, 394, 398, 405, 422, 427, 432, 435, 436, 444, 446, 448, 454, 455, 458, 461, 479, 486, 487, 490, 494, 513, 514, 515, 517, 518, 523, 572, 579, 581, 601, 632, 640, 642, 652, 655, 664, 666, 667, 679, 696, 703, 717, 723, 728, 731, 735, 738, 740, 745, 749, 762, 772, 779, 785, 786, 803, 806, 859, 866, 867, 870, 891, 899, 900, 908, 912, 913, 914, 920, 925, 926, 927, 928, 934, 937, 943, 946, 948, 970, 973, 982, 997, 1014, 1050, 1071, 1104, 1109, 1128, 1130, 1145, 1148, 1149, 1164, 1178, 1191, 1201, 1203, 1213, 1219, 1233, 1234, 1255, 1276, 1281, 1295, 1303, 1304, 1305, 1309, 1314, 1338, 1344, 1355, 1356, 1357, 1359, 1361, 1375, 1396, 1397, 1406, 1417, 1420, 1421, 1428, 1434, 1436, 1456, 1458, 1470, 1480, 1481, 1494, 1495, 1509, 1513, 1526, 1527, 1533, 1536, 1543, 1557, 1560, 1582, 1585, 1589, 1599, 1608, 1613, 1614, 1621, 1638, 1639, 1649, 1656, 1668, 1676, 1693, 1718, 1722, 1725, 1736, 1738, 1739, 1750, 1751, 1774, 1796, 1799, 1839, 1841, 1842, 1846, 1855, 1883, 1884, 1885, 1887, 1896, 1902, 1910, 1912, 1915, 1924, 1968, 1974, 2000, 2002, 2009, 2012, 2015, 2024, 2030, 2035, 2052, 2053, 2086

Extended Tune S.M.

51, 244, 249, 293, 336, 352, 423, 426, 431, 469, 493, 500, 506, 525, 539, 564, 606, 612, 644, 683, 700, 719, 787, 805, 839, 846, 978, 998, 1003, 1047, 1059, 1060, 1070, 1073, 1103, 1120, 1127, 1146, 1207, 1277, 1280, 1348, 1352, 1363, 1377, 1415, 1424, 1432, 1489, 1491, 1498, 1499, 1500, 1510, 1511, 1516, 1559, 1622, 1637, 1673, 1713, 1716, 1726, 1749, 1785, 1808, 1917, 1929, 1948, 1953, 1954, 1984, 1989, 2003, 2020, 2042, 2065

Fuging Tune C.M.

7, 14, 20, 42, 46, 53, 57, 58, 61, 195, 197, 200, 203, 215, 236, 237, 257, 271, 276, 279, 282, 283, 292, 297, 320, 326, 353, 360, 361, 372, 386, 393, 396, 404, 420, 442, 466, 468, 498, 499, 512, 521, 536, 537, 546, 568, 569, 586, 596, 602, 627, 641, 649, 657, 658, 681, 691, 710, 713, 716, 720, 727, 729, 766, 788, 790, 797, 804, 808, 810, 811, 818, 828, 843, 861, 864, 865, 890, 892, 894, 903, 907, 921, 977, 984, 1004, 1005, 1018, 1028, 1043, 1048, 1086, 1089, 1091, 1100, 1106, 1125, 1126, 1136, 1150, 1151, 1157, 1159, 1168, 1174, 1175, 1177, 1183, 1186, 1194, 1230, 1238, 1243, 1244, 1260, 1263, 1267, 1316, 1319, 1321, 1322, 1330, 1339, 1340, 1366, 1382, 1402, 1403, 1411, 1427, 1437, 1448, 1463, 1476, 1490, 1492, 1496, 1503, 1519, 1521, 1538, 1539, 1540, 1545, 1566, 1578, 1579, 1594, 1595, 1611, 1618, 1619, 1628, 1634, 1659, 1669, 1677, 1679, 1682, 1683, 1688, 1701, 1706, 1708, 1720, 1728, 1740, 1744, 1753, 1759, 1786, 1806, 1820, 1837, 1848, 1866, 1870, 1871, 1873, 1877, 1892, 1894, 1904, 1926, 1935, 1938, 1940, 1943, 1944, 1945, 1947, 1956, 1964, 1976, 1979, 1980, 1988, 1992, 2006, 2027, 2043, 2054, 2060, 2067, 2084

Fuging Tune L.M.

1, 12, 13, 17, 21, 45, 172, 199, 223, 243, 269, 272, 285, 294, 308, 314, 315, 321, 322, 323, 324, 332, 367, 373, 387, 395, 397, 449, 457, 501, 508, 522, 541, 549, 552, 577, 583, 584, 597, 604, 607, 610, 611, 620, 624, 673, 689, 690, 698, 706, 737, 775, 793, 798, 814, 819, 820, 821, 826, 836, 845, 849, 881, 901, 923, 935, 949, 952, 953, 1061, 1066, 1084, 1095, 1134, 1162, 1170, 1171, 1172, 1173, 1179, 1190, 1193, 1199, 1209, 1210, 1216, 1221, 1228, 1229, 1237, 1246, 1272, 1273, 1337, 1345, 1354, 1384, 1468, 1487, 1532, 1546, 1549, 1552, 1555, 1564, 1583, 1597, 1620, 1630, 1631, 1652, 1661, 1678, 1694, 1698, 1703, 1727, 1767, 1784, 1790, 1797, 1803, 1826, 1833, 1851, 1901, 1919, 1967, 1975, 1978, 1994, 2018, 2039, 2061, 2066, 2074, 2082

Fuging Tune P.M.

8, 15, 52, 194, 202, 219, 221, 265, 287, 289, 313, 377, 389, 390, 391, 399, 406, 408, 417, 471, 472, 483, 509, 527, 534, 598, 688, 708, 709, 741, 742, 743, 744, 815, 816, 831, 840, 863, 886, 888, 910, 959, 979, 980, 1020, 1032, 1033, 1080, 1090, 1154, 1158, 1161, 1163, 1206, 1222, 1262, 1326, 1332, 1346, 1347, 1349, 1379, 1383, 1390, 1410, 1439, 1449, 1452, 1479, 1482, 1486, 1507, 1520, 1522, 1523, 1591, 1596, 1675, 1757, 1824, 1854, 1867, 1888, 1913, 1946, 1955, 1983, 1990, 1993, 2029, 2083

Fuging Tune S.M.

28, 29, 193, 207, 248, 278, 295, 310, 424, 451, 459, 464, 477, 496, 497, 535, 540, 547, 605, 613, 663, 684, 685, 697, 734, 768, 777, 835, 862, 873, 879, 906, 995, 1016, 1055, 1056, 1057, 1058, 1075, 1105, 1110, 1111, 1225, 1313, 1329, 1333, 1364, 1365, 1414, 1451, 1467, 1547, 1548, 1567, 1577, 1629, 1647, 1665, 1680, 1714, 1724, 1770, 1773, 1780, 1781, 1782, 1828, 1830, 1836, 1893, 1930, 1966, 1970, 2013, 2022, 2023, 2041, 2063, 2071, 2072, 2073, 2077, 2085

Plain Tune C.M.

5, 18, 24, 25, 26, 27, 30, 56, 60, 188, 201, 208, 229, 230, 235, 239, 242, 247, 250, 251, 261, 306, 312, 327, 333, 334, 339, 340, 343, 345, 358, 363, 383, 407, 412, 416, 421, 434, 452, 453, 476, 511, 526, 529, 532, 560, 561, 566, 587, 600, 608, 609, 614, 615, 628, 646, 653, 656, 660, 675, 682, 771, 829, 842, 853, 871, 878, 955, 956, 957, 958, 963, 964, 1022, 1023, 1024, 1025, 1040, 1068, 1077, 1078, 1079, 1082, 1101, 1102, 1117, 1132, 1143, 1160, 1218, 1223, 1224, 1227, 1241, 1242, 1264, 1265, 1289, 1302, 1320, 1331, 1336, 1353, 1367, 1373, 1381, 1393, 1405, 1429, 1440, 1443, 1446, 1457, 1459, 1469, 1472, 1473, 1475, 1537, 1553, 1554, 1590, 1593, 1609, 1626, 1691, 1696, 1715, 1735, 1754, 1755, 1756, 1763, 1764, 1768, 1771, 1772, 1777, 1779, 1783, 1794, 1807, 1818, 1821, 1840, 1874, 1875, 1880, 1886, 1909, 1920, 1921, 1958, 1959, 1963, 2045, 2050, 2056, 2057, 2058, 2059, 2078

Plain Tune L.M.

32, 34, 37, 59, 179, 189, 190, 232, 240, 258, 259, 270, 284, 286, 309, 311, 316, 328, 329, 330, 335, 338, 366, 385, 392, 400, 409, 413, 414, 415, 510, 519, 524, 550, 551, 563, 625, 629, 633, 635, 636, 665, 668, 692, 699, 707, 712, 718, 736, 780, 781, 783, 784, 799, 812, 822, 841, 848, 850, 852, 856, 902, 911, 933, 960, 961, 962, 999, 1012, 1039, 1052, 1065, 1092, 1094, 1107, 1108, 1118, 1119, 1121, 1122, 1133, 1182, 1184, 1192, 1195, 1198, 1214, 1232, 1251, 1253, 1259, 1266, 1296, 1327, 1334, 1350, 1351, 1385, 1391, 1394, 1398, 1426, 1435, 1445, 1454, 1460, 1461, 1466, 1483, 1484, 1497, 1501, 1514, 1515, 1517, 1518, 1529, 1530, 1531, 1541, 1569, 1610, 1612, 1623, 1635, 1660, 1663, 1674, 1686, 1690, 1695, 1705, 1758, 1765, 1769, 1801, 1813, 1814, 1815, 1853, 1895, 1899, 1911, 1928, 1933, 1981, 1986, 1999, 2011, 2026, 2034, 2044, 2046, 2047, 2048, 2049, 2079

Plain Tune P.M.

16, 19, 23, 39, 43, 44, 47, 175, 183, 184, 198, 206, 241, 245, 274, 288, 302, 303, 325, 347, 354, 355, 359, 365, 410, 439, 443, 445, 450, 456, 462, 489, 492, 530, 531, 573, 575, 576, 578, 590, 603, 621, 634, 651, 661, 677, 704, 711, 725, 770, 789, 791, 792, 800, 802, 827, 830, 834, 838, 857, 869, 872, 874, 887, 897, 904, 905, 916, 924, 929, 936, 951, 965, 969, 981, 983, 985, 986, 987, 988, 989, 993, 1001, 1015, 1021, 1029, 1030, 1031, 1034, 1044, 1046, 1051, 1072, 1081, 1085, 1098, 1115, 1124, 1140, 1152, 1180, 1197, 1200, 1202, 1205, 1220, 1239, 1254, 1257, 1258, 1290, 1293, 1298, 1300, 1380, 1400, 1412, 1413, 1419, 1423, 1442, 1477, 1478, 1505, 1506,

1508, 1524, 1525, 1535, 1572, 1580, 1581, 1600, 1601, 1606, 1624, 1625, 1640, 1643, 1646, 1658, 1671, 1681, 1689, 1707, 1719, 1730, 1731, 1732, 1734, 1737, 1743, 1747, 1761, 1762, 1788, 1791, 1795, 1809, 1816, 1819, 1823, 1827, 1832, 1845, 1850, 1882, 1908, 1918, 1941, 1985, 1991, 1996, 2032, 2038, 2075, 2080

Plain Tune S.M.

35, 191, 192, 204, 213, 226, 246, 319, 331, 425, 465, 470, 484, 485, 495, 507, 533, 548, 585, 623, 643, 648, 678, 695, 714, 733, 739, 746, 817, 823, 884, 885, 893, 918, 1002, 1042, 1049, 1054, 1063, 1147, 1187, 1215, 1235, 1236, 1247, 1248, 1252, 1269, 1275, 1308, 1310, 1335, 1465, 1504, 1528, 1561, 1627, 1645, 1648, 1657, 1685, 1712, 1729, 1745, 1752, 1776, 1804, 1835, 1843, 1905, 1961, 1962, 1965, 1969, 1998, 2008, 2033, 2087

Set Piece

41, 62, 182, 185, 211, 220, 254, 260, 277, 280, 298, 304, 356, 362, 364, 402, 403, 428, 429, 430, 437, 460, 463, 481, 559, 570, 571, 588, 589, 591, 599, 618, 619, 626, 637, 662, 747, 760, 761, 763, 764, 824, 832, 847, 860, 931, 940, 941, 942, 945, 954, 966, 967, 990, 991, 1013, 1019, 1069, 1083, 1112, 1113, 1114, 1139, 1153, 1155, 1166, 1189, 1208, 1212, 1256, 1274, 1278, 1279, 1282, 1283, 1284, 1285, 1286, 1287, 1288, 1291, 1292, 1294, 1299, 1301, 1307, 1328, 1341, 1342, 1343, 1378, 1386, 1392, 1399, 1401, 1409, 1455, 1464, 1471, 1551, 1556, 1573, 1586, 1616, 1632, 1641, 1642, 1650, 1651, 1653, 1655, 1667, 1670, 1699, 1709, 1710, 1778, 1810, 1831, 1856, 1862, 1878, 1890, 1903, 1949, 1952, 1972, 1987, 2028, 2064

First Line

A

A blooming paradise of joy, 1100
A day of feasting I ordain, 1476
A span is all that we can boast, 2007
A virgin unspotted the prophet foretold, 982
Adore and tremble, for our God, 587
Again the Lord of life and light, 209, 1997
Against thy zealous people, Lord, 1568
Agonizing in the garden, 772
Ah, guilty sinner, ruined by transgression, 985
Ah! lovely appearance of death, 1658
Ah, whither rolls thou fair retiring light, 1343
Ah! whither shall I go, 1627
Alas! and did my saviour bleed, 656, 1006
Alas, my aching heart, 500
Alas, the brittle clay, 535, 879, 2063
Alas, the cruel spear, 1559
All hail the pow'r of Jesus' name, 502, 503
All hail! triumphant Lord, 1887
All hail, happy day, 857
All is hush, the battle's o'er, 969
All over lovely is my Lord and God, 1180
All things from nothing, to their sov'reign Lord, 1730
All ye bright armies of the skies, 457
All ye that pass by, to Jesus draw nigh, 928
All ye who faithful servants are, 1664
All you bright armies of the skies, 624
All you, who make the law your choice, 1693
Almighty God, eternal king, 2034
Almighty God whose boundless sway, 2036
Almighty king of heav'n above, 1164, 1293, 2038
Almighty maker, God, 1716
Almighty ruler of the skies, 286, 1911
Along the banks where Babel's current flows, 218, 219, 221, 222, 289, 389, 390, 391, 578, 1001, 1882
And am I only born to die, 590
And can this mighty king, 908, 1072
And I saw a mighty angel proclaiming, 68
And is the lovely shadow fled, 598
And is th'illustrious chieftain dead, 925
And must I part with all I have, 1381
And must this body die, 548, 787, 1016, 1110, 1111, 1313, 1648, 1770
And must this body faint and die, 594
And now the scales have left mine eyes, 252
And will the God of grace, 613

And will the judge descend, 606
Angels are lost in sweet surprise, 1844
Angels, roll the rock away, 146, 402, 936, 1668
Another six days work is done, 1636
Arise and bless the Lord, 1712
Arise, and hail the sacred day, 444
Arise, arise! the Lord arose, 1821
Arise, my gracious God, 1399, 2042
Arise my soul, my joyful pow'rs, 177
Arise, my tend'rest thoughts, arise, 580, 1853
Arise, O God, in thine anger, 567
Arise, O king of grace, arise, 298
Arise, O Lord, arise into thy resting place, 134
Arise, shine, O Zion, for thy light is come, 129
Arise ye bright nations and honor your maker, 462
Array'd in beauteous green, 1439
As lost in lonely grief, I tread, 677, 1031
As on some lonely building's top, 592, 1706, 1733, 2076
As pants the hart for cooling streams, 1403, 1617, 1848
As shepherds in Jewry were guarding their sheep, 667
As the hart panteth after the waterbrooks, 69
Attend our armies to the fight, 669
Attend, ye saints, and hear me tell, 1254
Aurora veils her lovely face, 1900
Aurora veils her rosy face, 543
Awake, awake, each tuneful heart, 1957
Awake, awake, put on thy strength, O Zion, 972
Awake my heart, arise my tongue, 57, 1760
Awake, my soul, and with the sun, 583
Awake, my soul, awake, 207, 1352
Awake my soul! awake mine eyes, 1184
Awake my soul! awake my eyes, 881, 1182
Awake my soul in joyful lays, 2082
Awake, my soul, to sound his praise, 345, 1537, 2014
Awake, our drowsy souls, 806
Awake our souls (away our fears, 1214
Awake, put on thy strength, O Zion, 971
Awake, ye saints, to praise your king, 61
Away, my unbelieving fears, 824

B

Back from the tomb, O ask her not, 1642
Be dark! Thou sun, in one eternal night, 1020
Be thou, O God, exalted high, 1518
Before Jehovah's awful throne, 570, 571
Before the rosy dawn of day, 671, 672, 1284, 1898

H

How soon, alas! must summer's sweets decay, 1816
How sweet the voice, how sweet the hand, 375
How sweetly along the gay mead, 916, 1307, 1738
How tedious and tasteless the hours, 176, 355, 1428, 1842
How vain are all things here below, 242
How vast must their advantage be, 1037, 1101, 1102
Hush, my dear, lie still and slumber, 509, 1480

I

I am come into my garden, my sister, my spouse, 77
I am not concern'd to know, 39, 494
I am the rose of Sharon and the lily of the vallies, 78
I am the saviour, I th'almighty God, 983, 1202, 1290
I beheld and lo, a great multitude, 882, 883
I charge you, O ye daughters of Jerusalem, 79
I give immortal praise, 2015
I hear the voice of woe, 1280, 1657
I heard a great voice from heav'n saying unto me, 754, 755, 756
I heard a voice from heav'n, 104, 758
I, in the burying place, may see, 766
I know that my redeemer lives, 111, 1226
I know thy judgments, Lord, are right, 407
I lift my soul to God, 1499, 1500
I love the Lord because he hath heard, 809
I love the Lord: he heard my cries, 1554
I love the volumes of thy word, 924
I love thy habitation, Lord, 1919
I send the joys of earth away, 373, 1268
I shall behold the face, 995
I was glad when they said unto me, 124
I will love thee, O Lord, my strength, 565
I will praise thee ev'ry day, 356
If angels sung a saviour's birth, 1151
If why I love my Jesus so, 1876
If your heart is unbelieving, 275
I'll lift my banner, saith the Lord, 1578
I'll lift my hands, I'll raise my voice, 933, 1384
I'll praise my maker with my breath, 288, 869, 937, 1071, 1130, 1303, 1346, 1347, 1410, 1505, 1506, 1757, 1762, 1867
I'll search the land, and raise the just, 966
I'm not asham'd to own my Lord, 1035, 1934
I'm tir'd with visits, modes, and forms, 1855
Immense compassion reigns, 723, 1154
In all my vast concerns with thee, 1964
In awful state the conq'ring God, 562
In deep distress I oft have cry'd, 515, 1442
In ev'ry land begin the song, 1261
In God the Lord I put my trust, 230
In pleasure's flow'ry path to stray, 1411
In the full choir a broken string, 1422, 1688
In thee, great God, with songs of praise, 561
In thine own ways, O God of love, 841
In this last solemn and tremendous hour, 1533
In vain the noisy crowd, 455
In vain the wealthy mortals toil, 635, 636
In vain we lavish out our lives, 1777, 1932

Indulgent God, with pitying eyes, 343, 1038, 1373, 1711
Infinite grace! almighty charms, 12
Infinite grief! amazing woe, 362, 958, 1000, 1471
Is any afflicted, let him pray, 80
Is this the anniversary so dear, 62
Is this the kind return, 1310, 1670
It is better to go to the house of mourning, 112
It is the Lord, our maker's hand, 1196

J

Jehovah reigns, his throne is high, 1604
Jehovah reigns, let all the earth rejoice, 118
Jehovah speaks! let Israel hear, 967
Jehovah! 'tis a glorious word, 1099, 1661
Jesus Christ is ris'n to day, Hallelujah, 1585
Jesus Christ the Lord's anointed, 264
Jesus drinks the bitter cup, 1750, 1751
Jesus is become at length, 185
Jesus is gone above the skies, 1826
Jesus is worthy to receive, 1626
Jesus, Lord of life and peace, 1456
Jesus, lover of my soul, 914
Jesus, my all, to heav'n is gone, 1800
Jesus! my shepherd and my friend, 1987
Jesus, once for sinners slain, 943
Jesus our God ascends on high, 977
Jesus, our soul's delightful choice, 1532
Jesus our triumphant head, 182
Jesus shall reign where'er the sun, 604, 630, 699, 850, 1153, 1165
Jesus, the saviour, from above, 1417
Jesus, the saviour, stands, 2020
Jesus, the vision of thy face, 804
Jesus, thy name we praise, 791
Jesus, where'er thy people meet, 1133
Jesus, who dy'd a world to save, 696
Jesus, whom ev'ry saint adores, 521
Join all the glorious names, 743, 744, 1051, 1725
Joy to the world, the Lord is come, 713, 855, 963, 1136, 1677, 1872
Judge me, O God, and plead my cause, 1571

K

Kind is the speech of Christ our Lord, 232, 269
King of Salem, bless my soul, 1646
Know ye not that a great man hath fall'n today, 764
Know ye not that there is a great man fall'n, 165

L

Laugh, ye profane, and swell, and burst, 1078, 1079
Let a broad stream with golden sands, 1792
Let all our tongues be one, 1075
Let all the earth their voices raise, 1152, 1375
Let all the earth-born race, 1379
Let all the heathen writers join, 1593, 1594
Let all the just to God, with joy, 473, 1048

Let angels above and saints here below, 904
Let diff'rent nation join, 1917
Let diff'ring nations join, 1414, 1969
Let earth and heav'n agree, 1281
Let earth and ocean know, 1989
Let everlasting glories crown, 1445
Let ev'ry creature join, 1415, 1489, 1647, 1776, 1828, 1954
Let ev'ry mortal ear attend, 81, 682, 947, 950, 1243
Let ev'ry tongue thy goodness speak, 1068
Let flowing numbers sweetly rise, 558
Let him, to whom we now belong, 1433
Let horrid jargon split the air, 965
Let Israel bless the Lord, 2073
Let mortal tongues attempt to sing, 848, 1815, 1986
Let not your heart be troubled, 113
Let others boast how strong they be, 346, 877
Let Pharisees of high esteem, 536
Let sinners take their course, 192, 423, 451, 497, 1577
Let strangers walk around, 507
Let the high heav'ns your songs invite, 413
Let the old heathens tune their song, 1312
Let the shrill trumpet's warlike voice, 121, 164, 1094, 1095
Let there be light! th'almighty spoke, 1113, 2010
Let tyrants shake their iron rod, 414, 415, 1228, 1229
Let us all fly to music this morning, 1191
Let us love, and sing, and wonder, 1356
Let Whig and Tory all subside, 681
Let Zion praise the mighty God, 501
Life is a span, a fleeting hour, 1265
Life is like a summer's day, 1044
Life is the time to serve the Lord, 449, 551, 1999, 2039
Life, like a vain amusement flies, 1150
Lift up your eyes, ye sons of light, 82
Lift up your heads eternal gates, 1441
Lift up your heads in joyful hope, 432
Lift up your heads, O ye gates, 554
Lift your voice, and thankful sing, 664
Like fruitful show'rs of rain, 840
Like sheep we went astray, 293, 623
Lo! he comes, in clouds descending, 1653, 2024
Lo! he cometh, countless trumpets, 572, 910
Lo! sorrow reigneth, and the nation mourns, 591
Lo! what an entertaining sight, 1870, 1909, 1914
Long as I live I'll bless thy name, 1126
Look down in pity, Lord, and see, 1674
Look up and see th'unwearied sun, 1019
Lord, dismiss us with thy blessing, 1841
Lord, hast thou made me know thy ways, 1405
Lord, hear my cry, regard my pray'r, 955
Lord, hear the voice of my complaint, 476, 1472, 1473
Lord, how secure and blest are they, 736
Lord, I am vile, conceiv'd in sin, 40, 481, 610, 1748
Lord, I will bless thee all my days, 273
Lord, I will not repine, 2008
Lord, in the morning thou shalt hear, 208, 1183, 1416, 1490, 1959
Lord, let thy servant now depart, 1082
Lord of the Sabbath, hear our vows, 1633

Lord of the worlds above, 178, 274, 422, 575, 651, 1050, 1239, 1436, 1513, 1827, 2030
Lord, thou hast been our dwelling place, 64
Lord, thou hast heard thy servant's cry, 1553
Lord, thou wilt hear me when I pray, 339, 1940
Lord, 'tis a pleasant thing to stand, 10, 773
Lord, we have heard thy works of old, 1618
Lord, what a feeble piece, 533
Lord, what a thoughtless wretch was I, 348, 819, 820, 821, 923, 1562
Lord, what is man, poor feeble man, 453, 1022, 1894
Lord, what was man, when made at first, 1784
Lord, when thou didst ascend on high, 1694, 1975
Lord, who's the happy man, that may, 1697
Loud hallelujahs to the Lord, 832, 1543, 1907
Loud let the tuneful trumpet sound, 186
Loud to the prince of heav'n, 1081
Love divine all loves excelling, 518

M

Majestic God when I descry, 1822
Majestic God, our muse inspire, 952, 1273
Majestyck God when I descry, 316
Make a joyful noise unto the Lord, 167
Man has a soul of vast desires, 1195, 1530, 1531
Man that is born of a woman, 752, 753
Man, born of woman, like a flow'r, 312
Mankind must all return to dust, 1272
Mark how it snows! how fast the valley fills, 1743
May peace within this sacred house, 1866
Meet and right it is to sing, 1856
Mercy and judgment are my song, 311
Methinks I hear the heav'ns resound, 1067, 2074
Methinks I see a heav'nly host, 291
Methinks I see an heav'nly host, 1684
Methinks I see my saviour dear, 358, 628, 1775
Methinks the last great day is come, 629
Might I enjoy the meanest place, 673
Mighty God, while angels bless thee, 1902
Mine eyes and my desire, 1329, 2013
Mourn, mourn, pharaoh and Ahab prevail in our land, 150, 151
Mourn, mourn, ye saints, as if you see, 519, 522
Mourn, mourn, ye saints, who once did see, 272, 1703
Muse, breathe the dirge o'er Delia's tomb, 761
Music descending on a silent cloud, 1213
Must friends and helpers drop and die, 964
Must friends and kindred drop and die, 1874
My beloved! haste away, 1599
My days are as the grass, 547
My feet shall never slide, 1349
My flesh shall slumber in the ground, 438, 1155, 1541, 1632, 1803, 1895
My friend, I am going a long and tedious journey, 705
My friends, I am going a long journey, 639
My God, accept my early vows, 2044
My God, how many are my fears, 1218
My God, my gracious God, to thee, 1400

O Jesus, our Lord, thy name be ador'd, 1719
O let thy God and king, 244, 564, 835, 1060
O Lord, I am not proud of heart, 871
O Lord, our fathers oft have told, 1244
O Lord our God most high, 1434
O Lord, our heav'nly king, 1491
O Lord, revive thy work in the midst of the years, 137
O Lord, thou art God from everlasting, 131
O Lord, thou art my God, and I will exalt thee, 106
O Lord, thou hast searched me out, 135
O Lord, to my relief draw near, 1623
O love divine! what hast thou done, 1034
O love! what a secret to mortals thou art, 1178
O! magnify the Lord with me, 1798
O, may the mem'ry of thy name, 1978
O may thy church, thy turtle dove, 953
O! now Amanda's dead and gone, 579
O praise God in his holiness, 126
O praise God, praise him in his holiness, 1916
O praise the Lord, all ye nations, 100
O praise the Lord and thou my soul, 853
O praise the Lord, O my soul, 115, 116
O praise the Lord of heaven, 85
O praise the Lord with one consent, 420, 1241, 1242
O praise ye the Lord, 166
O praise ye the Lord, prepare your glad voice, 183, 439,
 1332, 1525, 1624, 1896, 1955
O render thanks to God above, 1092
O sight of anguish, view it near, 436
O sing unto the Lord a new song, 130
O sing unto the Lord and praise his glor'ous name, 1858
O tell me no more of this world's vain store, 206, 655,
 1219, 1832
O that I could repent, 2033
O that the Lord would guide my ways, 615, 1973
O the sharp pangs of smarting pain, 1177
O! the sweet wonders of that cross, 516
O thou that hearest pray'r, unto thee, 152
O thou, that hear'st when sinners cry, 392
O thou, to whom all creatures bow, 86, 1492, 1763
O thou, whose hand the kingdom sways, 1555
O, 'twas a joyful sound to hear, 452
O wash my soul from ev'ry sin, 335, 798, 1833
O were I like a feather'd dove, 467
Of justice and of grace I sing, 228
Oft have I sat in secret sighs, 1708
Oft I am told the muse will prove, 1179
Often I seek my Lord by night, 1928
On ev'ry side I cast mine eye, 822
On Jordan's stormy banks I stand, 1793
On line of life our bodies hang, 775
On thee who dwell'st above the skies, 2026
Once more, my soul, the rising day, 1181, 1185, 1186, 1289
Onward speed thy conq'ring flight, 1359
Our bondage here shall end, 317
Our days, alas! our mortal days, 1392, 2043
Our days are as the grass, 1377, 1629
Our father, who in heaven art, 1004, 1005, 1920, 1921
Our God, our help in ages past, 1062

Our life contains a thousand springs, 865
Our life contains a thousand strings, 14
Our moments fly apace, 684, 1685, 1714, 1970
Our sins, alas! how strong they be, 281, 1570, 1897
Our states, O Lord, with songs of praise, 1904
Our term of time is sev'nty years, 898
Out of the deeps of long distress, 370, 1250

P

Pardon and grace and boundless love, 796, 942
Peace to his soul, the fatal hour is past, 589
Peaceful and lowly in their native soil, 1046
People and realms of ev'ry tongue, 1271
Perfect holiness of spirit, 1643
Pilgrim, burdened with thy sin, 951
Plung'd in a gulf of dark despair, 1328
Ponder my words, O Lord, 136
Praise the Lord, O my soul, 87, 125
Praise to God, immortal praise, 371
Praise ye the Lord; 'tis good to raise, 1391
Praise ye the Lord with hymns of joy, 250
Put not your trust in princes, 757

R

Raise monumental praises high, 1221
Raise your triumphant songs, 29, 663, 1003
Rejoice in glorious hope, 394
Rejoice, the Lord is king, 287, 725
Rejoice, ye righteous in the Lord, 1488, 1502, 1735, 1881
Rejoice, ye shining worlds on high, 552, 999, 1324, 1401,
 1418
Rejoice, you shining worlds on high, 322
Remember, Lord, our mortal state, 563
Remember now thy creator in the days of thy youth, 66
Return, O God of love, return, 842, 1615, 1768, 1779, 2019
Revive our drooping faith, 1348
Righteous art thou, O Lord, and upright, 163
Rise, great redeemer, from thy seat, 676
Rise, my soul, and stretch thy wings, 54, 448, 1412, 1420
Rise, saith the prince of mercy, rise, 836
Rivers to the ocean run, 1732

S

Sacred to heav'n, behold the dome appears, 1949
Salvation! O the joyful sound, 372, 788, 818, 1301, 1650,
 1679, 1778
Samuel the priest gave up the ghost, 751
Sanctify a fast; call a solemn assembly, 88
Sav'd from the ocean and tempest'ous skies, 1689
Save me, O God the swelling floods, 305, 537, 1811, 1837,
 1880, 1926
Say, mighty love, and teach my song, 863, 899, 900, 2000
See from the dungeon of the dead, 147
See the Lord of glory dying, 359, 1030
See the noon day cloth'd in darkness, 1413
See what a living stone, 1049, 1780, 1781, 1782

T

The Lord my pasture shall prepare, 263, 517, 1423

The Lord my shepherd is, 213, 496, 846, 1498, 1665

The Lord of glory reigns, he reigns on high, 741, 1145

The Lord reigneth, let the people tremble, 1861

The Lord reigneth; let the earth rejoice, 556

The Lord, the judge, his churches warns, 1797

The Lord, the sov'reign king, 525

The Lord, the sov'reign, sends his summons forth, 1021

The mighty Lord, the Lord hath spoken, 168

The moment a sinner believes, 1140

The op'ning heav'ns around me shine, 1360

The rising morning can't insure, 545

The saints shall flourish in his days, 722, 1620

The saviour calls; let ev'ry ear, 1595

The scatter'd clouds are fled at last, 304, 1739

The shining worlds above, 1161

The song of songs is Solomon's, 1721

The sound of the harp ceaseth: the voice of mirth, 759

The spacious firmament on high, 510

The spirits of the just, 768, 1547

The states, O Lord, with songs of praise, 939, 1496

The sun may set beyond the main, 505

The swelling billows know their bound, 1053, 1847

The voice of my beloved sounds, 172, 440, 670, 1710, 1952

The watchmen join their voice, 1467

The welcome news, 1941

The wond'ring world inquires to know, 1066

The world's foundations, by his hand, 1176

Thee we adore, eternal name, 921, 1129

Thee will I laud my God and king, 1157

Thee will I love, O Lord my strength, 1259

Then in the Lord let Israel trust, 716

Then jointly all the harpers round, 1546

Then let our songs abound, 1103

There is a glorious world on high, 915

There is a house not made by hands, 1659

There is a house not made with hands, 1873

There is a land of pleasure, 1014

There is a land of pure delight, 374, 974, 975, 976, 1687

There is an hour of peaceful rest, 1397

There the dark earth and dismal shade, 813

There the great monarch of the skies, 1457

There was an hour when Christ rejoic'd, 698

There were shepherds abiding in the fields, 117

Theron, among his travels found, 1662

These glorious minds, how bright they shine, 299, 940

Th'eternal speaks, all heav'n attends, 341, 1557

They that go down to the sea in ships, 680

Think, mighty God, on feeble man, 632, 688, 708, 731, 1098, 1104, 1390, 1449, 1478, 1809, 1974

This day is God's; let all the land, 1820

This is the day the Lord hath made, 702, 875

This is the glorious day, 1070

This life's a dream, an empty show, 33, 712, 1698

This spacious earth is all the Lord's, 868, 1358

Those glorious minds, how bright they shine, 650, 1611

Thou art my blest portion, thou dear Nazarene, 661

Thou art my portion, O Lord, 127

Thou art my portion, O my God, 1025

Thou giver of my life and joy, 418

Thou, Lord, by strictest search hast known, 582

Thou, O God, art praised in Sion, 94

Thou refuge of my weary soul, 1544

Thou, round the heav'nly arch, 1302

Thou sacred one, almighty three, 1425

Thou saith the first, the great command, 1663

Thou sun, with dazzling rays, 1799

Thou whom my soul admires above, 189, 190, 357, 631, 1758

Though beauty grace the comely face, 878

Though not with mortal eyes we see, 1671

Though troubles assail, and dangers affright, 929, 1477

Thousands of journeys night and day, 693

Thrice happy man, who fears the Lord, 1766

Thron'd on a cloud, our God shall come, 1263

Through all the changing scenes of life, 880, 1503

Through ev'ry age, eternal God, 1514

Throughout the saviour's life we trace, 1338

Thus far the Lord has led me on, 1529

Thus Gabriel sang, and straight around, 1217

Thus saith the first, the great command, 1663

Thus saith the high and lofty one, 381, 1141, 1169, 1398, 1408

Thus saith the ruler of the skies, 1097, 1575

Thus will the church below, 459

Thy mercies, Lord, shall be my song, 549, 1899

Thy mercy sweetens ev'ry soil, 9

Thy mercy, Lord, to me extend, 1039

Thy praise, O God, in Zion waits, 1790

Thy words the raging winds control, 602, 1340, 1950, 1951

Thy works of glory, mighty Lord, 1339

Time, like an ever-rolling stream, 907, 1865

Time! what an empty vapour 'tis, 326, 608, 609, 917

'Tis by the faith of joys to come, 428, 1447

'Tis by thy strength the mountains stand, 1485, 1538, 1539, 1540

'Tis done! the precious ransom's paid, 1545

'Tis finish'd! so the saviour cried, 475

'Tis finished, 'tis done, 1918

'Tis God that lifts our comforts high, 2040

'Tis not the law of ten commands, 653

'Tis pure delight without alloy, 195

'Tis with a mournful pleasure now, 647

To bless the Lord, let ev'ry land combine, 838

To bless the Lord, our god, in strains divine, 1596

To bless thy chosen race, 248, 424, 585, 1247, 1248, 1984

To bring the glorious news, 539

To God I made my sorrows known, 1802

To God in whom I trust, 777, 1905

To God the father, God the son, 17, 620

To God, the mighty Lord, 49, 50

To God, the only wise, 204, 1047, 1528

To God with mournful voice, 739

To heav'n I lift my waiting eyes, 1469

To him that chose us first, 1309

To Jesus, our exalted Lord, 1131

Author and Text Source

Addison, Joseph

9, 205, 263, 321, 323, 510, 517, 729, 1423

Allen, W.

948

Alline, Henry

482, 566

Anonymous

22, 32, 120, 147, 160, 162, 165, 174, 196, 198, 202, 212, 214, 220, 272, 275, 304, 312, 317, 341, 347, 359, 375, 378, 400, 418, 427, 432, 436, 437, 441, 443, 444, 445, 456, 458, 462, 505, 513, 519, 522, 544, 550, 558, 573, 594, 595, 597, 639, 640, 652, 679, 693, 694, 703, 704, 705, 738, 748, 760, 766, 769, 775, 783, 792, 795, 802, 822, 833, 849, 872, 886, 892, 916, 927, 931, 945, 953, 954, 982, 1007, 1014, 1019, 1030, 1036, 1043, 1046, 1067, 1091, 1113, 1124, 1151, 1164, 1191, 1197, 1208, 1209, 1232, 1246, 1254, 1256, 1272, 1282, 1288, 1292, 1293, 1300, 1307, 1326, 1343, 1344, 1355, 1394, 1405, 1411, 1413, 1425, 1468, 1533, 1542, 1546, 1548, 1556, 1557, 1569, 1571, 1573, 1579, 1580, 1585, 1587, 1602, 1610, 1613, 1621, 1638, 1642, 1646, 1654, 1669, 1671, 1674, 1689, 1691, 1703, 1719, 1722, 1730, 1738, 1739, 1747, 1816, 1821, 1823, 1839, 1841, 1856, 1866, 1876, 1877, 1901, 1910, 1918, 1924, 1941, 1949, 1952, 1972, 2008, 2010, 2035, 2038, 2055, 2074, 2086

Bakewell, John

934

Barbauld, Anna

209, 371, 1991, 1997

Barlow, Psalm

88: 16, 313, 677, 1031
108: 345, 1537, 2014
137: 218, 219, 221, 222, 289, 389, 390, 391, 578, 1001, 1882

Barnard, John

1291

Bay Psalm Book

148: 1524

Beddome, Benjamin

352, 459, 464, 465, 612, 1190, 1381, 2031

Bedford, A.

488

Beecher, Charles

985

Belknap, Psalm

122: 1607
137: 11

Bible

41, 63, 65, 66, 67, 68, 71, 74, 78, 79, 80, 86, 88, 91, 97, 98, 99, 101, 102, 103, 104, 106, 111, 112, 113, 117, 122, 123, 124, 129, 132, 133, 137, 141, 152, 153, 154, 159, 161, 163, 168, 169, 474, 542, 554, 567, 618, 619, 701, 751, 752, 754, 755, 756, 758, 759, 854, 882, 883, 971, 972, 1010, 1204, 1226, 1368, 1369, 1370, 1371, 1395, 1550, 1588, 1710, 1721, 1857, 1859, 1860, 1861

Bible, Psalm

11: 100
18: 565
23: 1392
30: 89
34 & 41: 70
41: 139
42: 69
44: 95
48: 557
68: 108
90: 64
93: 93
95: 105, 158
96: 1858
97: 556

Bible, Psalm *cont.*

100: 167
103: 115, 116
108: 84
116: 809
128: 138
133: 895, 896
133 & 122: 107
143: 75, 76, 110, 140
146: 757
150: 166
150 & Billings: 1916

Bible & Billings, William

150, 151, 1011, 1592

Bible & Watts, Isaac

753

Billings, William

44, 207, 227, 291, 316, 399, 414, 415, 454, 483, 546, 952, 965, 1023, 1024, 1228, 1229, 1235, 1236, 1273, 1684, 1822

Billings, William?

93, 485, 667, 681, 826, 852, 1042, 1166, 1355, 2036

Blacklock, T.

778

Book of Common Prayer

1849

Book of Common Prayer, Psalm

5: 136
19: 1805
60: 1927
65: 94
81: 90
90: 131
96: 130
100: 114, 128, 155
103: 87
104: 125
107: 680
119: 127
126: 96
127: 72
132: 134
133: 1906
139: 135
148: 85
150: 126

Byles, Mather

43, 109, 382, 491, 904, 1863

Byles, Samuel

1118, 1119

Cennick, John

489, 572, 910, 1800, 1968, 2029

Cleaveland, P.

142, 170

Cowper, William

508, 600, 1133, 1354, 1590, 1600

Crabbe, G.

951

Crossman, S.

1923

Dana, Mary

1676

Dodd, William

156, 157

Doddridge, Philip

13, 186, 201, 203, 238, 296, 343, 406, 413, 580, 606, 643, 654, 666, 797, 1038, 1065, 1081, 1160, 1170, 1171, 1172, 1270, 1285, 1363, 1373, 1382, 1439, 1532, 1581, 1633, 1666, 1667, 1680, 1711, 1742, 1853, 1938

Dwight, *Psalms*

18: 1596
19: 1434
70: 1555
88/2: 1977
145: 838
147/2: 1096

Enfield, William

1280, 1657

Montgomery, James

1712

Moore, T.

1723

Morton, Perez

85, 380, 504, 668, 1115, 1534, 1961, 2034

Needham, John

629, 1211

Newton, John

176, 185, 264, 278, 355, 356, 929, 1314, 1356, 1428, 1477, 1788, 1796, 1819, 1834, 1842, 1987

New Version of Psalms (Brady)

3: 1875
8: 1492, 1763
8 & Bible: 86
11: 279, 721, 996, 1225, 1462, 1563
13: 27, 236, 237, 499, 1619
15: 1697
16: 1628
19: 34, 333, 334
21: 1904
23: 187
24: 858, 1441
25: 777, 1905
27: 1756
29: 1253
31: 191
33: 473, 1048
34: 880, 1503, 1798
41: 257, 889
42: 1403, 1617, 1848
44: 1244
46: 303, 815, 816, 1479
47: 1981
51: 817
57: 1039, 1518
58: 271, 1818
61: 955
63: 1400
64: 476, 1472, 1473
67: 248, 424, 585, 1247, 1248, 1414, 1917, 1969, 1984
68: 387, 645
70: 1623
73: 2061
74: 468
80: 397
82: 1336, 1840
83: 1041, 1568
87: 970

88: 1466
89: 549, 1899
90: 898
92: 1446
93: 1121
95: 59, 315, 1404
96: 1734
97: 118
98: 710, 1759
100: 307, 364
105: 659
106: 1092
108: 1076
112: 255, 1686
113: 897, 1380
117: 1764
118: 1820
120: 515, 1442
122: 452
123: 2026
126: 2027
129: 1786
130: 695, 1275, 1335
131: 871
133: 1037, 1101, 1102
135: 420, 1241, 1242
136: 49, 50
137: 388, 1107, 1108
139: 582
142: 739
145: 1157
146: 853
147: 250
148: 48, 1158, 1220, 1458, 1526, 1527, 1946
149: 183, 439, 1332, 1525, 1624, 1896, 1955
150: 121, 164, 1094, 1095

Niles, Nathaniel

888

No text

603, 789, 1419, 1572, 1640

Occom, Samuel

1338

Oglivie, John

325

Ogilvy, John

47, 1304

Old Version of Psalms (Sternhold)

11: 230

12: 340
18: 20, 92, 727, 1087, 1088
47: 825
63: 1459

Oldys, W.

576, 728

Onderdonk, Henry

1707

Pasquin, Anthony

591

Peck, John

878, 1207, 1701, 1808, 2004

Perronet, Edward

502, 503

Phelps, Mr.

779

Pope, Alexander

579, 637, 638, 941, 1139, 1341, 1342, 1641

Relly, *Christian Hymns*

3: 344
5: 2, 1582
8: 1180
11: 1417
15: 231
16: 1178
17: 55, 1128
28: 2002
29: 661
40: 969
43: 410
55: 1599
58: 920
68: 791
69: 1693
84: 384, 866
87: 1085
94: 486

Richards, George

430

Robinson, Robert

581, 1838, 1902, 2005

Rowe, Elizabeth

671, 672, 1283, 1284, 1302, 1898, 1988

Rowson, S.

589

Scott, Elizabeth

806, 1887

Scott, Thomas

146, 402, 874, 936, 1668

Scottish Psalms **(Millar)**

137: 216, 217

Seagrave, Robert

54, 448, 1412, 1420, 1732

Smith, Mr.

761

Smith, Samuel

1359

Steele, Anne

180, 284, 318, 692, 801, 901, 915, 1131, 1156, 1265, 1306, 1460, 1544, 1595, 1936

Stennett, Samuel

363, 475, 691, 1636, 1793, 1995

Stoddard

1464

Tappan, W.

1397

Tate, Nahum

56, 276, 277, 396, 434, 646, 674, 790, 930, 1004, 1005, 1082, 1240, 1664, 1682, 1683, 1920, 1921

Taylor, Jane

256, 1305

Toplady, Augustus

906, 1953

8: 545
9: 656, 1006
11: 373, 1268, 1387
12: 944
14: 51, 495, 540, 998, 1055, 1056, 1057, 1058, 1059, 1063, 1299, 1637, 1843, 1948
15: 2016, 2017
16: 1851
19: 14, 346, 865, 877
21: 1312
23: 1438, 1704, 1767, 1982
27: 1426
28: 267, 337, 593, 1702, 1971
30: 477, 700, 1103, 1277, 1726
32: 301, 1367, 2070
34: 1264, 1958
36: 1551
38: 1922
39: 1392, 2043
43: 82, 179, 349, 1311
47: 173, 1278, 1789, 1903
48: 242
50: 1699, 1862
51: 1813, 1814
52: 1144, 2025, 2045
54: 1360, 1715
55: 921, 1129
56: 30
57: 736
58: 326, 608, 609, 917, 1865
59: 478, 1100
61: 327, 622, 903, 1321, 1322
62: 2006
63: 171, 200, 351, 528, 532, 771, 794, 909, 957, 1230, 1294, 1353, 2001
64: 1064
66: 374, 974, 975, 976, 1687
69: 253
72: 956, 1586, 1634
74: 1310, 1670
76: 1943
77: 799, 1678, 1890
79: 1328
81: 252
82: 177
83: 1097, 1575
84: 1559
86: 281, 1570, 1897
88: 372, 818, 1301, 1650, 1679, 1778
92: 353
93: 884, 885, 1965, 1966
94: 1754, 1755
95: 362, 958, 1000, 1177, 1471
96: 60, 568
101: 1393
104: 29, 663, 1003
106: 1008, 1317, 1956
107: 828, 864, 984, 2050
110: 548, 787, 1016, 1110, 1111, 1313, 1648, 1770

111: 53
122: 607, 1083
124: 653
129: 428, 1447
131: 1445
133: 309, 837
136: 1717
141: 894
142: 280, 310
146: 1195, 1530, 1531
148: 844, 1871
154: 268, 1765
158: 223, 1334, 2046, 2047, 2048, 2049
162: 283, 1603
163: 1644
166: 2064
167: 411
168: 1604
169: 265, 908, 1072, 2012

Watts, Isaac, *Hymns*, Book 3

1: 329, 330, 784, 1212
4: 466
6: 1826
7: 776, 962, 1386, 1810
8: 1018
9: 1075
10: 240, 516
12: 902
24: 463
30: 1315
32: 17, 620
38: 2015
39: 1309

Watts, Isaac, *Psalms*

2: 7
3: 1218
4: 339, 1940
5: 208, 1183, 1416, 1490, 1959
7: 292
8: 1491
8/1: 286, 1911
8/2: 1784
9/2: 676
11: 919, 1564
11 & NV11: 1709
13: 625
14/1: 574
16/2: 521
17 (**LM**): 33, 438, 712, 1155, 1541, 1632, 1698, 1803, 1895; (**SM**): 995, 1399, 2042
18/1: 1089, 1223, 1259
18/2: 320, 1493, 1942
19 (**LM**): 961, 1137; (**SM**): 1930; (**PM**): 446, 450, 534, 717, 887, 891, 913, 924, 1206, 1494, 1495
19/1: 1451, 1804, 1835

Watts, Isaac, *Psalms cont.*

19/2: 28, 1187, 1745, 1929
20: 1345, 1978
21: 561, 939, 1496
22: 520, 1074
22/2: 1132
23 (**CM**): 1565; (**LM**): 1483, 1497; (**SM**): 213, 496, 846, 1498, 1665
24: 45, 322, 552, 868, 1324, 1358, 1401, 1418
24 & 107: 999
25/1: 1499, 1500
25/3: 1329, 1752, 2013
26: 1919
27: 1427
27/1: 197, 1093, 1944, 1945, 1979
29: 1501
30/2: 1552, 1583, 2066
33/1: 1488, 1502, 1735, 1881
33/2: 715
34/1: 273
36 (**CM**): 1976; (**LM**): 1374; (**SM**): 193, 1729
39/2: 42, 229, 447, 1402, 1566, 1812, 1868, 1925, 2007
39/3: 922, 1443
42 (**CM**): 188, 627, 647, 1159; (**LM**): 31
44: 342, 1618
45 (**SM**): 244, 564, 746, 835, 839, 1060, 1105, 1504, 1673, 1893, 1962
45/1: 1937
47: 300, 977, 1106
48/1: 484
48/2: 506, 507, 823, 978, 1645, 2087
49 (**LM**): 813
50/1 (**CM**): 1263; (**PM**): 986, 987, 988, 989, 1021, 1846, 1850, 1854, 1888
50/2 (**PM**): 15, 19, 23, 175, 245, 369, 377, 398, 492, 530, 827, 834, 983, 990, 991, 993, 1015, 1202, 1262, 1276, 1290, 1452, 1508, 1509, 1536, 1589, 1591, 1824, 1883, 2075, 2080
50/3 (**LM**): 1797
51/1 (**LM**): 335, 781, 798, 1327, 1430, 1605, 1831, 1833
51/2 (**CM**): 660, 1440; (**LM**): 40, 224, 225, 376, 481, 610, 1748
51/3: 392
55 (**CM**): 467; (**SM**): 192, 226, 423, 451, 497, 1577
56: 569, 586
60: 669
61: 644, 1146, 1308, 1830
62: 1134, 1630, 1631
63 (**LM**): 933, 1384; (**SM**): 331, 719, 1054, 1510, 1511, 1567
63/1: 1174, 1175, 1362, 1825
65/2 (**CM**): 1485, 1538, 1539, 1540
65/3 (**CM**): 282, 641, 1741
66/1: 297, 658
68/2: 1694, 1975
69/1 (**CM**): 305, 537, 1811, 1837, 1880, 1926; (**LM**): 199, 367, 718, 1027, 1142, 1210, 1487
69/2 (**CM**): 1728
71/2: 1558, 1794, 1957
72/1: 722, 1620, 2037

72/2: 604, 630, 699, 850, 1153, 1165, 1271
73 (**LM**): 348, 819, 820, 821, 923, 1562; (**SM**): 319, 1465
73/1: 1444
73/2: 1194, 1512, 1609, 1692
77/2: 1260
80: 1084, 1173
83: 613
84 (**CM**): 1224, 1457, 1931; (**PM**): 6, 178, 184, 274, 422, 575, 651, 1050, 1239, 1436, 1513, 1827, 2030
84/2: 270, 673, 1251
89 (**LM**): 563; (**PM**): 632, 688, 708, 731, 1098, 1104, 1390, 1449, 1478, 1809, 1974
89/1 (**CM**): 247, 1696
89/2: 602, 720, 1188, 1340, 1950, 1951, 1963
90 (**LM**): 37, 38, 911, 960, 1052, 1198, 1199, 1514, 1517, 1576; (**SM**): 533, 535, 684, 879, 1685, 1714, 1970, 2063
90/1: 907, 1062
90/2: 1150
90/3: 842, 1615, 1768, 1779, 2019
92/1: 308, 385, 541, 584, 633, 726, 737, 1454, 1549, 1612, 1635, 1869, 1933, 2062
92/2: 10, 773
93/1 (**PM**): 741, 1145
93/2: 455, 601, 786, 803, 1163, 1222, 1295
94/1: 1267, 1330
95 (**CM**): 1125, 1318, 1453; (**LM**): 774, 1515; (**SM**): 336, 697, 805, 918, 1073, 1127, 1269, 1516, 1724, 1749, 1836, 2022, 2041
96 (**CM**): 1040, 1117, 1323, 1366, 1598, 1891, 2054, 2060; (**PM**): 514, 527, 1090, 1152, 1375, 1908
97/1: 409, 524, 1274, 1474, 2028
97/2: 457, 624, 807, 1829
98/1: 1463
98/2: 713, 855, 963, 1136, 1677, 1872
99/2: 873
100/1: 690, 860, 1351
100/2: 570, 571, 1450
101 (**CM**): 228; (**LM**): 311, 966
102 (**LM**): 1009
102/1: 592, 1706, 1733, 2076
102/2: 1196
103/1 (**LM**): 395, 812, 1337, 1597, 1864
103/2 (**LM**): 1801; (**SM**): 35, 547, 1377, 1629, 1785, 2077
103/3: 525
104: 314, 368, 616, 617, 687, 1017, 1053, 1176, 1847
105: 1077
106 (**SM**): 2073
107/2: 338
107/4: 332, 1339
111/1: 18
112 (**LM**): 1766; (**PM**): 1606
113 (**LM**): 366, 665; (**PM**): 365, 709, 1357, 1761
115 (**PM**): 241, 354, 735, 830, 859, 1029, 1205, 1258, 1535, 1795
116/1: 1554
116/2: 808, 810, 811, 1045
117 (**CM**): 215, 1331, 1886; (**LM**): 1231, 1261, 1385, 1939
117 & NV95: 1787
118 (**SM**): 1049, 1070, 1120, 1561, 1780, 1781, 1782
118/1: 1069

118/2: 1553
118/4: 702, 875
119/1 (CM): 560
119/2 (CM): 3
119/3: 1025
119/4: 412, 1783
119/5: 1879
119/7: 1593, 1594
119/11: 615, 1973
119/14: 407
119/16: 1437, 1519, 1947, 1992, 2067
121 (CM): 1469; (PM): 959, 1349, 1481, 1482, 1523, 1990
122 (CM): 386, 1521, 2084; (PM): 52, 405, 408, 531, 831, 1233, 1234, 1520, 1731, 1736, 1983, 2052, 2053, 2083
124: 258, 259, 1114, 1116
125 (SM): 1713
126 (CM): 46, 404, 498, 1168, 1297, 1316; (LM): 1584, 2069
129: 829
130 (CM): 370, 716, 1250; (LM): 1388
132 (CM): 298, 1135; (LM): 143, 144, 553, 555
133 (CM): 1870, 1909, 1914; (PM): 8, 417, 621, 634, 745, 749, 840, 1298, 1396, 1406, 1522, 1675, 1681, 1912, 1913, 1915; (SM): 862
134: 211
135 (CM): 61
135/2: 1296
136 (LM): 793, 1994; (PM): 1486
139/1 (CM): 1964; (LM): 935
139/2 (CM): 511, 512, 730, 1123; (LM): 1061, 1461
139/3 (LM): 1660, 1695
141: 2044
142: 1802
144 (LM): 856, 1431, 2068
144/2: 453, 1022, 1894
145 (LM): 1376, 1616
145/1: 1126
145/3: 1068

146 (PM): 288, 742, 869, 937, 1071, 1130, 1303, 1346, 1347, 1410, 1505, 1506, 1507, 1639, 1757, 1762, 1867
147 (CM): 657, 1245, 1720, 1740, 1744, 1817, 2051, 2056, 2057, 2058, 2059
147/1: 870, 1391
147/2: 501
148 (LM): 832, 845, 1099, 1661, 1907; (PM): 642, 1032, 1033, 1080, 1161, 1379, 1383, 1470, 1543, 1625, 1799, 1993; (SM): 1364, 1365, 1415, 1489, 1647, 1776, 1828, 1954, 2003
148/2: 350
149 (SM): 1989

Wesley, Charles

21, 181, 194, 233, 234, 287, 394, 426, 435, 479, 518, 523, 590, 598, 725, 824, 857, 867, 905, 912, 914, 926, 928, 973, 979, 980, 1034, 1148, 1149, 1200, 1201, 1203, 1255, 1281, 1433, 1608, 1627, 1649, 1653, 1658, 1750, 1751, 1774, 1845, 1878, 1884, 1885, 2024, 2032, 2033

Wesley, Samuel

1545, 1574

White, J.

1020

Williams, W.

1421, 1601

Young, Edward

145, 148, 149

Topic

Addresses to Christ

262, 306, 347, 384, 526, 626, 724, 844, 861, 866, 1086, 1249, 1312, 1319, 1328, 1429, 1456, 1466, 1555, 1599, 1626, 1753, 1771, 1772, 1871, 1892, 1935, 2020, 2021

Addresses to the Holy Spirit

309, 837, 1254, 1438, 1581, 1700, 1704, 1767, 1958, 1982, 1985

Adoption

246, 648, 1109, 1424, 1791

Afflictions of the Church

11, 214, 216, 217, 218, 219, 221, 222, 289, 388, 389, 390, 391, 578, 1001, 1041, 1084, 1107, 1108, 1173, 1244, 1568, 1834, 1882

Ascension and Exaltation of Christ

45, 82, 179, 181, 182, 233, 234, 293, 300, 322, 349, 359, 479, 486, 520, 552, 562, 623, 858, 867, 868, 977, 999, 1030, 1074, 1097, 1106, 1132, 1148, 1149, 1311, 1324, 1358, 1401, 1417, 1418, 1422, 1441, 1559, 1575, 1688, 1694, 1975, 1998

Atonement

464, 465, 519, 522, 928, 934, 1600

Baptism

231, 894

Beauty of the Church

244, 459, 558, 564, 746, 835, 839, 1060, 1105, 1504, 1673, 1893, 1962

Birth of Christ

210, 261, 276, 277, 290, 291, 396, 430, 431, 432, 434, 435, 436, 437, 457, 490, 539, 624, 667, 674, 710, 713, 790, 807, 826, 843, 855, 857, 886, 920, 930, 963, 973, 982, 1040, 1067, 1117, 1136, 1139, 1151, 1217, 1240, 1323, 1326, 1366, 1598, 1651, 1677, 1682, 1683, 1684, 1717, 1734, 1759, 1829, 1872, 1891, 2054, 2060, 2074

Characters and Offices of Christ

264, 294, 502, 503, 723, 743, 744, 780, 1051, 1138, 1154, 1361, 1407, 1680, 1725, 1800, 1839, 2018

Charity

70, 71, 139, 954

Christ

173, 1144, 1278, 1789, 1813, 1814, 1903, 2025, 2045

Christian

27, 54, 236, 237, 242, 252, 292, 335, 362, 373, 392, 448, 467, 489, 499, 515, 538, 569, 586, 625, 644, 777, 781, 798, 799, 817, 842, 880, 893, 906, 914, 955, 958, 1000, 1069, 1146, 1147, 1177, 1214, 1259, 1268, 1308, 1327, 1329, 1360, 1387, 1412, 1420, 1430, 1437, 1442, 1460, 1471, 1499, 1500, 1503, 1519, 1590, 1605, 1615, 1619, 1644, 1664, 1678, 1699, 1715, 1732, 1752, 1768, 1779, 1830, 1831, 1833, 1855, 1862, 1890, 1905, 1947, 1953, 1968, 1992, 2013, 2019, 2023, 2067

Christian Church

10, 215, 298, 303, 342, 484, 506, 507, 604, 613, 630, 675, 699, 722, 773, 815, 816, 823, 850, 932, 953, 978, 1064, 1135, 1153, 1165, 1231, 1261, 1271, 1331, 1385, 1479, 1578, 1618, 1620, 1645, 1697, 1787, 1886, 1937, 1939, 1981, 2086, 2087

Christmas

73, 102, 117, 123, 132, 133, 433

Church Meetings

46, 273, 404, 498, 1168, 1297, 1316, 1584, 1798, 2069

Communion

81

Communion with God

58, 135, 187, 213, 496, 846, 884, 885, 952, 1194, 1273, 1286, 1459, 1483, 1497, 1498, 1512, 1565, 1609, 1665, 1692, 1754, 1755, 1851, 1965, 1966, 2016, 2017

Creation and Providence

13, 14, 93, 205, 250, 263, 314, 316, 319, 332, 346, 368, 473, 517, 616, 617, 676, 687, 729, 793, 865, 870, 877, 959, 1017, 1028, 1039, 1048, 1053, 1061, 1113, 1164, 1170, 1171, 1172, 1176, 1293, 1339, 1349, 1374, 1378, 1391, 1423, 1444, 1461, 1465, 1469, 1481, 1482, 1488, 1502, 1518, 1523, 1730, 1735, 1822, 1847, 1852, 1881, 1990, 1994, 2010, 2038

Day of Judgment

15, 19, 21, 23, 32, 68, 175, 245, 369, 377, 378, 398, 409, 460, 492, 493, 524, 530, 572, 577, 605, 629, 654, 701, 797, 827, 828, 834, 849, 864, 872, 882, 883, 910, 981, 983, 984, 986, 987, 988, 989, 990, 991, 992, 993, 994, 1015, 1020, 1021, 1124, 1202, 1207, 1262, 1263, 1274, 1276, 1290, 1452, 1474, 1508, 1509, 1536, 1589, 1591, 1653, 1655, 1656, 1797, 1808, 1819, 1824, 1846, 1850, 1854, 1883, 1888, 1941, 2024, 2028, 2050, 2075, 2080

Death and Resurrection

4, 5, 26, 37, 38, 200, 267, 312, 317, 327, 337, 351, 360, 361, 374, 383, 416, 421, 429, 505, 528, 532, 543, 544, 546, 548, 563, 566, 573, 588, 590, 593, 594, 595, 596, 597, 598, 622, 632, 635, 636, 637, 638, 640, 686, 688, 693, 704, 708, 731, 760, 761, 762, 763, 765, 766, 767, 768, 771, 775, 782, 787, 794, 795, 804, 813, 814, 878, 890, 898, 903, 909, 911, 957, 960, 964, 974, 975, 976, 1009, 1016, 1023, 1024, 1052, 1078, 1079, 1098, 1104, 1110, 1111, 1160, 1167, 1198, 1199, 1227, 1230, 1235, 1236, 1256, 1265, 1272, 1294, 1313, 1321, 1322, 1325, 1353, 1390, 1411, 1421, 1448, 1449, 1468, 1478, 1514, 1517, 1533, 1547, 1569, 1576, 1587, 1601, 1638, 1641, 1642, 1648, 1658, 1659, 1669, 1676, 1687, 1689, 1701, 1702, 1770, 1809, 1873, 1874, 1900, 1901, 1918, 1923, 1938, 1971, 1974, 1995, 2001, 2004

Dedication

72, 124, 142, 143, 144, 169, 170, 553, 554, 555, 556, 557, 972

Depravity and Fall of Man

40, 223, 224, 225, 376, 481, 574, 580, 610, 1334, 1707, 1748, 1784, 1792, 1853, 2046, 2047, 2048, 2049

Dominion of Christ

287, 725

Doxology

17, 41, 618, 619, 620, 1004, 1005, 1309, 1315, 1920, 1921, 2015

Easter

97, 111, 145, 146, 147, 148, 149, 1226, 1588

Election

60, 568, 698

Exaltation of Christ

185, 443, 691, 772, 905, 1065, 1081, 1281, 1608, 1887, 1987

Faith

36, 113, 191, 203, 230, 275, 280, 283, 284, 310, 318, 344, 352, 414, 415, 428, 454, 476, 550, 692, 824, 915, 1013, 1225, 1228, 1229, 1447, 1472, 1473, 1603, 1623, 1628, 1654, 1708, 1746, 1747, 1863, 1961, 2011

Family Worship

228

Fast Day

63, 64, 75, 76, 88, 96, 99, 110, 131, 136, 140, 150, 151, 152, 163, 565, 567, 1010, 1550, 1927

Fear and Hope

9, 16, 31, 69, 188, 238, 313, 400, 468, 627, 647, 677, 711, 822, 929, 1031, 1122, 1159, 1218, 1237, 1403, 1477, 1484, 1532, 1544, 1579, 1617, 1848, 1875, 1889, 2036

Funeral

66, 91, 104, 112, 165, 171, 589, 639, 662, 705, 750, 751, 752, 753, 754, 755, 756, 757, 758, 759, 764, 925

Gospel

198, 968, 1439

Grace

206, 251, 549, 643, 655, 666, 836, 1140, 1219, 1832, 1899

Hell and Heaven

281, 299, 514, 527, 650, 940, 1090, 1152, 1190, 1306, 1375, 1397, 1570, 1611, 1793, 1897, 1908

Hosannas to Christ

738, 904

Humility

418, 508, 579, 748, 871, 1179, 1246, 1354, 1649, 2033

Intercession of Christ

7, 375, 944, 1118, 1119, 1356, 1551

Invitations and Promises

101, 103, 253, 381, 445, 461, 682, 733, 734, 801, 946, 947, 950, 967, 1012, 1141, 1169, 1243, 1398, 1408, 1595, 1610, 1614, 1777, 1932, 1991, 1996, 2035

Jewish Church

49, 50, 338, 387, 645, 653, 659, 829, 970, 971, 1077, 1092, 1260, 1296, 1486, 1786, 2027, 2073

Joy and Rejoicing

195, 248, 424, 477, 478, 482, 585, 700, 736, 1100, 1103, 1247, 1248, 1277, 1363, 1726, 1984, 2082

Justification

268, 1435, 1558, 1765, 1794, 1806, 1957

Knowledge

2065

Law and Gospel

249, 529, 678, 1002, 1215, 1432, 1445, 1455, 1463, 1467, 1663, 1773, 2071, 2072, 2085

Liberality

255, 257, 889, 1280, 1573, 1606, 1657, 1686, 1766

Life and Ministry of Christ

201, 1382, 1556

Lord's Day

28, 208, 308, 331, 385, 541, 584, 633, 702, 719, 726, 737, 875, 933, 1054, 1174, 1175, 1183, 1187, 1362, 1384, 1400, 1416, 1451, 1454, 1490, 1510, 1511, 1549, 1567, 1612, 1633, 1635, 1636, 1745, 1790, 1804, 1820, 1821, 1823, 1825, 1835, 1869, 1929, 1933, 1959, 2062

Lord's Supper

240, 329, 330, 363, 463, 466, 516, 776, 784, 902, 962, 1018, 1075, 1212, 1386, 1810, 1826, 1841

Love

107, 256, 403, 425, 518, 536, 714, 863, 895, 896, 899, 900, 1037, 1101, 1102, 1178, 1870, 1906, 1909, 1914, 1922, 2000

Magistracy

271, 311, 561, 966, 1336, 1496, 1818, 1840, 1904

Marriage

138

Masonic

1112, 1718, 1949

Missionary Meetings

2037

Moral Law

1693

Morning and Evening

207, 545, 583, 671, 672, 683, 685, 881, 1019, 1026, 1181, 1182, 1184, 1185, 1186, 1189, 1284, 1289, 1302, 1343, 1352, 1409, 1529, 1898, 1940, 2044

Music

485, 941, 1213, 1341, 1342, 1464

New Year

1255, 1878

No Text

603, 789, 1419, 1572, 1640

Ordination

86, 120, 134, 153, 1368, 1369, 1370, 1371

Pardon

57, 295, 370, 469, 470, 500, 695, 707, 716, 802, 1250, 1252, 1275, 1333, 1335, 1388, 1622, 1760

Patriotic

456, 458, 591, 740, 770, 779, 888, 939, 1011, 1043, 1208, 1209, 1344, 1592, 1972

Perfections of God

18, 20, 29, 35, 61, 92, 108, 129, 137, 180, 193, 227, 241, 247, 265, 288, 297, 328, 354, 365, 366, 395, 411, 420, 455, 504, 510, 511, 512, 547, 582, 587, 601, 602, 649, 658, 663, 665, 709, 715, 720, 727, 730, 735, 739, 741, 742, 786, 803, 812, 825, 830, 838, 853, 859, 869, 873, 897, 908, 935, 937, 1003, 1029, 1068, 1071, 1072, 1087, 1088, 1096, 1121, 1123, 1126, 1130, 1145, 1157, 1163, 1188, 1196, 1205, 1216, 1222, 1241, 1242, 1258, 1295, 1303, 1320, 1337, 1340, 1346, 1347, 1350, 1357, 1372, 1376, 1377, 1380, 1410, 1425, 1434, 1491, 1492,

Perfections of God *cont.*

1505, 1506, 1507, 1535, 1597, 1604, 1616, 1621, 1629, 1639, 1696, 1729, 1757, 1761, 1762, 1763, 1785, 1795, 1801, 1802, 1844, 1864, 1867, 1950, 1951, 1963, 1964, 1976, 2012, 2064, 2077

Perseverance

204, 340, 427, 1047, 1314, 1405, 1528, 1713, 1723

Prayer and Praise for the Church

296, 559, 1238, 1607

Prudence

22, 39, 494, 1042, 1381

Public Worship

6, 8, 52, 178, 184, 197, 211, 270, 274, 386, 405, 408, 417, 422, 452, 531, 575, 621, 634, 651, 673, 745, 749, 808, 810, 811, 831, 840, 862, 1045, 1050, 1093, 1224, 1233, 1234, 1239, 1251, 1298, 1396, 1406, 1427, 1436, 1457, 1513, 1520, 1521, 1522, 1675, 1681, 1731, 1736, 1827, 1912, 1913, 1915, 1919, 1931, 1944, 1945, 1979, 1983, 2030, 2052, 2053, 2083, 2084

Redemption

55, 177, 220, 341, 343, 410, 488, 783, 791, 997, 1038, 1085, 1128, 1180, 1203, 1257, 1373, 1557, 1560, 1711, 1845

Regeneration

611, 1192, 1193, 1348, 1643, 1967, 2078

Repentance

523, 606, 612, 656, 660, 912, 951, 1006, 1008, 1200, 1201, 1305, 1310, 1317, 1440, 1475, 1476, 1646, 1670, 1671, 1705, 1727, 1956, 2031

Resignation

194, 278, 542, 576, 614, 728, 876, 1300, 1674, 2008, 2026, 2040

Resurrection of Christ

302, 402, 406, 444, 521, 646, 696, 806, 936, 943, 1143, 1291, 1585, 1668, 1807, 1943

Safety and Triumph of the Church

24, 25, 43, 393, 848, 1279, 1359, 1815, 1866, 1980, 1986

Saints and Sinners

33, 279, 438, 560, 600, 712, 721, 874, 919, 985, 995, 996, 1155, 1267, 1330, 1399, 1462, 1541, 1563, 1564, 1627, 1632, 1698, 1709, 1803, 1895, 2042

Salvation

186, 372, 379, 661, 788, 792, 800, 818, 926, 948, 969, 1014, 1211, 1270, 1301, 1580, 1650, 1679, 1774, 1778, 1960, 2002, 2009, 2032

Sanctification

615, 1973, 2079

Scripture

34, 333, 334, 412, 446, 450, 534, 703, 717, 887, 891, 913, 924, 961, 1137, 1206, 1494, 1495, 1593, 1594, 1783, 1879, 1930

Seasons of the Year

212, 282, 501, 641, 657, 1091, 1245, 1253, 1285, 1485, 1501, 1538, 1539, 1540, 1548, 1666, 1667, 1720, 1740, 1741, 1742, 1744, 1817, 1877, 2006, 2051, 2055, 2056, 2057, 2058, 2059

Secular

62, 109, 174, 196, 202, 304, 401, 491, 513, 679, 945, 965, 1046, 1166, 1413, 1662, 1739

Sickness and Recovery

407, 592, 922, 1443, 1552, 1553, 1554, 1583, 1706, 1733, 2066, 2076

Sincerity

127, 471, 472, 1025

Solomon's Song

1, 77, 78, 79, 172, 189, 190, 232, 243, 269, 357, 440, 480, 631, 670, 706, 949, 1066, 1266, 1710, 1721, 1758, 1876, 1910, 1928, 1952

Sufferings and Death of Christ

2, 12, 199, 260, 266, 272, 305, 358, 367, 380, 475, 537, 599, 628, 668, 718, 732, 747, 785, 796, 847, 942, 1007, 1027, 1034, 1142, 1210, 1338, 1394, 1487, 1545, 1574, 1582, 1691, 1703, 1728, 1750, 1751, 1775, 1811, 1837, 1880, 1926

Thanksgiving

53, 65, 67, 74, 80, 83, 84, 85, 87, 89, 90, 94, 95 98, 105, 106, 114, 122, 125, 128, 130, 141, 154, 155, 156, 157, 158, 159, 160, 161, 162, 167, 168, 258, 259, 320, 324, 353, 356, 371, 419, 462, 474, 669, 680, 809, 841, 854, 856, 916, 931, 938, 1089, 1114, 1116, 1131, 1191, 1204, 1221, 1223, 1292, 1307, 1345, 1389, 1431, 1493, 1534, 1546, 1738, 1805, 1857, 1858, 1859, 1860, 1861, 1916, 1942, 1978, 2068

Time and Eternity

42, 229, 301, 326, 447, 449, 453, 533, 535, 551, 608, 609, 684, 879, 901, 907, 917, 921, 1022, 1062, 1129, 1197, 1367, 1392, 1402, 1566, 1602, 1685, 1714, 1812, 1816, 1865, 1868, 1894, 1925, 1970, 1999, 2007, 2039, 2043, 2063, 2070

Times and Seasons

286, 339, 581, 1156, 1911, 1936

Trust and Confidence

119, 176, 355, 394, 397, 426, 441, 487, 509, 769, 852, 1035, 1036, 1082, 1134, 1254, 1288, 1428, 1433, 1446, 1480, 1542, 1571, 1630, 1631, 1660, 1695, 1722, 1737, 1788, 1796, 1842, 1934, 1977, 2061

Universal Praise

44, 47, 48, 56, 100, 115, 116, 118, 121, 126, 164, 166, 183, 235, 239, 285, 307, 321, 323, 325, 345, 350, 364, 382, 399, 413, 439, 442, 483, 525, 570, 571, 642, 664, 681, 690, 694, 778, 832, 833, 845, 860, 892, 927, 1032, 1033, 1076, 1080, 1094, 1095, 1099, 1115, 1158, 1161, 1220, 1232, 1283, 1287, 1304, 1332, 1351, 1355, 1364, 1365, 1379, 1383, 1395, 1414, 1415, 1426, 1450, 1458, 1470, 1489, 1524, 1525, 1526, 1527, 1537, 1543, 1596, 1624, 1625, 1647, 1661, 1672, 1712, 1719, 1764, 1776, 1799, 1828, 1849, 1856, 1884, 1885, 1896, 1902, 1907, 1917, 1946, 1954, 1955, 1969, 1988, 1989, 1993, 2003, 2014, 2029, 2034

World

30, 348, 652, 819, 820, 821, 923, 1195, 1393, 1530, 1531, 1562, 1613, 1924

Worship

3, 51, 59, 192, 209, 226, 254, 315, 336, 423, 451, 495, 497, 540, 607, 697, 774, 805, 918, 956, 979, 980, 998, 1049, 1055, 1056, 1057, 1058, 1059, 1063, 1070, 1073, 1083, 1120, 1125, 1127, 1133, 1269, 1299, 1318, 1404, 1453, 1515, 1516, 1561, 1577, 1586, 1634, 1637, 1716, 1724, 1749, 1756, 1769, 1780, 1781, 1782, 1836, 1843, 1948, 1997, 2022, 2041

Youth and Old Age

689, 851, 1044, 1150, 1162, 1282, 1652, 1690, 1743, 1838, 2005, 2081